DATE DUE			
JUL 8 '81			
FEB 16'84			
OCT 31 '84			
JUL 14 '85			
AUG 15 '85			

The Religion of
the Chinese People

Explorations in Interpretative Sociology

GENERAL EDITORS

PHILIP RIEFF
Benjamin Franklin Professor of Sociology
University of Pennsylvania

BRYAN R. WILSON
Reader in Sociology, University of Oxford
Fellow of All Souls College

Also in this series

MAX WEBER AND SOCIOLOGY TODAY
Edited by Otto Stammer
Translated by Kathleen Morris

THE SOCIAL FRAMEWORKS OF KNOWLEDGE
Georges Gurvitch
Translated by M. A. and K. A. Thompson

FROM SYMBOLISM TO STRUCTURALISM
Lévi-Strauss in a Literary Tradition
James A. Boon

LUCIEN LÉVY-BRUHL
Jean Cazeneuve
Translated by Peter Rivière

GURVITCH
Georges Balandier
Translated by M. A. and K. A. Thompson

Forthcoming

THE CARNETS OF LÉVY-BRUHL
Translated by Peter Rivière

FALSE CONSCIOUSNESS
Joseph Gabel
Translated by M. A. and K. A. Thompson

Marcel Granet

The Religion of the Chinese People

Translated, edited
and with an Introduction by
MAURICE FREEDMAN

Harper & Row Publishers
New York, Evanston, San Francisco

*First published in 1922 by Presses
Universitaires de France (Paris),
as* La religion des Chinois, *and
translated by arrangement*

LIBRARY OF CONGRESS CATALOG CARD NUMBER: 74–33106

STANDARD BOOK NUMBER: 0–06–136172–0

Set in Plantin (text) and Albertus (display)
Printed and made in Great Britain
by The Camelot Press Ltd., Southampton

Contents

This English version of her husband's book
La religion des Chinois
is, by permission, dedicated to Mme Marie Granet,
member of the Resistance
to the German Occupation of France,
and its historian

Editorial Preface

The Introductory Essay explains why I have translated this book. My decision to undertake the translation was made as a result of a few weeks' work in Paris towards the end of 1972 when I was collecting material upon Granet in connexion with a study of the Western perception of Chinese religion. I have to thank the Social Science Research Council (London) for the grant that made it possible for me to work in Paris.

The translation is dedicated to Mme Marie Granet, who stands at the head of the list of people to whom I acknowledge my indebtedness. She gave me the run of her husband's library (still very much as it was when he died), supplied me with copies of printed and unprinted documents, spoke to me about her husband and his work, and introduced me to many of his pupils. No admirer of Marcel Granet could have been more handsomely rewarded. With Mme Granet's name I must link that of her son, Dr. Jacques Granet.

The other people to whom I should like to express my gratitude for help are: Dr. Hugh Baker, Mme Suzanne Bidault, M. Paul Demiéville, M. Georges Dumézil, M. Jacques Havet, Dr. David Hawkes, M. Clemens Heller, Mrs. S. C. Humphreys, M. Max Kaltenmark, M. Victor Karady, M. André Leroi-Gourhan, M. Claude Lévi-Strauss, Professor Piet van der Loon, Dr. Steven Lukes, M. Jean-Pierre Peter, M. Rolf-Alfred Stein, Mlle Alberte Tang, Mme Nicole Vandier-Nicolas, and Mme Françoise Wang. My wife shared my work in Paris and by her constant help with the translation saved me from many errors; those that remain are my own.

In translating Granet I have tried to keep close to his style, wherever possible retaining his punctuation and use of capitals and italics. In the Introductory Essay and Editorial Notes I have translated passages from the French where I thought it would be particularly useful to do so. The Editorial Notes are meant to serve several purposes—among them to link up points in the text with the general body of Granet's work, to show some of the sources of his ideas, and to comment upon a few problems of translation. The date of publication is given every time one of Granet's works is cited in order to help the reader bear in mind the chronology of his writings. For convenience, page references to works reprinted in *Etudes sociologiques sur la Chine* are given to that book.

M. F.

All Souls College, Oxford
March 1974

Introductory Essay

Marcel Granet, 1884–1940 Sociologist

Nobody familiar with French thought between the Wars is likely to be surprised to see a book by Marcel Granet in a series devoted to sociology, but it might at first sight seem odd that a work entitled *The Religion of the Chinese People* should appear as a contribution to 'interpretative sociology'. It looks more like sinology or ethnography. As a matter of fact, even if it had been merely either of those things, it would have been worth translating, for it is to my mind the best single brief work on its subject. Yet its significance goes deeper. It is an important document in the annals of Durkheimian sociology. And it was written by a genius.

Granet composed the book in six weeks in 1922. He had been back in France from his war service barely three years. His wife was for the moment teaching in a lycée in Tonnerre (Yonne) to which he travelled frequently from Paris to see her and their infant son. When Maurice Solovine invited him to write a short book for the series 'Science et Civilisation', he seized the opportunity to make profitable use of his life as a commuter separated from his books and papers. It appears that he wrote *La religion des Chinois* in the train and during moments of his intermittent domesticity in Tonnerre.[1] The book has several features that distinguish it from all the other works he wrote. First, it lacks a scholarly apparatus—which I have tried to supply in the Editorial Notes, not as a sort of long-distance criticism, but mainly in order to connect up this odd-man-out among his books with the richly documented scholarship that had gone before it and was yet to come.

[1] I shall cite written evidence on Granet's life whenever I can. Many of the statements I shall make, however, are based upon my conversations with his pupils and associates, and above all, with his widow, Mme Marie Granet, in Paris in November 1972. Some of my remarks are, of course, speculative, but I think that the manner in which I have expressed them shows that I do not offer them as incontrovertible assertions of fact

Although because of the nature of the series to which it was a contribution the book was deprived of references and a critique of the sources upon which it was based, Granet certainly looked upon it as a major component of his *œuvre*, and was later constantly to cite it in the notes to his more technical writings. Second, and more important, the book is the only study that Granet ever wrote which attempted to take in the whole sweep of Chinese history and the full range of its religious developments. Yet a third unique feature of the book may also stem from the peculiar circumstances of its composition: in none of his other writings does Granet make more than passing and anecdotal use of his experiences in China; it may well be that the special conditions in which he wrote *La religion des Chinois* relaxed the constraint he imposed upon himself to abide by the textual sociology which he took as his vocation.

It must surely occur to an anthropologist to wonder why Granet made so little use of his observations of Chinese life. Present-day sinologists, for their part, are more concerned with the fact that none of the work he lived to publish, other than *La religion des Chinois* (which in any case non-French sinologues tend to overlook), deals except in a casual way with the imperial China that followed the Han dynasty. Prehistoric, 'feudal', and early imperial China appear to have engrossed his energies. And that chronological restriction, now out of tune with sinological interests (but in accord with the sinological preferences evident earlier in the century), has earned him some neglect by students of China. But in fact, as this book demonstrates, Granet had taken the measure of Chinese history as a whole, and often set himself down to lecture in Paris upon the history of Chinese civilization to the present—although, as one of his pupils put it to me, by the time the end of the academic year had arrived he had reached only the T'ang dynasty, and had got so far only by galloping the last stretch of the course. In his last days he was actively working upon a book that was to have illustrated Chinese conceptions of majesty with data drawn from the history of the eighth and ninth centuries: *Le Roi boit. La Reine rit. Notes sur le folklore ancien de la Chine.* Yet in fact the work had been planned no later than 1929, as we can tell from the reference made to it (p. 234, fn. 1) in *La civilisation chinoise*, 1929. We know enough about *Le Roi boit* from Professor Stein's account of it to realize that if Granet had lived to bring it to its published form it would have marked, for his writings, a leap forward in time. Underlining the unity of Granet's work, Stein says that *Le Roi boit* was to have crowned it: 'Peu d'œuvres ont été élaborées avec autant d'esprit de suite que celle de Granet. Arrivé à la sinologie au moment où il était déjà formé à la sociologie, il a, dès le début, envisagé une grande enquête sur la constitution de la société et notamment de la famille chinoise. Avançant pas à pas, il a procédé systématiquement à l'édification de ce monument. *Le Roi boit* devait la couronner'.[2] But one might observe that, dying suddenly at the age of fifty-six, Granet is unlikely to have thought of that book as the culmination of his life's work. Had he lived, he might well have taken further strides towards the present, and in so doing have filled in some of the outlines sketched in *La religion des Chinois* with the passionately intense scholarship of his technical writings.

In France, Granet's work has by no means been forgotten. After the War his most important papers were collected in *Etudes sociologiques sur la Chine*,[3] 1953; as we have seen, his distinguished pupil Stein published an account of *Le Roi boit;* his two complementary essays in *haute vulgarisation, La civilisation chinoise*, 1929, and *La pensée chinoise*, 1934, were reprinted; and *La religion des Chinois* was itself reprinted in 1951. The Norwegians brought out his Oslo lectures, *La féodalité chinoise*, in 1952. His pupils, by no means all of them professional sinologues, have kept his memory green—although, partly no doubt because of the nature of his teaching and his apparent failure to explain to his sinological audiences the precise character of his sociological premises and reasoning, he has had no true successors in his combination of the roles of sinologue and sociologist. French sinology is now less sociological than when he lived, French sociology only half-aware of the significance of his labours.

In the English-speaking world, Granet's reputation was first generally established by the translation of *La civilisation chinoise* (1929) in 1930 and of *Fêtes et chansons* (1919) in 1932.[4] The present translation apart, the only other of Granet's works to appear in English is his essay 'La droite et la gauche en Chine'.[5] The Edwards translation of *Fêtes et chansons* (*Festivals and Songs of Ancient China*) naturally commanded attention because of Granet's striking contribution to the interpretation of the *Shih Ching*, 'The Book of Odes'; but the impact made by the English version of *La civilisation chinoise* (*Chinese Civilisation*) would doubtless have been greatly enhanced if it had later on been matched by a translation of *La pensée chinoise*, 1934, its major partner, in which Granet's analytical and expository powers are dazzlingly displayed.

[2] R. A. Stein, 'Présentation de l'œuvre posthume de Marcel Granet: "Le Roi boit" ', *Année Sociologique*, third series, 1952, published 1955, p. 9.

[3] Details of Granet's works will be found in Part 1 of the Bibliography at the end of this book.

[4] There appears to have been another English translation of this book circulating in Paris but I have not seen it.

[5] It is about to be published as I write this Introduction: Rodney Needham, trans., 'Right and Left in China', in Needham, ed., *Right and Left: Essays on Dual Symbolic Classification*, University of Chicago Press, Chicago and London, 1973.

(It would, however, offer a daunting challenge to a would-be translator.) Some glimpses of that work have since 1963 been afforded to the English reader in C. Wright Mills's essay 'The Language and Ideas of Ancient China: Marcel Granet's Contribution to the Sociology of Knowledge',[6] but that essay is perhaps more remarkable for the date at which it was composed (1940) and for its assault on American sociological provincialism (as seen by Mills) than for its exposition of Granet's achievement. It follows that readers who must rely upon Granet in English have only an inadequate sample before them. I hope that *The Religion of the Chinese People* will by its conciseness and amplitude be able to exemplify and recapitulate the whole range of Granet's work.[7] That hope may be thought to be misplaced, given that the book falls in the first half of Granet's career as a writer. But I may echo what Stein has justly said about the unity and continuity of that scholarly vocation. The book now translated into English recurs to all the major themes in the work published from 1912, and, more suprisingly, foreshadows nearly all those to come. Granet's *œuvre*, of which *La religion des Chinois* was for him an important element, is in effect a series of overlapping discussions of a group of central problems in Chinese social organization and thought. The treatment of a theme sometimes changes as time goes on; a 'fact' in an earlier work is dropped; new data are fed into the models; the image of the development of Chinese society grows more complex as study follows study. But as one reads the books and papers in the order in which they were written, one is overwhelmed by the impression that one is the witness of a gradual unfolding over a range of nearly thirty years of a plan designed in great detail at the beginning of the man's career. I shall show presently that the plan was formulated very early on, and certainly before Granet set foot in China.

Students of China apart, scholars in the English-speaking world are not generally alert to the significance of Granet's work[8] except in so

[6] In Mills's *Power, Politics and People, the Collected Essays of C. Wright Mills*, ed. Irving Louis Horowitz, Oxford University Press, London, Oxford, New York, 1963.

[7] In Part 1 of the Bibliography at the end of this book mention is made of translations of Granet's work into languages other than English. The latest is an excellent Italian version of *La religion des Chinois: La religione dei cinesi*, ed. Bianca Candian, Adelphi, Milan, 1973. The appearance at about the same time of two translations of this book (never before translated, as far as I can discover) suggests a heightened international interest in Granet, which, I suspect, is likely further to increase.

[8] An important exception is Mrs. S. C. Humphreys, the ancient historian. See her 'The Work of Louis Gernet', *History and Theory, Studies in the Philosophy of History*, vol. 10, no. 2, 1971. That paper, by its account of Gernet, the classical scholar and a fellow-Durkheimian of Granet, is a major contribution to our understanding of the ramifications of Durkheimianism into the periphery

far as anthropology has drawn upon it in its studies of kinship—and in doing so has unwittingly underlined the way in which Granet's concentration upon sinological questions was, as I shall say more fully later, a method of discussing humanity at large. It is indeed ironical that the English-reading sociological public will have learned more about Granet from the translation of Lévi-Strauss's *Les structures élémentaires de la parenté* than from any other source, for that is a work which, for all the homage it pays to Granet's inspiration and the care it gives to expounding the development of his ideas about kinship and marriage in China, does not, in my view, sufficiently appreciate the broad base of Granet's sociological learning and the generality of his aims.[9]

of the sociological world. Mrs. Humphreys's remarks on Granet are very much to the point, and I should like to record my indebtedness both to the paper and to its author for inspiration and help. The parallelism between Gernet's work on Greece and Granet's on China, to which Mrs. Humphreys draws our attention, could be made even more dramatic by a systematic confrontation of passages from their work, when we should see how deep the Durkheimianism bit. Let me illustrate by a few quotations from Louis Gernet and André Boulanger, *Le génie grec dans la religion*, Albin Michel, Paris, 1970 (first published 1932, La Renaissance du Livre, Paris) which, with little modification, could be slotted into Granet's writings on China. 'Une bonne part de la religion officielle de la cité est héritée de cultes agraires. C'est un fonds primitif qui se reconnaît là (p. 36). ... Chœurs de garçons et chœurs de filles, dans la religion populaire, sont plus qu'un souvenir de coutumes matrimoniales; on les voit affrontés dans un dessin élémentaire que reproduit encore, à une époque tardive, une danse mimée où les troupes se répondent: "Où sont mes roses, et les violettes, où ma belle ache?—Voici les roses, et les violettes, et la belle ache." Les joutes avec fruits paraissent attestées ... (p. 42) ... Riches de sentiment, et d'une gravité qui, dans les foules proches de la terre, n'exclut pas plus les bouffonneries et la licence qu'une grâce rude, les fêtes paysannes ont été un milieu de vie religieuse ... La nature participe de la vie des hommes ... La nature est de la fête, elle favorise les échanges des hommes et leur dépense allègre. Expressions isolées et fugitives d'un vieux fonds d'idées et de sentiments: le commerce est magnifié où sont engagés, par les réunions saisonnières, les individus, les groupes, les sexes, les générations successives. Une pensée globale inspire les gestes et les symboles (pp. 41–44) ... Il n'y a pas à insister sur l'importance des lieux sacrés qui sont fréquemment les montagnes, les fleuves, les sources, les bois, etc. Il y a lieu de penser qu'ils doivent leur qualification à des usages paysans (p. 47) ... dans un fonds de religion populaire singulièrement persistant, l'idée de Terre-Mère est restée l'élément principal (p. 55).' One could go on.

[9] Claude Lévi-Strauss, trans. James Harle Bell and John Richard von Sturmer, ed. Rodney Needham, *The Elementary Structures of Kinship*, Eyre and Spottiswoode, London, 1969, chaps. 19–22. And cf. E. R. Leach, *Rethinking Anthropology*, London School of Economics Monographs on Social Anthropology no. 22, Athlone Press, London, 1961, pp. 73ff.; and see note 67 in the Editorial Notes to the translation below.

In a less dramatic and effective fashion Granet has passed into the consciousness of English-speaking anthropology through Radcliffe-Brown, who, it is clear, often referred to him in his teaching in Chicago and Oxford, but failed to inscribe him adequately in his writings. In a public lecture he gave in London in 1951 (and at which I probably heard Granet's name pronounced for the first time in my life) Radcliffe-Brown offered what I take to be an exposition of Granet's ideas on ancient Chinese kinship and its connexions with basic notions of universal order, although the brief account is not entirely accurate.[10] It is possible that, had the Japanese war against China not taken place, the investigation that Radcliffe-Brown planned for a Chinese anthropologist would have made an important ethnographic extension of Granet's work.[11] As matters stand, then, Granet may well appear to anthropologists (in both the French- and English-speaking worlds) as a kinship theorist *malgré lui* and who yet stands away from any China that the profession interests itself in. It is necessary to trace the origins of the perplexing situation in which Granet can be described by sinologists as a sociologist and by sociologists as a sinologist, with justice on both sides.

He was born in 1884. After a highly successful career at school (at the Lycée d'Aix-en-Provence and at Louis-Le-Grand in Paris) he entered the Ecole Normale supérieure in 1904 as an historian. He followed a conventional course of study, embracing philosophy and law as well as history, but to these established subjects he added sociology. It will be recalled that Durkheim had begun teaching in Paris in 1902; in 1904–5, Granet's first year there, Durkheim delivered his first course at the Ecole Normale, on education. It was intended for all

---

[10] 'The Comparative Method in Social Anthropology', the Huxley Memorial Lecture for 1951, reprinted in A. R. Radcliffe-Brown, ed. M. N. Srinivas, *Method in Social Anthropology*, University of Chicago Press, Chicago, 1958, pp. 124f. Radcliffe-Brown's use of the word 'clans' to refer to the units between which brides were exchanged does violence to Granet's conceptions—perhaps in the interests of brevity.

[11] *Op cit.*, p. 124: 'The evidence is that the system of marriage was one where a man married his mother's brother's daughter, or a woman of the appropriate generation of his mother's clan. According to my information this kind of organization, which apparently existed forty centuries ago in that region [the Yellow River], still survived there in 1935, but the investigation of it that I had planned to be carried out by Li Yu I was unfortunately prevented by the Japanese attack on China.' On Radcliffe-Brown in China, see my 'Sociology in and of China', *The British Journal of Sociology*, vol. 13, no. 2, June 1962, pp. 107f., and 'A Chinese Phase in Social Anthropology', *id.*, vol. 14, no. 1, March 1963, p. 12. I recall from my last conversation with Radcliffe-Brown, a few months before he died in 1955, that the Chinese problem sketched in his Huxley Memorial Lecture was still lively in his mind.

students at the University of Paris hoping to be *agrégés* in the faculties of sciences and letters.[12] Granet became a Durkheimian before he ever dreamt of China. He was *agrégé* in history in the competition of 1907,[13] and in August of that year was appointed to teach history in the Lycée at Bastia.[14] But he was to return to Paris after one academic

[12] For information on Durkheim I have relied heavily (as everyone must now do, and gratefully) upon Steven Lukes, *Émile Durkheim, His Life and Work, A Historical and Critical Study,* Allen Lane, The Penguin Press, London, 1973. For the facts now being invoked, see especially pp. 379, 619.

[13] For details see chap. V. Langlois, 'Agrégation d'Histoire et de Géographie, concours de 1907', *Revue Universitaire,* vol. 16, pt. 2, no. 9, 15 Nov. 1907.

[14] I have checked the details of Granet's career in his personal file in the Archives Nationales in Paris. The only published account of his life in French, as far as I can discover, is in Edouard Mestre, 'Marcel Granet (1884–1940)', *Annuaire 1940–1941 et 1941–1942. Ecole Pratique des Hautes Etudes, Section des Sciences religieuses,* Imprimerie Administrative, Melun, 1941. Dying under the German tyranny, Granet was deprived of the usual crop of obituaries, but doubtless various sinological jealousies had something to do with the silence— at least, that is a view held by some in France. After the War a brief obituary was published in the *Année Sociologique,* 3rd series, 1940–48, vol. 1, and two appreciations of his work, the Preface by Louis Gernet and the Introduction by R.-A. Stein, in Granet's collected papers, *Etudes sociologiques sur la Chine,* 1953. On 5 December 1955 a set of memorial addresses was given in Paris (I have copies of those by Mme N. Vandier-Nicolas and Henri Lévy-Bruhl, which I have read with profit) but they have not appeared in print. Hitherto, the only comprehensive account in English has been Marion J. Levy, Jr.'s 'Granet, Marcel', in *International Encyclopedia of the Social Sciences,* vol. 6, ed. David L. Sills, Macmillan and Free Press, Chicago, 1968, but it is chiefly an appreciation of Granet's work and is weak biographically. The fullest survey of Granet's intellectual career is in fact Yang K'un's 'An Introduction to Granet's Researches', in Chinese, *Peking University School of French Studies, Social Science Quarterly,* Peking, 1943; it has been of very great service to me in my work on Granet, and I have to thank Dr. Hugh Baker for help with it. And see Yang K'un, 'Marcel Granet: An Appreciation', *The Yenching Journal of Social Studies,* Peking, vol. 1, no. 2, Jan. 1939. The same issue of that journal contains Witold Jablonski, 'Marcel Granet and his Work'. Yang K'un and Jablonski are important witnesses to Granet's teaching. On the latter see P. Demiéville, 'W-A. Jablonski (1901–1957)', *T'oung Pao,* vol. 45, nos. 4–5, 1957. Yang was much closer to his master in combining sinological and ethnological interests, but I do not yet know much about him beyond the two papers cited above. A list of 9 of his papers in Chinese, dating from 1932 to 1943, appears at pp. 519f. of Ping-yuen Yu, *Chinese History, Index to Learned Articles, Volume II. Based on Collections in American and European Libraries,* Harvard-Yenching Library Bibliographical Series I, Harvard University, Cambridge, Mass., 1970. One of the articles listed there is a further piece on Granet (1942), but I have not yet seen it. And cf. Yang K'un, 'An Introduction . . .', pp. 23f. G. William Skinner, ed., *Modern Chinese Society, An Analytical Bibliography, 1. Publications in Western*

year, being admitted to the Fondation Thiers in 1908. Having been a member of one elite establishment, the Ecole Normale, he now entered another. In the following year he was joined there by Marc Bloch and Georges Davy.

When exactly he conceived the idea of turning himself into a student of China I cannot discover; but the general circumstances are known, and it is likely that the event they surround took place at the very beginning of his career at the Fondation Thiers. As a student there he started out with an interest in feudalism; it is said that he planned to write a study of the notion of honour in the feudal period. The story goes that Lucien Herr, the Librarian of the Ecole Normale (a man who as a scholar and a socialist exerted enormous influence upon generations of *normaliens*),[15] advised him, when he thought of widening his researches to take in the Japanese case, to seek the advice of Chavannes, then apparently the nearest he could get in Paris to an expert on Japan. Chavannes counselled him to begin with Chinese as the necessary first step towards Japanese studies, but (as one version of the oral tradition has it) warned him that he would probably get entangled in Chinese, never to reach Japanese. If that part of the story is true, then Chavannes saw justly that means would become end. Perhaps, too, by the power he exercised over his new pupil, he in effect willed that conversion, for although Granet eventually registered to learn Chinese at the Ecole des Langues orientales vivantes,[16] he was in fact supervised by Chavannes.[17]

During his three years as *pensionnaire* pursuing his researches at the Fondation Thiers we are able to watch the evolution of his interests. In the first Director's report on his work, Granet is shown as a student of European feudal institutions moving towards the study of the Far East. In the third and last such report, Granet stands fully committed to China.

1909: 'M. Granet has undertaken to study as historian and jurist the law of persons in feudal society. He has devoted this first year to the study of texts on French feudalism ... At the same time, working under

---

Languages 1644–1972, Stanford University Press, Stanford, Calif., 1973, p. 418, gives Yang's year of birth as 1901 and lists his doctoral dissertation, 1934, at the Université de Lyon, on the ancestor cult in its relation to ritual succession and inheritance.

[15] Cf. Charles Andler, *Vie de Lucien Herr (1864–1926)*, Rieder, Paris, 1932.

[16] Where the language was taught by Arnold Vissière.

[17] Jablonski, *op. cit.*, p. 242, asserts: 'To Durkheim Granet is indebted for his interest in feudal China ...' But in its context the statement is ambiguous, for it may mean either that Granet was led by Durkheimianism to the study of feudal China or that Durkheim himself steered him in that direction. If the latter, then I think the evidence, such as it is, is contrary. But I suspect that Jablonski intended the former meaning. Had Durkheim recommended Granet to study an exotic society, it would have been more likely to be Japan

M. Chavannes's direction and at the Ecole des langues orientales, he is preparing himself to tackle texts dealing with the Far East. He sees that from now on his task will be to show the feudal lord at home and at his suzerain's court, in the latter setting merged in a group of peers, in the former, head of a group of vassals. A double set of social obligations flows from this partly double life; and when these obligations conflict, the sentiment of honour then intervenes, in order to cut through the difficulties. That is the theme for which M. Granet will seek illustrations, first in ethnographic sources, then in the literature on the Far East.'[18]

In his second year, 1910, Granet has reached the Chinese family (i.e. kinship) as a problem: 'He is seeking his field of observation not only in France but in Japan and China ... He is slowly unravelling how and to what extent the feudal group has taken the place of the family; in what way the form of the family in a given civilization explains the form taken by feudalism within it; finally, what conflicts of obligation spring from the co-existence of two institutions both aiming at the same end: mutual protection.—From that collection of inquiries M. Granet has separated off a part which is more complete than the rest in order to make it the subject of a special study: that which deals with the organization of the Chinese family.'[19]

1911: 'M. Granet, setting out with the idea of studying the law of persons in feudal society, and realizing the need to extend his observations to Japan and China, has more and more circumscribed his subject, as was fitting, and, finally, intends to present a study of the Chinese family. In this connexion he has found special texts in many collections containing the formulae of rites which have remained the basis of Chinese society. Such rituals offer the interest that they inform us on the religious aspect of phenomena, which aspect constitutes its inmost nature. By means of these rituals M. Granet is studying the Chinese family chiefly through mourning regulations; for the dead of a family are at least as real and important members of it as the living; and the fact of being bound by such observances on the occasion of the death of such persons is precisely what indicates kinship and its degree. The family is a mystical consubstantiality of the dead and the living. The essential elements of its constitution are linked to that principle. Kinsmen are people who participate in the same sacra. The pivot of the family is the senior branch, heir to the cult; people are kin to the extent that they are close to one another in the cult ceremonies, etc. Two particularly important texts, one dealing with mourning and

[18] *Annuaire de la Fondation Thiers 1910*, n.s., Imprimerie Gaignault, Issoudun, 1910, p. 14.

[19] *Annuaire de la Fondation Thiers 1911*, n.s. Imprimerie Gaignault, Issoudun, 1911, pp. 9f.

the other with marriage, have seemed to M. Granet worth translating. He intends the translation of the latter to be his *thèse complémentaire*. M. Granet's work, intelligently conducted, has aroused the lively interest of specialists; and leaving the Fondation Thiers, M. Granet has been given a scholarship to go to China . . .'[20]

These reports bear witness to decisive moments of Granet's development as a scholar. In his three years at the Fondation Thiers he put Durkheimian sociology to work in the analysis of ancient Chinese society and fastened upon the family and ritual as, for him, the central problems to be tackled. In the Editorial Notes to this translation I have marked a number of passages for which the Durkheimian inspiration can be documented, and there is no need to labour the point that all his life Granet looked back to Durkheim and Chavannes as joint and equal masters. To them he dedicated *Fêtes et chansons*, 1919. The persistence through his work on China of the themes of ritual and the family is a more remarkable fact. By 'ritual' we must understand 'ritual and myth', and by 'family', 'kinship and marriage'. In talking to his pupils in the 'thirties (and perhaps in earlier years, but for the 'twenties I lack the evidence), Granet seems to have divided his teaching into the *mythique* and the *juridique* (meaning by the latter chiefly the rights and duties of kinship and marriage), and was disappointed when, as appears generally to have been the case, he could not hold their interest equally in both: the kinship often bored those who were entranced by the myth and the ritual. They were no doubt especially adrift in the complexities of the arguments we can now read in *Catégories matrimoniales*, 1939, not having been prepared for them by a clear statement of the underlying sociological principles and their intellectual origins. In a sense, as I think the book now translated illustrates, religion for Granet was at the intersection of the *mythique* and the *juridique*. But by not making his sociology sufficiently explicit in his teaching, he failed to pass on that special vision to his pupils . . . But I must not move too far out of my chronological account.

The scholarship (*mission*) referred to in the Director's last report on Granet as a *pensionnaire* at the Fondation Thiers was a government grant for study in China; and Chavannes had procured it. French political and academic interest in China was high. Granet installed himself in Peking to spend under two years there in 1911–13. The point of his going to China was not to study Chinese life as it was lived, as one might imagine if one were not aware of his background; it was, certainly, to get some idea of what the country was like; but the overriding aim was to study the Chinese classical texts in the setting where Chinese studied them, a sort of field work (as we might now say)

[20] *Annuaire de la Fondation Thiers 1912*, n.s., Imprimerie Gaignault, Issoudun, 1912, pp. 7f.

upon scholarship. In Peking he came to know André d'Hormon, a Frenchman who had been established there for some five years and upon whose knowledge of Chinese and Chinese scholars he appears to have been able freely to call.[21] Mestre, who as Granet's pupil and colleague in Paris had a thorough acquaintance with his work, writes of the Peking years that Granet then put himself to school with the Chinese literati less in order to gain enlightenment from them than to train himself further in the art Chavannes had already taught him of making use of the learned commentaries on the texts—to confront texts and their interpretations. 'Il sonde le commentateur; il note, par exemple, le "parti pris de symbolisme où les lettrés se sentent tenus comme par une obligation professionnelle"; il s'empare de ce qu'il leur arrive de dire malgré eux, des enseignements sur l'histoire ou les moeurs qui leur servent à justifier leurs interprétations. Il prépare ainsi ses premiers travaux, ceux où il utilise principalement les chansons de l'amour du Livre des Vers . . .'[22] When Chavannes wrote to Granet after a long silence to demand some account of his work at the public expense, he received a paper that so surprised and impressed him that he sent it off for publication in the *T'oung Pao*: it was Granet's first sinological publication,[23] 'Coutumes matrimoniales de la Chine antique', 1912; it

[21] He was born in 1881. Making only a couple of short visits to France (the first of them in 1919-20, when he was present at Granet's defence of his doctoral theses), d'Hormon spent 48 years in China, returning finally to France in 1955, when he took up residence in the Abbaye de Royaumont with the part of his library he had been allowed to bring out of China. He died in 1965 in his eighty-fourth year. He was a man of great literary distinction, with a very deep knowledge of Chinese. He and Granet kept in touch; they held each other in high esteem. I suspect, but I cannot decisively establish, that d'Hormon played a crucial role in Granet's studies in Peking. Unfortunately, d'Hormon surrounded himself by a screen which is very difficult to penetrate. Little has been written on him, but see Paul Demiéville, 'Aperçu historique des études sinologiques en France', in Demiéville, *Choix d'études sinologiques (1921–1970)*, Brill, Leiden, 1973, pp. 471f. The paper was originally published in *Acta Asiatica*, vol. 11, Tokyo, 1966.

[22] Mestre, *op. cit.*, pp. 39f. But it is to be noted that the very method that in Peking brought him close to Chinese scholarship (and probably through d'Hormon) was, after his stay in China, to alienate him from Chinese scholars, except for the very few who became his pupils in Paris. Cf. Yang K'un, 'Marcel Granet: An Appreciation', *op. cit.*, p. 227: 'Unfortunately, Granet has no personal connection with our Chinese scholars. His method of work differs entirely from that of Chinese sinologues of the old type and the new.' For a not unexpectedly sharp reaction from an unsympathetic Chinese scholar see V. K. Ting, 'Professor Granet's "La Civilisation Chinoise"', *The Chinese Social and Political Science Review*, vol. 15, no. 2, July 1931.

[23] The first work he ever printed was a socialist pamphlet, *Contre l'Alcoolisme, Un programme socialiste*, 1911.

contained the core of the argument later worked up into *Fêtes et chansons*, 1919. Since the last work Granet himself published was entitled *Catégories matrimoniales*, 1939, one is forced by the parallelism to realize the *juridique* framework within which he organized his labours.

Unhappily, very little has survived of Granet's correspondence, but there still exists a copy of a long letter he wrote to friends from Peking, dated 5–8 March 1912, in which he gives an account of his experiences during the troubles of the Chinese Revolution. He describes the evacuation of his hotel when it was threatened: 'We pack up: the 24 historians, in their frail cases, decorated with green characters, make a shaky structure. The Année sociologique is in my hand bag. I stuff my suitcases.'[24] The books he saved may symbolize to us—I suppose he meant them to symbolize to his friends—the twin objects of his intellectual contemplation: Chinese texts (he means the Twenty-Four Dynastic Histories, impedimenta of formidable bulk) and his run of the *Année Sociologique* from which he appears never to have been parted. The latter was for him a kind of encyclopaedia and source-book which he constantly studied and marked. The numerous markings in the set still in his study at Sceaux (and which is almost certainly the very same set he had with him in Peking) have enabled me to pick out the passages and themes that especially caught his attention. That evidence is a simple confirmation of what we already know: kinship and ritual (but widening into general religious topics) preoccupied him.[25]

About Granet as an observer of China there are, among social scientists at the present day, two symmetrically opposite myths. One, which I have myself heard in the United States, has it that Granet never was in China to observe it. One may see how a hurried reading of his work might lead to that mistaken conclusion. The other myth casts Granet in the mould of the modern field worker. Poirier, in a history of

[24] The letter was addressed to René and Lucienne Gosse. A typescript copy was made available to me by Mme Granet.

[25] Cf. Yang, *op. cit.*, p. 230: 'When I saw Professor Granet in his home for the first time, on November 14, 1928, he advised me to read *L'Année Sociologique*. He told me that the section on general sociology did not deserve much attention because of its philosophical tendency; but he recommended that I read well the section on religious sociology, saying that he read it often and found some things that were highly significant.' It will be seen that Granet's close interest in kinship does not emerge from this anecdote—nor from the article as a whole. The passage proceeds: 'Then, talking to me about Mauss, he insisted on my taking his lectures and on my reading his entire works, and reading them several times . . . he advised me to give at least two months to each of two articles by Mauss: "*Les Variations Saisonnières des Sociétés Eskimos*" and "*Essai sur le Don*".' But to a European student his first recommendation for non-sinological reading was Westermarck on Moroccan marriage!

ethnological thought, contrasts among the great French founders of the subject in modern times, those (such as Durkheim, Lévy-Bruhl, and Mauss) who gazed at the world from their armchairs, with those who worked out their theories upon the basis of their experience in the field—he lists Granet, Griaule, and Leenhardt.[26] The truth, of course, is that while Granet was a sensitive observer of what lay about him in China, and at a poignant moment in its history,[27] he was no more conventionally 'in the field' in Peking than a Chinese scholar could be said to be who spends a couple of years in Paris studying French literature or history—or perhaps, studying French scholars studying French literature or history. In any case, whatever the weight we give to Granet's firsthand experience of China, I do not think we should err in saying that what he made of that country rested almost entirely upon what he had decided about it before he ever left France.

Upon his return to Paris in March 1913 he resumed his career as schoolmaster by being appointed to teach history in the Lycée de Marseille and then in October at the Lycée de Montpellier. But in December of that year he moved up the academic ladder to become 'Directeur d'études pour les religions d'Extrême-Orient' at the Ecole Pratique des Hautes Etudes, replacing his teacher Chavannes who had resigned that post. The first lecture he gave at the Ecole Pratique (a sort of inaugural lecture) was published as 'Programme d'études sur l'ancienne religion chinoise', 1914; it was a manifesto; but in fact he did not give the course he had advertised ('d'une part d'exposer les *Rites de l'eau*, d'autre part d'expliquer le chapitre *Le mariage des nobles* du YI-LI') because the only student who, by virtue of his knowledge of the language, was capable of taking an active part in the course left for China.[28]

'Programme d'études . . .' was intended to inaugurate his career as a teacher of Chinese civilization, and indeed it lays down some of the basic principles of method by which all his work was to be guided. In order to understand the Far East, one must study China, the country which provided the whole region with its civilization. In order to study traditional Chinese institutions, it is useful to study them as far back as possible in the past. And the three approaches proposed in this first

[26] Jean Poirier, 'Histoire de la pensée ethnologique', pp. 126f. in Poirier, ed., *Ethnologie générale*, Encyclopédie de la Pléiade, NRF, Paris, 1968; and see in the same volume the same author's 'Ethnologie juridique', p. 1120.

[27] That moment is also caught in the very finely constructed novel, first published in 1922, by Victor Segalen, *René Leys*, N.R.F., Gallimard, Paris, 1971. On Segalen, see Henry Bouillier, *Victor Segalen*, Mercure de France, Paris, 1961; but the interrelations among the French writers and scholars in Peking at the time have yet to be worked out. There appears to have been a connexion between Segalen and d'Hormon.

[28] *Annuaire* of the *Ecole Pratique des Hautes Etudes* [1914–1915] Paris, 1914, pp. 61, 81f.

statement of aims involve, first, an examination of the ancient dictionary *Shuo Wen*; second, the study of the chapter in the *I Li* on the marriage of nobles; and third, an analysis of the texts, of different times, relating to the rites connected with water and rain and the customs bearing on them. In short, the method rests upon textual and linguistic analysis coupled with a sociological penetration into the ancient popular religion lying behind the official religion for which the texts themselves officially speak. The ethnographic element in the method is, however, more apparent in this early formulation than it was later to be: 'Since we seek to reconstruct ancient popular beliefs, the data from modern folklore will often be of use to us. Sometimes a recent Chinese text, at other times the researches of a foreign observer will come to our aid. The observations carried out on indigenous peoples, the populations of the Chinese South and West, will above all be very useful to us, because these peoples in their slower development have better preserved the popular customs common to the whole area of Far Eastern civilization.'[29]

Because his eyesight was bad, Granet had not done military service, but in December 1914 he was called up, to begin a military career of some distinction and which led him circuitously back to China. Serving in the infantry he was twice wounded, three times mentioned in despatches, and awarded the Croix de Guerre. In the autumn of 1917 he was pulled out of the front (his regiment was in the Verdun sector) and posted to an officers' training camp—where he failed, possibly by design; he was apparently content to remain a sergeant. He himself never heard the story, which if accurate throws some light on the social workings of the Durkheim school, that his removal from the fighting was due to an intervention made by Lévy-Bruhl, then in the office of the Minister of Munitions, Albert Thomas. During all the bloody years he fought on the Western Front, Granet pursued his Chinese studies and researches, using every leave of absence to bring his two doctoral theses to completion. It is awesome evidence of his devotion to his calling. His two theses were in fact ready by the time he left France unexpectedly in 1918.

In September of that year he was astonished to find himself posted to General Jeannin's staff in Siberia—his standing as an orientalist must have had something to do with the posting, but, as we shall see, he could make no use of his Chinese in his new theatre of war. He made his way to Vladivostok (and thence to Irkutsk) across the United States and the Pacific. He found himself attached as an instructor to one of the Czech contingents and appears to have written a military manual for them. He was demobilized in Siberia and moved down into China, where he spent two or three months living with d'Hormon in Peking while he awaited a boat back to Europe. That was his second and last visit to

[29] *Op. cit.*, pp. 237ff.

China; another was later planned for the time when his son would have finished his school education, but the Sino-Japanese war apparently prevented it. [30]

Soon after his return to France, June 1919, he married and resumed his academic life. He was examined for his doctorate in January 1920. Hearing that Sir James Frazer was in France, he procured his appointment to the 'jury' of examiners; but an eye-witness of the event reports that, nervous of speaking French, Frazer said not a word.

La religion des Chinois, 1922, falls in the period when Granet was harvesting some ten years of sinological work. *Fêtes et chansons* was published in 1919 and its complement (as a thesis and intellectually, *juridique* balancing *mythique*) *La polygynie sororale et le sororat dans la Chine féodale* in 1920. In fact, the bulk of the papers reprinted in *Etudes sociologiques sur la Chine* belong to those years: 'Quelques particularités de la langue et de la pensée chinoises', 1920; 'Le dépôt de l'enfant sur le sol', 1922 (but written in 1920); 'La vie et la mort, Croyances et doctrines de l'antiquité chinoise', 1920–21; and 'Le langage de la douleur d'après le rituel funéraire de la Chine classique', 1922. His courses at the Ecole Pratique resumed in 1919–20 with lectures on ancient Chinese practices connected with birth, childhood, and

---

[30] In a letter to his future wife, dated 27 December 1918 from Irkutsk, Granet wrote wryly: 'Sous prétexte de chinois, on m'a envoyé, je crois, en Sibérie pour me punir de ne point savoir le russe et, pour me l'apprendre, on me mit avec des Tchèques: ils parlent, après tout, une langue slave. Car je suis instructeur d'un groupement tchécoslovaque . . .' (From a photocopy of the letter supplied to me by Mme Granet.) A later letter from Irkutsk, 26 January 1919, may be quoted to show that there was at least one moment in his career when Granet had second thoughts about his vocation: 'Je m'ennuie effroyablement et fais un peu de chinois, pour me consoler. Mais l'érudition est une chose qui me paraît de piètre intérêt et j'ai le grand projet de lâcher Paris et d'aller faire de l'enseignement secondaire en province . . . Quand j'aurai des enfants, j'en veux faire des paysans et des braconniers, des hommes libres. (Si ce sont des filles, ma foi, je ne sais pas trop ce que j'en ferai.)' (From a copy of the letter given to me by Mme Granet.) Granet was born into a professional family; his father was an engineer, his grandfather a landowner; he knew the countryside of southern France. The hint of romanticism about peasants is echoed, I think, in *La religion des Chinois*. Cf. note 69 below.

After his return from China in 1919, Granet hardly ever went abroad; he seems to have had little taste for travel. He made two brief trips, to Frankfurt and Cambridge, and a longer one, in 1936, to Oslo when he delivered the series of lectures that were to be published posthumously as *La féodalité chinoise*, 1952. The visit to Cambridge was made in 1937; Granet delivered the Jane Harrison Memorial Lecture for that year, on the subject 'La bataille des cadeaux dans les usages chinois' (of which no copy has survived, it would seem), and was a guest of Newnham College. I thank the Principal of Newnham College, Mrs. Jean Floud, for finding the information for me on the Cambridge visit.

majority, and classes on the *I Li* texts dealing with majority. It was a pattern of instruction he was to pursue at the Ecole Pratique until he died. In the first few years of the 1920s his theme was mourning, but supplemented in 1923–24 by marriage rites. In 1924–25 and 1925–26 he turned to kinship and marriage in the *I Li*, in 1926–27 to the *Chuang Tzu* and an ancient calendar, in 1927–28 to the *Huai Nan Tzu* and the calendar; while in the decade 1928–29 to 1938–39 he treated various themes in Taoism in both lectures and *explications de textes*. In his last year, 1939–40, he gave a series of lectures on the K'un Lun 'mountain' in the *Shan Hai Ching*, and for his *explication de textes* took two T'ang sources on the Feast of Lanterns.[31]

His teaching at the Ecole Pratique was the most severely sinological part of his career as an academic, and addressed to very small numbers of advanced students. But in 1920 he began also to teach at a somewhat lower level when he was appointed to deliver a course on the history of Chinese civilization at the Sorbonne, which he continued until 1925–26. In 1926 he was elected to the chair of Geography, History, and Institutions of the Far East at the Ecole Nationale des Langues orientales vivantes,[32] which was from then on the major theatre of his less technical teaching. In the same year he was appointed Director (Administrateur) of the newly created Institut des Hautes Etudes chinoises. He was very active.[33]

[31] See the *Annuaires* of the *Ecole Pratique des Hautes Etudes, Section des Sciences religieuses*, for the years *1920–1921* and *1921–1922*, Paris, 1920 and 1921, and for the years *1922–1923* to *1940–1941 et 1941–1942*, Melun, 1922 to 1941.

[32] In the curriculum vitae Granet submitted as a candidate for this chair (among the papers in his personal file in the Archives Nationales) he mentions as being in preparation a book entitled *La Chine et l'Asie centrale* to appear as vol. 35 in the series 'L'Evolution de l'humanité', the collection edited by Henri Berr. In fact, that 'volume' in the end proved to be *La civilisation chinoise*, 1929, and *La pensée chinoise*, 1934, and one is led to wonder about an unrealized book which, to go by the title, seems to point to a more conventionally historical approach than Granet adopted in his major publications.

[33] Granet's courses in the Sorbonne 1920–21 to 1925–26 followed the same pattern as those at the Ecole Pratique. In 1922–23, for example, under the general title of Chinese Civilization, he lectured on the Chinese family and analysed texts relating to the ancestor cult. And again, from 1926–27 his instruction at the Institut des Hautes Etudes chinoises took the same form: in 1929–30 his course on Chinese Civilization there was divided into three parts—1. lectures on 'Le système du monde dans les croyances chinoises'; 2. the study of texts taken from the mystical philosophers and poets; 3. exercises in translation. While the teaching at the Ecole Pratique was intended to stimulate advanced work, that at the Sorbonne and the Institut was primarily for students presenting themselves for certificates and diplomas in Chinese studies. At the Ecole des Langues orientales, on the other hand, the emphasis was different. Here, in 1929–30 for

In this spare account of his academic life little emerges on Granet as sociologist. The students whom he taught were not destined for sociological careers, and even those with general ethnological interests were few in number. One of these last was Yang K'un, who busied himself not only with the small circle about Granet but also with the much larger one around Mauss. The two outstanding members of the ethnological world who studied under Granet were Georges Dumézil and André Leroi-Gourhan.[34] But, of course, there was another side to Granet's academic life in a broader sense. He numbered Mauss among his intimates and moved within the band of social scientists tracing their ancestry to Durkheim, his own teacher. He was a regular attender at sociological meetings and for a time in the 'thirties was President and Vice-President of the Institut Français de Sociologie. Yet little of this active sociological life is reflected in his writings, except in so far as it informs his interpretations of China. In fact, I have been able to find only three publications (short reviews and the early socialist pamphlet on the drink problem apart) on other than sinological matters. The first belongs to the same year, 1922, in which he published *La religion des Chinois*. Entitled 'Le droit et la famille', it is a review article dealing with Fauconnet's *La responsabilité*, Davy's *La foi jurée*, and the fifth edition of Westermarck's *The History of Human Marriage*. Had the piece been anonymous, one might have supposed it to be the work of a well-informed and keen-minded Durkheimian launched upon a

example, he lectured to the first-year students on the history of China, and to those in the second and third years on 'le rôle de la Chine contemporaine dans l'économie et la politique générales'. The courses referred to in this note are listed in *Livret de l'étudiant, Année scolaire 1922–1923, l'Université de Paris et les établissements parisiens d'enseignement supérieur*, Bureau de Renseignements à la Sorbonne, Paris, and the corresponding issue for 1929–30, when the Presses Universitaires de France, Paris, are given as the publishers.

[34] The testimony they give of Granet's powerful intellectual influence upon them may be exemplified by what the first has written about it. Dumézil describes how, having come to a point in his studies of Indo-European mythology at which he felt the need to take a fresh turn, he hurriedly learnt some Chinese in order, in 1934, to join Granet's small class at the Ecole Pratique. (His fellow-students there were Mme Vandier-Nicolas, Kaltenmark, and Stein; one could hardly imagine a more gifted collection of four students!) '. . . pendant trois ans . . . j'ai écouté, regardé ce grand esprit extraire, avec autant de délicatesse et de respect que d'énergie, la substance conceptuelle de textes au premier abord insignifiants, voire insipides.' And in the spring of 1938, of a sudden, Dumézil's new work on comparative mythology took shape. Georges Dumézil, *Mythe et épopée**. *L'idéologie des trois fonctions dans les épopées des peuples indo-européens*, Gallimard, Paris, 1968, pp. 13f. Dumézil has given a fuller account of his acquaintance with Granet—and furnished a document of capital importance to students of Granet's work—in a preface, written in 1969, for the Italian translation of *Danses et légendes*, which has not yet appeared.

conventional sociological career. In fact, this was the only time Granet
published a review of any length of a non-sinological work—and even
his notices of books on the Far East were astonishingly few and terse.
He did not like reviewing. Besides, we may suspect that he was determined to concentrate his energies upon the accomplishment of the plan
he had worked out for himself early in his life.

The second non-sinological paper was one he contributed to a symposium on Durkheim's sociological work; it was published in 1930.
'La sociologie religieuse de Durkheim' is of course less important to us
here for the adequacy of the appraisal it makes than for the evidence it
affords on Granet's reading of Durkheim. I shall look at it from that
point of view. Early on it contrasts the principles of the Durkheimian
sociology of religion with the postulates of the 'religious psychology'
at work among anthropologists and historians of religion. The latter are
concerned with biographical accounts or with explanations resting upon
either 'psychologie courante' or 'théories élaborées à partir de la simple
réflexion psychologique: ces historiens de métier ne semblent point
avoir l'idée qu'à chaque société correspond une psychologie inconnue
que le savant doit d'abord découvrir et expliquer.' As for the anthropologists, for all their evolutionary ideas, they lack a sense of history
and development. The sociological analysis of religion must enrich
psychological knowledge by imbuing it with the idea that it is social
life itself which has always been a great creative agent of rules of behaviour, sentiments, ideas, and psychological realities.[35] Those Durkheimian postulates are, of course, the very foundation of Granet's work
on Chinese religion: 'society' must be put in the forefront; it must be
shown at work through time (although this is arguably more Granetian
than Durkheimian); the ideas of a foreign society are to be patiently and
meticulously analysed from within and not smothered and blurred in
the rubrics derived from a general psychology (that is, a set of assump-
tions about man at large in fact based upon our understanding of
ourselves).

Granet turns to the question of delimiting religion, underlining
Durkheim's refusal of conventional definitions and his recourse to the
'sacred', and discusses the significance of the fact that in *Les formes
élémentaires de la vie religieuse* Durkheim was concerned with one body
of data, relying upon a complete and critical evaluation of them. That
analytical study of the sources led him to make real discoveries, as for
example when he maintained, against Frazer, that the Arunta did not
in fact represent the most primitive form of Australian culture.[36] It
is as though Granet were invoking Durkheim to validate the patient
amassing and analysis of Chinese texts, and suggesting that things can
be said on the basis of them that nobody has said before.

[35] *Op. cit.*, p. 288.   [36] *Ibid.*, p. 289.

Against the theories of animism and naturism Durkheim proved, first, that the worship of the dead, so far from being primitive, appears only in developed societies, and second, that the great forces of nature are divinized only late on.[37] We shall see in Granet's account of Chinese religion that the ancestor cult comes late, the ancestors, along with other supernatural entities, having emerged from an undifferentiated mass associated with the Holy Places of the earliest peasant society.

The radical opposition of sacred and profane has its origins in the contrast between two states of social life. 'La vie profane correspond à des moments où l'activité sociale est ralentie, les hommes vivant dispersés; les périodes de congrégation sont, au contraire, le moment d'une activité intense, fructueuse, réconfortante, pendant laquelle la conscience individuelle s'exalte et, pour ainsi dire, se surpasse.' Religious ideas take their strength and their reality from the fact that they express the highest hopes conceived by a group of men when, in order to recreate their social bonds, they put out their greatest effort.[38] The world of Durkheim's Australia and that of *Fêtes et chansons* are one.

Durkheim showed that mankind will never be able to do without festivals and assemblies in which the individuals brought together reaffirm in common their common sentiments. And since religion is a social reality, the study of religious symbols, far from being a learned pastime, is a scientific study essential for comprehending mankind. Durkheim could make us see how the sociology of religion allows us to understand the formation of categories of thought: categories of force, time, space, and so on, and above all, of totality.[39] La pensée chinoise.

I do not mean to imply by this little exercise that Granet was nothing more than a slavish follower of his sociological master, any more than he was of his other master, Chavannes. He could at times be un-Durkheimian, as when he refused to heed the master's strictures on the theory of group marriage. But there was a basic trust in the Durkheimian inspiration and loyalty to Durkheim's ideas that prevented any radical departure and inhibited criticism. This last point is best illustrated by the manner in which Granet handled the work by Durkheim and Mauss on primitive classification. In his splendid translation and edition of that essay, Needham, in drawing our attention to the shortcomings (to put it no stronger) of the use made by Durkheim and Mauss of their sources on China and the faultiness of their reasoning, understandably writes: 'It is a remarkable puzzle that Granet not only does not go into this matter, but even writes that Durkheim and Mauss's few pages on China "mark a date in the history of Chinese studies" . . .'[40] I think

[37] *Ibid.*, p. 290.   [38] *Ibid., loc. cit.*   [39] *Ibid.*, pp. 291f.
[40] Rodney Needham, trans. and ed., Emile Durkheim and Marcel Mauss, *Primitive Classification*, Cohen and West, London, 1963, especially pp. xxif. The quotation from Granet is from *La pensée chinoise*, 1934, p. 29, fn. 1.

it is pretty clear that Granet was not very interested in the source upon which his mentors were mainly relying: J. J. M. de Groot's *The Religious System of China*,[41] towards which he maintained a somewhat disdainful air even as he took from it (and from De Groot's *Les fêtes annuellement célébrées à Emoui*)[42] bits of ethnography relating to modern China. Granet's sources were the Chinese texts. He obviously wanted to pay respect to the Durkheimian inspiration without bothering with the particular argument on China advanced by men whom he more than admired. The remark quoted by Needham falls in a long footnote which Granet opens with a coquettish denial that he knows anything about sociological theory or theories (and that at a time when he was closely connected with the Institut Français de Sociologie). Then, in the context of a rhetorical question asserting the first job of sociologists to be the discovery of facts, he suggests the possibility that he himself has pointed to some facts hitherto overlooked. The basis for their discovery is to be found in the study by Durkheim and Mauss on primitive classification. He concludes the note with a tribute to his teacher: if he has carried out the analysis of Chinese categories to arrive at a correct interpretation on the basis of the Chinese data, his best reason for thinking the analysis to be correct is that it brings out 'la prééminence de la catégorie de totalité' upon which Durkheim insisted in *Les formes élémentaires*. The tribute is to a basic sociological postulate (whether we agree with it is another question) and its fruitfulness for his own work.[43]

[41] Brill, Leiden, 1892–1910.

[42] The French translation by C. G. Chavannes (not to be confused with E. Chavannes, Granet's teacher), Annales du Musée Guimet, Paris, 1886, of the Dutch original published in Batavia (Java) and The Hague, 1881–83. Cf. in the Editorial Notes below, note 134, for an example of Granet's use of De Groot's ethnography.

[43] The essay by Durkheim and Mauss is earlier referred to in 'Quelques particularités de la langue et de la pensée chinoises', 1920, p. 149 in *Etudes sociologiques*; in *Fêtes et chansons*, 1919, p. 249, fn. cont., in the context of the emergence of the concepts of *yin* and *yang* within the primitive festivals of China; and in *Danses et légendes*, 1926, p. 615, where Durkheim and Mauss (but the work is not named) are said to have recognized 'par une intuition admirable' the kinship between Chinese and primitive classifications. *Intuition*: admirable choice of word! . . . It is perhaps worth adding that Mauss reverted to the Chinese evidence for the argument of the essay on classification in his review of the fifth volume of De Groot's *The Religious System of China*, 1907, in *Année Sociologique*, 1906–9, vol. 11, 1910, which he concluded, p. 233, with the paragraph: 'On remarquera enfin un texte qui met en relation les "cinq sortes de *ku* (maléfice), les cinq notes de la gamme, et les *noms de clans*". Nous n'osions pas espérer jamais trouver pareille corrélation entre l'ancienne organisation des clans et le système de classification que nous avions étudié. Il est vrai que le texte est de l'époque des Ming, par conséquent tardif, et que l'arithmétique

The third of Granet's main non-sinological writings is the record of his intervention in a long debate on the teaching of sociology held at the beginning of the 'thirties in several meetings of the Institut Français de Sociologie. The debate began with two statements by Fauconnet.[44] At the meeting held on 18 June 1932 Granet, speaking from the chair, ventured to offer his objections to Fauconnet 'although I am in no way a philosopher and absolutely unqualified to teach Sociology'.[45] He spoke as an historian,[46] placing stress upon the need to avoid merely illustrating the narrow theory put forward by one teacher and upon the necessity of treating sociology as a young and unformed subject. He turned to the different requirements of students in the Facultés and the Ecoles Normales primaires.[47] It seemed to him that the teaching of sociology ought to consist essentially in the treatment of selected problems in order to illustrate the sociological progress already achieved.[48] Were he himself to be teaching the subject he would begin with its history before passing to selected problems, of which he offered as examples suicide and potlatch. It was Durkheim's *Le suicide* and not *Les règles de la méthode sociologique* or *La division du travail social* which had conquered him. The problem of suicide was one of those in which it was easiest to bring home the fact that social phenomena are total phenomena; in the study of it quantitative methods could be

---

mythologique y domine.' Mauss is presumably referring to p. 850 where De Groot translates a Ming text as follows: 'There are families who offer incense and sacrifices (to that vermin) in the same way as they do to their domestic ancestors. It is also called k u. The sickness caused by it the world calls k u disease; this may vary, in connexion with the clan-names [surnames], according to the five musical notes, so that the five varieties of k u are mentioned.' It was not very much to go on.

[44] 'Enseignement de la Sociologie', *Bulletin de l'Institut Français de Sociologie*, ère Année (1930–31), pp. 69–72, and 'L'enseignement de la Sociologie', *Bulletin* . . . , 2e Année, Fasc. 1 (1931), pp. 5–31.

[45] *Bulletin* . . . , 2e Année, Fasc. 3 (1932), p. 99. Granet's speech is at pp. 98–107.

[46] *Op. cit.*, p. 107: 'Voilà mes observations que m'ont inspirées ma faible expérience et mes préjujés d'historien'. And cf. p. 99, where he speaks of 'une éducation et . . . des habitudes d'historien'.

[47] In this context, *ibid.*, p. 102, Granet makes a remark that must set up some resonance in the minds of many of his readers at the present day, although a few may conclude that the situation is now in part reversed: 'Il y a lieu de craindre, à mon avis, que l'ensemble de la Sociologie ne passe pour une tentative de justification d'institutions ou de mœurs qui, pour beaucoup de jeunes esprits, paraissent démodées. L'idée que la Sociologie est "réactionnaire" ou "conservatrice" a été exprimée pour que nous ayons à compter avec une espèce de méfiance sentimentale à laquelle il ne faudrait pas donner l'apparence d'être fondée.'

[48] *Ibid.*, p. 103.

combined with qualitative; and there was a considerable body of literature on it. Parallel arguments were adduced in favour of potlatch, including the fact that the discovery of the phenomenon by sociology had led to its being found in societies in which hitherto it had lain unnoticed.[49] Granet is against encyclopaedism, undue systematization, and dogmatism. Sociology being only in the making, it ought to be taught cautiously and critically. One could not have asked more of someone who actually taught the subject! And yet the speech tells us something by indirection about Granet as a teacher of *sinology*: he must try to take social phenomena as total; he must select problems and work at them in depth; he must at all costs avoid superficial comparison.

There are two major passages in Granet's *œuvre* where we may further study his views on sociological method. The first in time is to be found in *Danses et légendes*, 1926. In the long Introduction to that intricate and difficult book, the full significance of which lies beyond the scope of this essay, Granet sets out to justify a method of analysis which, in essence, consists of two steps: first, the establishment within the corpus of Chinese texts of a group of mythic themes, which, by imposing themselves upon generations of Chinese writers, compels them to set arrangements of the scraps of 'history'; second, a reading of those themes as keys to the development of Chinese history—in this case the emergence of chieftainship and urban life from the ancient segmentary society. 'I should be happy if my work were to lend credit to the idea that the antiquity of Chinese civilization (or civilizations) ought not to be underestimated simply because the literary documents at our disposal were drawn up late. I think, on the contrary, that I have made it apparent that there is a way (despite the defects in the documents and with the help of justified extrapolations) of writing a *developmental history* of Chinese institutions. China knew a purely segmentary organization; it created a monarchical organization of society and a quasi-monarchical organization of the family; intermediate types . . . are to be found in between . . . The establishment of the lordly power proper to a political chieftain and of the lordly power proper to a family head can be studied in China, still better perhaps than in Rome—*studied in developmental terms and in their interconnexions*. After having practised, with the organization based upon clans, a system of alternating total prestations which provided the general mechanism of social life—after having passed through the potlatch system and created chiefdoms—China came to build a feudal system resting upon the principle of exchanges regulated by protocol . . . There was doubtless some profit in disengaging these successive aspects of Chinese civilization. Some people still claim to confine Sociology to "Peoples without history" (thus holding in reserve the argument against it that it can

[49] *Ibid.*, pp. 104–106.

attain only logical classifications or statistical perspectives). Now, only the use of sociological analysis has allowed the discovery of a whole order of facts which, it would seem, illuminate the development of one of the great peoples of history. The method has long since proved its heuristic value, but one still hears talk of "the Dogmas of the Sociological School". Perhaps a workman should express his gratitude when he has made use of an efficient tool and one which he has not himself invented.'[50]

And in that context[51] Granet rejects what he ironically calls 'ethnographic erudition'. The same Durkheimian refusal to engage in indiscriminate comparison,[52] the same Durkheimian insistence upon the close analysis of a body of data under sociological inspiration, and the same preference (less Durkheimian and perhaps more original) for treating society across time[53] characterize his posthumously published lectures on Chinese feudalism.

Durkheim was Granet's master, Mauss, whom he revered, his most intimate academic friend. There is no doubt that with Mauss he argued out over the years many of his sociological ideas. Yet, to go by his writings, he was closer intellectually to the uncle than to the nephew. The model upon which China was worked out—a total China, so to say, however limited chronologically and topically in the event—had been laid down in Granet's understanding of Durkheim's lectures, monographs, and reviews. And the ethnographic direction taken by Mauss's gradual development of his uncle's ideas seems in most respects to have left Granet's Durkheimianism unchanged. Or rather, the form of the Durkheimian doctrine to which he continued to adhere was that which, if we accept Condominas's analysis, belonged to a period of the master's work as yet unaffected by Mauss's validation of ethnographic evidence.[54] It was not that Granet failed in his later years to understand (presumably encouraged by Mauss) the advances made in ethnographic

[50] *Danses et légendes*, 1926, pp. 58f.   [51] *Ibid.*, p. 55.

[52] *La féodalité chinoise*, 1952, p. 16: 'On sait que la comparaison est l'arme de choix des sociologues. On sait encore que ceux-ci, du moins dans l'école française, se refusent à manier cette arme sans précaution. Ils se refusent à diluer l'analyse des faits par des rapprochements tumultueux empruntés aux civilisations les plus disparates, aux âges et aux milieux les plus différents.'   [53] *Ibid.*, pp. 4f.

[54] Georges Condominas, 'Marcel Mauss, père de l'ethnographie française, I, A l'ombre de Durkheim', *Critique*, no. 301, June 1972, pp. 130f. The change in Durkheim's attitude towards data drawn from ethnographic studies had already been noted in Claude Lévi-Strauss, 'Ce que l'ethnologie doit à Durkheim', *Annales de l'Université de Paris*, vol. 30, no. 1, 1960, pp. 47ff. (reprinted in Claude Lévi-Strauss, *Anthropologie Structurale deux*, Plon, Paris, 1973). And on the contrast between uncle and nephew see Lévi-Strauss, 'French Sociology' =chap. 17 in Georges Gurvitch and Wilbert E. Moore, eds., *Twentieth Century Sociology*, The Philosophical Library, New York, 1945, p. 527.

method and the value of the accumulating anthropological evidence; his remarks in *La féodalité chinoise*[55] make that plain. Yet he never reached the point of turning that recognition into a reason for changing his own style of work.

It needs to be noticed that Granet's intensive study of the Durkheimian canon and the *Année Sociologique* in general was largely limited to the earliest works and in any case to the publications appearing before he left for China in 1911. Certainly, he read the later work, but, except for *Les formes élémentaires*, I do not think he read it with that close attention which was in effect the basis of his sociological education.

If we take Lukes's summary of the Maussian extension of Durkheim's work, which seems to me to be substantially just, then Granet emerges as for the main part a sociologist in the earlier vein. Lukes writes that on the whole 'Mauss's theoretical contributions result from putting Durkheimian sociology to work, de-emphasizing its least acceptable features (the latent mysticism of the group, the crowd psychology, the identification of historical origin and analytical simplicity) and demonstrating its considerable explanatory power.'[56] Granet certainly put Durkheimianism to work, but he retained a good deal of the 'least acceptable features' listed parenthetically in the quotation from Lukes, as the book now translated I think illustrates. Yet the Editorial Notes to the translation trace a few of the Maussian inspirations (there are others), and I must not give the impression that I imagine that the relative importance for Granet of Durkheim and Mauss can be precisely stated. The difficulties are obvious.[57]

Granet's total fidelity to textual sociology, the concentration upon the printed text as the prime source, is highlighted by his occasional treatment of data drawn from observations on China made by other scholars. As for his own observations in China, we have already seen that he largely kept them out of his published work, and I suspect that he also excluded them from his teaching. In *Fêtes et chansons*, 1919, he refers quite often to De Groot's *Les fêtes annuellement célébrées à Emoui*, but he is totally sceptical of the value of an analysis (he calls it the folklorist's method) that, as he interprets it, confines itself to the description of facts as they are stated by native informants or expressed

[55] p. 3.
[56] Steven Lukes, 'Mauss, Marcel', in *International Encyclopedia of the Social Sciences*, vol. 10, ed. David L. Sills, Macmillan and Free Press, Chicago, 1968, p. 80.
[57] In 'Marcel Granet: An Appreciation', *op. cit.*, Yang K'un is quite sure that Mauss's 'influence on Granet is deeper and more fruitful than Durkheim's'. But although I greatly respect Yang's opinions, it does not seem to me that the evidence he adduces amounts to more than testimony to the profound admiration Granet had for his friend; and that is quite a different matter.

in the language of a particular school.[58] Some people, he says, starting from facts now to be observed, draw up catalogues. (He refers to Grube and Wieger.) Sometimes they ascribe a positive value to informants' statements: if the latter say that a particular rite is to chase away demons, that is taken as the origin of the custom (De Groot). Or an explanation is sought by recourse to a fashionable theory such as Naturism or Animism: 'il suffit de constater qu'une fête se place aux environs d'un solstice ou d'un équinoxe pour la déclarer tout de suite fête solaire; puis, de la définition donnée, on s'ingénie à déduire toutes ses caractéristiques'[59] (De Groot).

But the striking aspect of Granet's attitude to ethnographic data on the Han population (as distinct from the aboriginal peoples) of China is not, of course, that he rejects the poor method exemplified in De Groot's work; it is that he himself is not driven to a keen and studied analysis of those data by what he takes to be the correct method. No, the riches are in the Chinese texts. One might argue that, given the paucity of the ethnographic data on China available to him at the time he was writing, he made the right decision. But one suspects that the main motive for the decision was the wish not to be distracted from the task he had set himself of wrestling with the texts (and their commentators) to fight his way through to a revelation of their meaning.[60]

His early work contains a number of references to comparative ethnographic data, chiefly on the peoples on the periphery of China. *Fêtes et chansons* has an Appendix (III) of 'Notes ethnographiques'. The data are presented, as one might have suspected, to strengthen the evidential value of his statements about China and not to serve the purpose of comparative sociology.[61] In the later work the comparative references fall away. That fact might be read to testify to a growing

---

[58] *Fêtes et chansons*, 1919, p. 3 (*Festivals and Songs*, p. 3).

[59] *Ibid.*, p. 2 (*Festivals and Songs*, p. 2).

[60] In *Fêtes et chansons*, 1919, p. 5 (*Festivals and Songs*, p. 5), he justifies his concentration upon the ancient evidence by saying that, while in some cases the modern data are better for research into the foundations of a belief, that is not so in the present instance. And he adds, with a turn of phrase one comes to recognize as a feature of his style: 'J'étudierai le passé directement parce qu'il est plus facile à connaître; simple question de fait.'

[61] Note *Fêtes et chansons*, 1919, p. 29 (*Festivals and Songs*, p. 28), where Granet says that in the course of the study he will where necessary use non-Chinese sources, preferably drawn from the folklore of the area of Far Eastern civilization. But alongside that pronouncement it is useful to read his earlier remark, pp. 4f., that when, as in the adduction of a Hakka song, we establish a similarity between contemporary custom and an ancient one, we are not to assume that one is a copy of the other: both came into being in analogous conditions; and he instances a Lolo song (*Festivals and Songs*, p. 4). But cf. his earlier statement in 'Programme des études . . .', 1914, pp. 237f.

Ccp

impatience with anything non-Chinese, but I believe that it may have a different meaning: the non-Chinese ethnography was coming to him from, so to say, a private source, and was being absorbed into his thinking about China. In 1931 Edouard Mestre, formerly his pupil (although older by some months), was appointed to teach with him in the Ecole Pratique as 'maître de conférences pour les religions de l'Indochine'; the post was a new one. While Mestre took part in the ordinary sinological teaching, he also gave courses on various aspects of South-East Asian cultures, not only on religion, and not only on French Indo-China (where he had started life as a customs officer). Granet's academic ties with Mestre were very close. It is clear that when the ideas incorporated finally in *Catégories matrimoniales*, 1939, were being worked out, they were thoroughly discussed not only with Mauss but also Mestre, who would seem to have been the only one of Granet's pupils to show great interest in that side of his work. It is obvious that Mestre was reading the ethnographic literature on both the non-Han peoples of China and on mainland South-East Asia. He must certainly have been responsible for, as I may put it, Granet's continuing ethnographic education. In the year 1936–37 Mestre lectured on the marriage customs of the Kachin and on those of the peoples of northern Indo-China. He spoke on what Leach was later to call the structural implications of matrilateral cross-cousin marriage among the Kachin.[62] The

[62] *Annuaire 1937–1938, Ecole Pratique des Hautes Etudes, Section des Sciences religieuses*, Melun, 1937, pp. 34–37. P. 35: 'La coutume Katchin recommande le mariage avec une cousine, fille d'un oncle maternel; c'est donc, que toute alliance matrimoniale entre deux familles engage, dans quelque mesure, leurs générations futures. Pareille coutume tend à garantir la pérennité des foyers et, par suite, il semble que le mariage (promis d'avance), avec la fille d'un oncle maternel, convienne particulièrement pour le fils dernier-né qui est, chez les Katchin, celui qui succédera au père.' And note Mestre's last course, 1949–50, on marriage alliance among the Kachin, Garo, and Khasi, in which he states that in view of the rudimentary form of the ancestor cult among the Kachin, Granet's speculations on their closed marriage circles were unfounded. 'Le circuit des cinq familles nobles n'est fermé que parce que ce milieu est fermé. Il s'agit en réalité d'une confédération de chefferies unies entre elles par des alliances matrimoniales; le nombre de cinq est purement contingent ou, du moins, il est sans rapport avec un nombre correspondant de générations d'ancêtres.' -*Annuaire 1950–1951* ..., Melun, 1950, pp. 33f. He had independently reached a conclusion forming part of Leach's argument in 'The Structural Implications of Matrilateral Cross-Cousin Marriage', 1951, in Leach, *op. cit.*, especially pp. 84f. Mestre's anthropological importance has not anywhere been dealt with, as far as I can see. He published little. His name of course appears in Granet's work and it is registered in one anthropological classic: Mauss, 'Essai sur le don . . .', *Année Sociologique*, 1923–24, n.s., vol. I, 1925, p. 159, fn. 2, where along with Granet he is thanked for help on the subject of Chinese contracts. And cf. Marcel Mauss, *Oeuvres 3. Cohésion sociale et divisions de la sociologie*, ed. Victor Karady, Editions

next year he lectured on the marriage customs of the Naga.[63] Some at least of the ethnographical reticence shown by Granet in *Catégories matrimoniales* must have been due to his absorbing the benefits of Mestre's researches.[64]

I think it is clear that Granet set out to make what he took to be a total analysis of Chinese society and thought. We cannot possibly say what he would have been able further to achieve had he lived beyond the age of fifty-six, but it is certainly reasonable to assume from what we know of what he did during three intensively lived decades of scholarship that 'totality' would have continued to mean something in effect restricted: restricted in historical time and in range of sources. His work was, in addition, marked by a more purely sociological restriction: the great variety of Chinese civilization has so far as possible to be reduced to a few basic principles of thought and order (as we may judge most clearly from *La pensée chinoise* and the book now translated), such that development over time (however stressed) produces not so much novelty as the gradual unfolding of principles laid down early in history. Those principles, so to say, tend to press down all contingent innovation into a basic pattern. One can understand easily enough that a totalizing simplification of China would be unlikely to commend itself to sinologists for whom the continuous change and creativity of Chinese culture are self-evident. Perhaps that is what lies in part behind Demiéville's interesting summary of Granet's achievement in his 'Aperçu historique des études sinologiques en France', where he says *inter alia*: 'C'était un maître original et caustique . . . Il y a chez lui du philosophe, parfois du poète. Il témoigne d'une réaction contre les tendances historicistes et l'excès de philologie qui avait caractérisé le XIXe siècle . . . Granet annonce en sinologie ce qu'on appelle aujourd'hui la méthode structuraliste.'[65]

One can see how Granet looks like a sociologist to the sinologists. If he seems to sociologists to be a sinologist it is because of what appears

---

de Minuit, Paris, 1969, p. 61, where in a passage from the *Annuaire* of the Ecole Pratique, Section des Sciences religieuses, 1925, Mauss records the fact that Mestre has given an excellent account of exchange in the *kula* region. On the sinological side see Rolf-Alfred Stein, 'Edouard Mestre (1883–1950)', *Annuaire 1951–1952, Ecole Pratique des Hautes Etudes, Section des Sciences religieuses*, Paris, 1951. [63] *Annuaire 1938–1939* . . . , Melun, 1938, pp. 50f.
[64] In the footnote to p. 211 of *Catégories matrimoniales*, 1939, Granet acknowledges Mestre's help.
[65] Demiéville, *op. cit.*, pp. 106f. In her paper on Gernet, *op. cit.*, pp. 195f., Mrs. Humphreys lays stress on the connexions between Granet's work and that of Lévi-Strauss, drawing attention not only to the obvious influence of *Catégories matrimoniales* upon *Les structures élémentaires de la parenté*, but also to what she calls the 'even more striking parallels between Granet's analyses of Chinese thought and Lévi-Strauss's work on myth and classification systems'. And see

to be his narrow concentration upon China. I say 'appears to be'; I think that, all appearances to the contrary, Granet was a universalizing humanist for whom the study of Chinese civilization was a way of breaking out of the confines of European provincialism and of exploring alternative cultural worlds. In a few lines of *La féodalité chinoise* he sums up what Western anthropologists would recognize as coming close to their credo: 'By its extent, its duration, its mass, Chinese civilization is one of the most powerful creations of mankind; none other is richer in human experience. Yet it is infinitely less familiar to the public than the Mediterranean civilizations ... Nevertheless, every cultivated man is today aware of the narrowness of the world circumscribed by *classical studies*. Why should China remain alien to him if nothing human should remain alien? Man will know himself only if he knows all the ways of being human. To achieve that, he must leave home in order to find himself.'[66]

Of course, it may be objected that by confining himself to one non-European civilization, Granet was in fact denying the humanism to which he laid claim. But it must be understood that, while making a special case for China, on the grounds of its length of documented history and richness of experience, he was seeing it as only one among the many cultures being explored by members of the Maussian circle and whom he himself helped to encourage in their collective universal learning. Yet there remains a contradiction, which indeed lies at the core of much anthropological striving. China was to be studied because it was basically other and unique: in a particularly forceful passage of *La pensée chinoise*, 1934, Granet characterizes the civilization he was studying by the formula 'neither God nor Law'.[67] And yet somehow it could be used as a model of and for all cultures, including his own. I have no doubt that he found in China, *his* China, many of the qualities that he wished for Civilization. And fully to understand what he read into China we should need to take into account not only his Durkheimian sociological heritage but also his deeplying atheism[68] and his unswerving adherence to democratic socialism.[69]

Editorial Note 22 below on Granet's structural analysis of mourning ritual. The theme demands a careful and detailed treatment which would be out of place here, much as I should like to speculate on 'La pensée française'.

[66] *Op. cit.*, pp. 1f. Gernet's Préface to *Etudes sociologiques*, 1953, especially pp. xiif., discusses Granet's sociology very sensitively.

[67] See Editorial Note 144 below.

[68] He was not a convert to atheism; he was brought up in it. One of his pupils put it to me that, as a result, while he had in full measure *l'esprit mythique*, to which he himself attached importance, he lacked *l'esprit religieux* that Mauss, for example, possessed. The proposition might well be considered at length.

[9] About which I do not yet know enough. It might be argued that there was

Granet's rejection of explicit comparison must be seen in that light. At one level, and that the obvious one, he set out to use sociological (Durkheimian) method to write the developmental history of Chinese society and culture. At another level, aiming further, he overleapt comparison in order to reach, through the intensive study of one civilization, an understanding of humanity at large. That grand and veiled enterprise, which too has its Durkheimian inspiration, especially in *Les formes élémentaires*, was brought home to me by an event reported by one of Granet's pupils. One day, she told me, Granet declared to his class (and knowing by hearsay of his superb style as a lecturer, one may recapture the drama of the announcement): 'La Chine, je m'en fous. Ce qui m'intéresse, c'est l'Homme.' (If I must translate: 'I don't give a damn about China. What interests me is Man.')

He died in late November 1940. He had taken over from Mauss, at the latter's insistence after the fall of France, the headship of the Fifth Section of the Ecole Pratique, and in that role he was summoned to an interview with an official of the new regime he detested. The encounter must have been highly disagreeable. He died as he returned home from it. Mauss wrote his epitaph: 'Marcel Granet, 1884–1940, Historien de la Chine'. One wonders whether he would have been content with that insufficiently ambiguous description, however complimentary his loyal friend intended it to be.[70]

---

a populist streak in his socialism that was responsible for the emphasis laid, especially in this book, on the peasant origins of Chinese civilization. Cf. note 30 above.

[70] Terry Nichols Clark, *Prophets and Patrons: The French University and the Emergence of the Social Sciences*, Harvard University Press, Cambridge, Mass., 1973, got to me too late for me to be able to use it in writing this essay. Granet makes only a fleeting appearance in the book (see especially pp. 47, 219), but it furnishes some of the institutional background for the study of his activity within the Durkheimian camp.

The Religion of
the Chinese People

Preface

*Here is a man with whom one can
talk; one does not talk to him;
one wastes a man. Here is a man
who cannot be talked to; one talks
to him; one wastes one's words.*

The Analects of Confucius, XV, 7[1]

This book is made up of four chapters followed by a conclusion. The second and third chapters deal respectively with the feudal and official religions. They bring together the facts scattered here and there concerning the greatest historical event of the Chinese past: the foundation of national unity in the shape of the Empire. Before the empire, that is, before the second century B.C., the country was divided into confederated domains[2] linked more by some uniformity of civilization than by the closeness of their political ties. The uniformity was complex, and there were spheres within it sufficiently distinct to allow of differentiation. But that task remains to be done, and in the picture I offer of *feudal religion* I have not sought to take regional peculiarities into account. I have wanted to define the general form of religious life in the various domains. I must add that this general form runs some risk of being a particular one because of the drawback that the documents come almost entirely from a State situated in Shantung, the State of Lu. There is very good reason for thinking that, from feudal times, the customs of Lu were taken as *normal*; but it is true that it was above all in the imperial era that they were accepted as *norms*. It follows from this that in the attempt to establish the development of Chinese religion as a whole the obligation upon us to describe feudal religion on the basis of that of the State of Lu is no great disadvantage. And since feudal religion in the form it took in Lu was conceived as a model for those who presided over the elaboration of the rites later followed by the official classes, it deserves to be known in detail. The chapter devoted to it will be the longest in the book. Worship and beliefs will be studied in their principal forms in order to prefigure their future, and also to show their relations with the social organization in the period when they formed the basis of religious life. They were above all the cults and beliefs of urban settings, or better put, the cults and beliefs of the courts established in the towns of the various domains. The chapter will therefore open with a description of urban and noble life.

Similarly, the third chapter will begin by describing a special milieu: one displaying a particularly corporate character and made up of a clearly enough defined class whose members are customarily designated by the name of *literati*. They were grouped in rival schools whose teachings were doubtless sufficiently distinct; practical circumstances brought the School of Lu to the forefront, the School whose master was Confucius. Although Confucius lived during the feudal period, I shall examine Confucian thought at the moment when the influence it exercised was effective and served to maintain the structure of an established religion, the support of which appeared necessary to the nascent Empire. It is sometimes called *Confucian religion*, but one might say of it that it was also imperial or even national. It merits that latter name by its extent and chiefly because it was an excellent expression of the national character, if at least we define it by reference to the middling classes of society. In truth, it was the religion of the literati; it was a class religion as much by virtue of its professional origins as by that of the character of its adepts. I have called it *the official religion*. This characterization will at once explain why I am less eager to enumerate the mythological creations—most of them enjoyed only a mediocre success—which correspond to the development of this artificially formed system of worship, than to expound the moral and psychological aspects of the religious usages practised by the influential classes of the Chinese nation. I shall therefore chiefly study the success of what one might call the 'ritual formalism' of the *haute bourgeoisie* of China. It is odd that we can justify the somewhat large place devoted in this account to a religion without a clergy, a religion whose dogma has no real importance, a religion based simply upon social conformity and founded upon moral positivism.

The place accorded to Buddhism and Taoism will be correspondingly restricted, and I shall have to deny any place to a number of imported religions: Manichaeism, Nestorianism, Islam, etc. As for these latter, I have found it easy to resign myself to the situation: to study their history in China would serve rather to complete their total history, with the aid of the Chinese evidence, than to convey knowledge of the religious life of China. But this remark is not true for Buddhism, while the case is quite other with Taoism. This last name is used to designate an ancient and complex movement of thought. In olden times it seems to have corresponded to a stream of philosophical ideas in which a sectarian spirit is immediately perceptible. This metaphysics is then seen to have inspired a clergy and activated a cult: a religion appeared which strove to become national and which always kept the appearance of a sectarian religion. And just as, from a metaphysical point of view, Taoism had all the appearance of expressing a specifically native conception of the world, so, once formed into a religion, it was the natural refuge for the popular customs and traditions banished by the official religion in its progressive desiccation. If that view is correct, Taoism ought to have taken up a good part of this book; my excuse is that I can hardly assert that I believe it to be correct: Taoism is unknown.[3] The same excuse would not work for Buddhism. But symmetry justifies my not giving more room to it than to Taoism. The reason is not one of pure form: if I consider it under its properly Chinese aspect (the only relevant one here) I do not think it inexact to define Buddhism as a sectarian movement (of foreign origin, but that is of little importance) tending to make good the deficiencies of the official religion. I have given the title of 'Religious Revivals in China' to the fourth[4] chapter, devoted to Buddhism and Taoism. I shall examine them both, I admit, chiefly in their complementary role, and in that they point to the needs of religious life that the official religion in China did not satisfy for anybody, unless it be the literati. So that it is necessary to say something about the struggle kept up by the supporters of the State religion against the devotees of the sectarian religions. The victory of the former must be noted, as must be the trend to syncretism that resulted from the conflict.

In modern China the syncretic tendency passes as the rule of religious life, symbolized in the formula, constantly reiterated, of *the three religions*. I am brought now to speak of the manner in which I have conceived my closing and opening chapters. For various reasons, they are the chapters in which the part played by the personal equation is the largest.[5] My first chapter takes for its subject *peasant religion*. The fact which with the foundation of national unity dominates Chinese history is the creation of urban life and the establishment of the feudal hierarchy. But in order to reconstruct peasant religion and the condition of China when society was completely rural, it is necessary to proceed inductively. It happens (at least, so I believe) that by an extraordinary chance a document[6] allows us to carry out the exercise of induction in satisfactory methodological conditions. Everything in history is conjectural. And so how are we to proceed? Without this introduction in which I try to show what the ancient religious foundation of the race was, by what means could we understand either the development of the official religion in its two successive forms, a development brought about by abstraction, schematization, and impoverishment of the primitive foundation, or the tactics of the sects which, at the expense of this impoverished religion, sought to revive the religious spirit and which gave to their conquering faith a national face or a popular air by borrowing broken-down elements of belief and worship from that same ancient foundation ? And perhaps, trying to describe the present state of religious life by questioning the peasant masses, the very stuff of the country, we should rediscover that same foundation as a whole. My last chapter deals with present-day religion. There could be no question here of enumerating the practices and beliefs observable today in the whole of China. Since it was necessary to choose and all choice is arbitrary, I have gone to the extreme. I have chiefly made use of personal observations in the attempt to define the attitude of a modern Chinese to what we call religion: I have tried to give the measure of *religious sentiments* in the China of our times. All I can say about my own observations is that they are made in good faith. Does the best faith in the world lead to the truth ? I shall not assert that it does in a book which takes religion as its theme. Bringing the book to a close, I have pointed to a problem which interests a certain number of Chinese as well as some Westerners: what future is in store for religion in China? It was fitting that the question be posed. Ought I really to have answered it ? It is unnecessary to say that a historian of religion cannot fancy himself to possess the gift of prophecy.

Chapter One

Peasant Religion

Rural life

The opposition between urban and rural life is an essential feature of Chinese society.[7] That ancient opposition—the simultaneous existence of towns and villages is attested by the oldest documents—was doubtless more marked in antiquity than it was later to be. In the historical times of the feudal period, countrymen, in contrast to town-dwellers, preferred the left to the right;[8] as we know, nothing so much distinguishes two population groups as the principle of orientation they have adopted. We have no right, for the time being, to think that the distinction was based upon a difference in race;[9] nor does it seem to have corresponded to a separation into closed castes: there were constant exchanges between the two parts of the population, and examples abound of historical personages passing from one to the other. The opposition was linked with mode of grouping and style of life. In the texts, products of urban settings, it is expressed in opinions which would suggest an inequality of value. Rural life was opposed to urban life as peasant life to noble life. The essential point is that the countrymen, the ordinary people, the plebeians, had the customs that were proper to them; a fact marked by the aristocratic Rituals in the saying: 'The Rites do not go down to the common people.'[10]

We should not know those common customs were it not that there has been preserved for us in an Anthology of poems a whole collection of songs which became estimable in the eyes of the courtiers in the towns of the domains by the symbolic use they made of them. These songs, more or less reworked by and deformed at their hands, are made up of themes, poetic sayings, in which the rustic inspiration makes itself felt. When these themes are grouped together, sociological analysis can succeed in reconstructing a picture of rural life in its broadest outlines.[11] But however methodical the work of reconstruction may be, and even when it is subsequently confirmed by the examination of the traces left by popular usages in the learned literature, the picture obtained can be only a general picture. It is valid for the Chinese lands as a whole and for a vast period of poorly defined time: it eliminates local and historical peculiarities: a defect which is, after all, minor and which is felt only by historical fanatics enamoured of individual facts and chronological precision. There is less risk that the reconstruction incorporates oddities: the defect would then have been more serious and it needs to be pointed out.

At the beginning of the feudal period (which came to an end roughly in the second century B.C.; it had begun six centuries earlier and possibly even before that), probably also at its close, certainly before it had begun and perhaps still after it had ended, in the collection of countries making up the Chinese Confederation (that is to say, the middle region of the Yellow River, mainly in its eastern part, apparently also in some of the border territories to the south), this is what life was more or less like in the countryside.

The peasants occupied villages situated on high ground and usually enclosed by quickset hedges. Some of them were cave-dwellers, and perhaps all of them had been so in ancient times. Most commonly they built their houses in the shape of a kiln, out of mud and rammed earth. The walls and the roofs were so thin that a rat or a sparrow could pierce them.[12] A square opening in the middle of the roof allowed the smoke of the hearth to pass out and the rain to fall through and be collected. On the south side a door opened to the East and a little window to the West. The house was just one room. In the South-West corner, the darkest, the grain was stored; there too people slept, on straw or reed mats. Every house had its own compound. Round it was an orchard planted principally with mulberries. The low-lying lands were kept for cultivation; the furrows crossed, running from East to West and South to North,[13] and the fields were square, separated by the uncultivated edges that were used as paths and where small huts were built; these last sheltered the workers who lived there to watch over their harvests and who never left their fields except during the dead season. They saw their wives only at meals, which were brought by them with the help of their children. As long as the rains allowed work to go on, the peasants drew from the fertile alluvium hemp, peas, and cereals, principally millet, which were their staple foodstuffs. When the grain was threshed and stored, they returned to the village, repaired their roofs, blocked the cracks in the walls, and shut themselves up in their houses during the hard and dry cold of the winter: they rested, as did the soil, worn out by the effort of production. But for the women on the other hand it was then by no means the dead season: they spun hemp and wove clothes. The two sexes took it in turns to labour: the work, regulated by an alternating rhythm, was modelled on the succession of the wet and dry seasons well marked on the plains of eastern Asia.[14]

Throughout the year, in the fields cultivated in common as in their shut-off villages, the peasants had dealings only with their kinsmen. A village enclosed a close-knit and homogeneous great family. Ties of blood, natural filiation, did not introduce true divisions into this large community: a nephew was not less than a son nor a father more than an uncle. Domestic life itself induced no exclusive sentiments: all the young people of one generation, brothers or cousins (it was all one) married women who were equally sisters or cousins. In this huge family maternal affection itself did not take on an appearance of jealous affection: if anybody was preferred it was the children of the eldest sister. In like fashion, all the aunts were called *mothers*: the mother most respected was not the woman who gave one birth but the woman who by her age (or her husband's) occupied the rank of mother of the family. Indeed, age and generation were the sole principles of classification within the domestic community,[15] which was led, or better still, represented by the oldest member of the most senior generation. This latter was called *head* or *father*. That term, which has the meaning of 'chieftain', was used after the family name, which seems also to have been that of the village. The name, emblem of the community, was the sign of a sort of identity of substance, specific and incommunicable, which, maintained by commensality, was the very essence of this kind of kinship.

The large undivided family, which, as the days went by, was self-sufficient and lived in isolation, was, however, neither completely independent nor always closed. The alternating distribution of work went with a strong opposition between the sexes expressed also by the prohibition on marriage within the group of kinsmen. In each generation one half of the children, all those of one sex, had to leave the familial village to go to marry into a neighbouring village, being exchanged against a group of young people of the same sex and of another name. It is possible that the exchange was in the first place of boys, since the name was in ancient times passed down through women and the house always remained a feminine thing,[16] the husband arriving originally as son-in-law never having occupied it as its master. But from the time that the texts inform us of directly, the exchange was of girls: the most pathetic plaint in the old songs is that of the bride forced to go to live in a strange village.[17] The essential point was that marriage was made by a crossing of families, just as the fields were made by a crossing of furrows.[18] By this practice each hamlet received a group of hostages from a neighbour and in turn furnished it with one. These periodic exchanges, by which a family group obtained pledges giving it a hold upon another group, also caused a foreign influence permanently to penetrate its inner life. They made evident the dependence of the domestic communities and the supremacy of the local community, a wider grouping of another kind.

The complex unity of this higher grouping did not rest upon sentiments as simple as those lying at the base of domestic solidarity: these other sentiments did not arise from constant contact, from identity of interests, from common work, and daily commensality. From day to day the individual belonged completely to his family, and the awareness of this belonging entailed an habitual feeling of opposition towards neighbours. It was only on exceptional occasions that family egoism could feel itself mastered by the vision, then sudden and dazzling, of higher interests never clearly seen in ordinary circumstances. Their rhythmic life provided the Chinese peasants with these occasions at two points in the year: when they finished and when they began domestic work and labour in the fields, when men and women, their activity alternating, changed their mode of life, at the beginning of spring and at the end of autumn. The weaving done or the grain harvest brought in, each family group was put in possession of an abundance of riches: these were moments of joy, moments when the harshness of practical concerns was relaxed, moments favourable to large gestures, propitious to generous exchanges, welcome periods of large-scale social intercourse. And it was not at all an interchange that sought only direct and material advantage: each family, proud of the fruits of its labour, wished to display its Fortune; neighbouring groups came together in a communal assembly, each inviting the others to make use of all its riches: it won recognition of its prestige by its generosity. In these solemn meetings of families usually withdrawn into themselves and shut up within the circle of their daily cares, each of them, becoming aware of its power at a time of plenty and feeling it to be increased by its public display, lost its usual feelings of enmity towards the neighbouring families at the moment when its self-confidence was carried to its highest point. The interpenetration of the different groups was more intense, more moving, more intimate, and more absolute for their isolation and self-containedness being in normal times more complete.[19]

The gatherings of rural communities consisted in powerful orgies in which were affirmed, at one and the same time, the strength of family grouping and that of political grouping. Marking the beat of the rhythm by which female and male work alternated, the gatherings had the character of great sexual festivals in which were effected the matrimonial exchanges by which each group permanently held hostages from all the others and sent them delegates: these festivals of peasant harmony were also festivals of marriage and of fertility. Marking the time of rustic work, inaugurating the success to come, celebrating the success achieved, they were moreover great agrarian festivals in which orgies of food were mingled with sexual orgies. They snatched people suddenly away from their monotonous lives; they sharply awoke within them the profoundest hopes to be conceived by an agricultural people; they excited the creative activity of inner life to the highest degree. The practices and beliefs born of this extraordinary activity governed the development of Chinese religion: public and family cults, ancestor and agrarian cults, even the cult of heaven, emerged from these festivals of human and natural fertility in which the domestic spirit was revealed in all its strength while the sense of society was created.

Holy places and peasant festivals

The assemblies of rural communities were held in special places: they were beyond the cultivated fields in a part of the territory withdrawn from domestic appropriation and profane use, on land that was holy for everybody. The location of these Holy Places is quite well marked out for some parts of China; but all I can describe is the general appearance, the ritual landscape of the Festivals. For the unfolding of their traditional ceremonies, they required a terrain variegated with woods, water, vales, and heights. There the crowd of pilgrims spread themselves, come from afar, often in carts, dressed in seasonal clothes that were freshly woven and of which the dazzling newness declared the prosperity of each family. In their finery, the womenfolk, usually invisible and shut up in their hamlets, showed themselves in groups and shone like clouds. With their sprigged robes, their grey or madder-red head-dresses, they appeared as beautiful as the mallow or cherry blossom. Groups of people made or renewed relationships. Drawing one another by the sleeve, taking one another by the hand, they gave themselves up to the joy of meetings long and impatiently awaited and which had to be of short duration. In the enthusiasm of these solemn assemblies they moved up and down in all directions over the terrain, filling it with their happiness and feeling that happiness fed by the memories recovered at their contact with the witness of all the potent joys of their race. They wished to make this beneficent contact as intimate as possible; from it there seemed to come to them a prodigious enlargement of their inner life. They experienced the presence of a tutelary power whose sanctity sprang from every corner of the landscape, blessed forces which they strove to capture in every way. Holy was the place, sacred the slopes of the valley they climbed and descended, the stream they crossed with their skirts tucked up, the blooming flowers they plucked, the ferns, the bushes, the white elms, the great oaks and the wood they took from them: the lit bonfires, the scent of the nosegays, the spring water in which they dipped themselves, and the wind that dried them

DCP

as they came from bathing, all had virtues, unlimited virtues;[20] all was a promise given to all hopes. And the animals which teemed and also held their seasonal assemblies, grasshoppers gathering under the grass, the arrested flights of birds of passage, ospreys[21] gathered together on sandy islets, wild geese calling to one another in the woods, all were part of the festival and shared in the holiness of the place and the moment. Their calls, their chases, were signals, emblems, a language in which men heard an echo of their own emotions. They felt themselves strong by their harmony with the natural order. Their festivals opened and closed the rainy season. Were the festivals regulated by the first and last rainbows to appear? Or did they regulate their appearance? In these gatherings where rural concord was forged in rhythmic time, all, exalted by a sentiment of joyous power, imagined that they cooperated in the harmony of Nature. Their creative joy turned into a need to worship from which the earth set aside for their gatherings benefited, divine land where everything merited a cult, the great isolated trees, the little woods, the pools, the confluences of rivers, the gushing fountains, the mounds, the split stones, and the rocks which seemed to bear the imprints of giant footsteps.

But moving out of the routine of their daily lives (doubtless hard and brutal, certainly wretched and empty of thought) the peasants of ancient China did not pass without a transitional stage into such a state of religious exaltation: they were not immediately ready for the great surges of emotion when they came from their homes to the communal Festival, for they were still heavy with the spirit of their own territory, saturated with family egoism, full of suspicion towards the stranger. The different groups approached one another not without some fear; each was moved by the prestige of the other; but did they not need to uphold their family honour? Shyness was disguised under a bantering air; the bands confronted one another mockingly and exchanged challenges. Then it was that the Festival began; the whole of it was spent in a series of contests; the variety in the Holy Place provided ample matter to the thrust of the game which, once unleashed, sought to unfold. Bird-nesting (for example of swallows) was the object of tournaments, as was the gathering of firewood and simples, and there were battles of flowers. Then there were races along the stream and the hillsides, foot-races, cart-races, boat-races, and especially the crossing of fords by opposing groups, their clothes raised to the waist, with much provocation and bantering. Confidence and joy sprang from all this emulation; the family spirit stripped itself little by little of its aggressive timidity in every band which had some success and was made aware of its resources. Challenges gave way to gifts: the groups exchanged plucked flowers and pledges of friendship which they undertook to keep until the next meeting. Brought together by their peaceful contests, the neighbouring families began suddenly to feel an intense need for communion, and peasant harmony, a creation once more renewed and with an entirely fresh strength, was born of the contests in the Holy Place.

The contests produced this rejuvenation of the social pact because they brought into confrontation the youngest forces in the community and could be ended in the most intimate of communions. The ancient Festivals were above all festivals of initiation, which brought into social intercourse young people hitherto shut up in the hamlets of their families: betrothals and marriages were there contracted to the benefit of the community and under its control: they reduced the exclusiveness of local groups. The bands opposed in the contests were made up of young people who must not be either from the same village or of the same sex, and who (at least in the spring) for the first time attended the gatherings at the Holy Places and who before that had never met. We might not be able to imagine what their emotions were; they had such potency that on each occasion the young people burst into poetry, recovering the primary forms for the expression of feelings. When they faced one another in the contests in opposed lines their rivalrous action was always regulated by rhythm; whatever the contest, it had the appearance of a duel of dance and song. The challenges, brief vocal images accompanied by mime, flew alternately from one band to another, forming poetic couplets. Their themes were obligatory and all taken from the ritual landscape: the beasts which also seemed to take part in the Festival in the Holy Place, by their cries and their movement in the chase, provided numerous models for the images sketched by voice and gesture. These pictures were quite other than reproductions of gestures and cries: they were descriptive formulae infinitely surpassing in richness a simple sequence of onomatopoeic sounds with immutable values. What they reproduced were the signals of the Festival, already endowed with a symbolic meaning and rich in all the traditional sentiments of the assembly; and, besides, employed by the alternating choruses that opposed one against the other, they formed by their being paired a complete phrase whose elements, balancing term for term, took from their place in the total design a special syntactic function and all the properties of an abstract sign.[22] But in their contests the choruses did not merely create a language for expressing the sentiments springing from their face-to-face opposition; what they created was a stirring language: their mimed and sung formulae had a constraining force, for they were made up of emblems which, furnished by the Holy Place, seemed to possess a power to command. When in their contests the young people represented wild geese, partridges, and quails seeking their mates, they strove to make one another obey the order to unite which was the reason for their assemblies. With all the images of the ritual landscape, flowers, foliage, the rainbow joining two regions of Space, springs flowing together, they composed a litany of seasonal saws by means of which they linked their wills together and placed one another under a spell. Little by little, by the effect of this long incantation, feelings of sexual modesty and family spirit were muted within them. The power of the poetry finally brought them together, and they no longer resisted the duty to unite.

Their first unions were celebrated in the Festivals of Spring, but they could set up house only after the Autumn Festivals. As long as the work in the fields lasted, even old couples were kept apart; nor were suitors allowed to join their betrothed except by night and furtively. They jumped the hedges and, hiding from their kin, courted each other; especially at full moon, they sang their aubades, taking great care not to be surprised by cock-crow. These meetings at night were doubtless chaste. The opposition of the sexes was so strong that a long preparation and favourable times were needed to bring them together; sexual union seemed so frightening that it was forbidden for long periods. But when it was allowed and regulated, when in the spring festivals all the young people of the community came together for the first time, what a unique and moving moment it was! They were poetically inspired and, not being able any longer to sing once they were married, they knew of a sudden how to improvise dances and songs in the traditional spirit of their race. They made all of surrounding nature take part in their powerful emotions; boys and girls assembling on the holy earth imagined that their youthful unions cooperated in the revival of nature, when in the Holy Place the ice on the rivers melted under the breath of spring, when the waters came to life and the springs, long dried up, spurted forth, when finally the soft fertile rain fell and the dew appeared, when the precocious flowers came up in damp corners, in the time of new foliage, of plumtrees and flowering peachtrees, of swallows returning, while the magpies built their nests and singing the birds chased one another in pairs. All the hopes of fertility mingled in their breasts: while the eggs they swallowed, the meteors they caught sight of, the bunches of plantains they gathered up in the laps of their skirts, the flowers they offered each other as betrothal pledges seemed to them to embody the principles of motherhood, they believed further that their springtime nuptials were propitious to universal germination, that they called forth the seasonable rain, and that, finally, by desacralizing the earth, forbidden to human work during the winter, they now opened the fields to fertilization. Sanctified witness of their magnificent labours, the Holy Place appeared to contain an infinite creative power endlessly renewed by the Festivals.

In these festivals of springtime and youth, sexual communion was the central rite, and at all times the word for spring signified the idea

of love. When could love have had more efficacious strength than in its
fresh newness? The sexual rites of the spring festivals hardly needed
to be rounded off by a communion of food; they sufficed, after all, for
betrothals. But when people entered upon domestic life, they were
chiefly preoccupied with establishing an identity of substance in order
to make life in common possible. A great orgy of drink and food was
the essential feature of the Autumn Festivals. Sexual practices were
then secondary; thus, these were not the festivals of initiation and
inauguration; they were the festivals of harvest and the return to the
hamlets. They quite early took on a special character and the appearance of village festivals; girls and boys doubtless continued to assemble
in the Holy Place there to sing and dance, but the centre of the ceremony
was shifted to the floor where the grain was threshed. There neighbouring families invited one another to great feasts. Hosts and guests
were separated into two bands, as in the love-song contests, and formed
up in lines. The opposition of local groups was first expressed in this
fashion. But each of them knew the benefit to be got from not jealously
keeping the products of its own fields: it would not have dared to be
the first to taste the fruits of its harvest, and it first of all felt the need
to consecrate its new-won riches by using them with generosity. These
acts of generosity were a matter of some moment for the honour of the
family, which drew from them an omen of plenty. Was it not necessary,
in order to be confident of the future, for present prosperity to be
recognized by all? Besides, none was the loser by it, since nobody
would have wished to be put to less expense than his neighbour. By
these alternate acts of prodigality, all thought to enrich themselves
with the truest form of wealth: mutual esteem and faith in the happy
Fortune of their country. They killed lambs and brought jars of wine;
they drank and ate their fill. In this unusual commensality all became
aware of a sort of intimacy, different from that underlying kinship, and,
so to speak, of a less everyday essence, but which yet seemed of higher
value, so much did feeling spring vigorously from the intoxication of
these junketings. On both sides they drank toasts to each other from
wine-cups made of rhinoceros horn: 'Ten thousand years of life! Life
without end!' And everybody returned thanks.

And the workers in the fields gave thanks to the tilled land. Accompanying themselves on clay tambourines, they sang of their labours
and of the days of the year gone by; they called upon all the helpful
forces of Nature to take part in the communion feast; in their dances
they represented the animals which to them seemed beneficent: cats
and leopards. In their religious fervour they got to such a pitch of
excitement that a town philosopher could then say of them that 'they
were all as though mad'.[23] But the excitement was very different from
that which animated the spring gatherings. At the festivals of plenty it

was the heads of villages, the elders, who presided, and the celebrations appeared as festivals of old age. And they appeared too as festivals of 'the ageing year'. While spring signified 'love, union, joy', autumn signified 'death, separation, mourning'. An end was put to cultivation; earth was sacralized; 'old things', worn out by service, were taken leave of; they were exhorted to go, like men, to their winter quarters, withdrawing into their original dwellings according to their kind. The time of cold and drought was come; the water was invited 'to withdraw into its channels'; wand of hazelnut wood in hand, in mourning attire, the old saw the year out to its end. In this way the dead season was established by a festival of old age, just as spring had been by the festivals of youth. And the rural communities, by sanctifying their time-honoured harmony, had once again succeeded in ensuring the order of Nature.

Ancient beliefs

The sense that the natural world and human society are closely bonded has been the basic element of all Chinese beliefs. We have been able to see how this sense could come about. Among Chinese peasants the life of feeling became intense, the creative power of the mind truly showed itself, only on the occasion of the Festivals of Spring and Autumn; now, these gatherings stamped time with the rhythm by which the work in the countryside was divided up and which coincided with the rhythm of the seasons. The communities gathered together, at the very moment when consciousness of the social bond could surge up within them, noted infallible recurrences in Nature: the thought of harmony dominating their hearts appeared to them as a reality with two closely linked aspects, human and natural order. But they distinguished the Order of the world from the desires of their hearts no more than they thought of society independently of its natural setting. It was a completely emotional conception which was to be turned into a system of dogma only after a slow process of reflection. In peasant thought it was only the basis (scarcely perceived in itself) of the efficacy common to all the practices at the times of the festivals, an always dual efficacy, reaching men through things and conversely reaching things through men, an indefinite and indeterminate efficacy in kind and essentially religious. Everything in the Holy Place, everything in the Festivals was indifferently good for everything; all the acts and formulae of the contests were as signals and orders for the collectivity of beings; all things to be seen in the Holy Place were constraining symbols for men. But whether human or natural emblems, none appeared endowed with a particular value, none was conceived for a special end. The jumping of grasshoppers seemed to govern a whole body of social rules: the season of marriages in common, their celebration in the sacred vales, the practice of marrying out of the family and within the same stock, the dances of the contests, the courting procedures, the prohibition of jealous behaviour, the rules of fertility. And the crossing of the stream by the young people achieved all in one the lustration necessary for all fertility, the reincarnation of souls floating down the stream, the arrival of the rains, and the transition from one season to another. Fed by strong and confused emotions, an emblematism was the core of all beliefs and all worship.

The basis for organizing these confused facts intellectually and practically was the Calendar. From the song contests were born not only a great number of emblematic formulae but also the art of formulating the seasonal themes. What the peasants observed in natural recurrences provided, once put into poetic form, an important body of calendrical sayings; analogous in form to the symbolic themes of the Festivals, stereotyped, conventional, obligatory in character, and, besides, rich in themselves in traditional wisdom, these sayings too seemed to possess a constraining power. The harvest in, to give thanks to all things and, before the new year, to give them their leave for the winter, the Chinese peasants sang in chorus the labours and the days of the year now past; the poetic patchwork of their sung calendar, reciting to them their future tasks, presaged their success and promised them the continued help of Nature. Such a song was testimony of past obedience, a vow of future obedience to the law which obliged men and things to bring their actions into harmony. It is significant that the Chinese attributed this poem to their most venerated legislator: the Calendar was and remained the supreme law, valid at once for human society and the natural world. But as soon as the seasonal sayings, the observations and the prescriptions, emblems common to all species of beings and signals ordering every action, were arranged in an organized calendar, each took from the very fact of its position a capacity to become the distinct sign of a particular meaning and a special efficacy. Thus it was that the reappearance or the retreat of hibernating animals, the hawk changed into the ring-dove or the ring-dove changed into the hawk, were no longer simply emblems of Spring and Autumn but actually the signal for the return to the village or for going out into the fields, for the close of hunting or for its opening. Symmetrically, as soon as the religious practices ordered by these signals were removed from the concerted action of the Festivals, they lost their indistinct values: each, appearing to pursue a particular end, seemed to have been thought out for this special use. There came a time when the crossing of the stream served only to procure rain and when it was considered a sort of mimetic rite specially conceived for that fixed end.

The creation of a Calendar was a task of religious organization that

called for the help of directive thought. That thought was provided by
the concepts of *yin* and *yang*, principles whose concurrent action
constituted both human and natural order. *Yin* and *yang*, whose
philosophical fortune was to be very important, quite early on became
cosmological entities for astronomers; in the beginning they were
merely elementary principles of classification. They were above all
two orders, female and male. All things belonged to one or other of them,
or rather, the totality of one class formed a female grouping, *yin*, that
of the other a male grouping, *yang*. But these concrete categories were
also active principles. Space was made up of the opposition of *yin* and
yang, Time of their alternation. These real and sexuate principles,
brought face to face and alternating, were the very stuff of Totality,
whose Order they moreover expressed. Nature was so represented. The
idea people had of the natural world being, from the first, joined with
that they had of the human world, the structure of society must be
the model upon which they conceived the general structure of the
World.[24] Now, in peasant society, division by sex was the essential
division, always perceptible in the elementary unit, the family, in which
husbands and wives were of different names and different essences. And
that is why *yin* and *yang* were in the first place two sexual groupings.
Male and female activities had to be conducted in distinct places and at
distinct times; and for that reason *yin* and *yang* worked in opposition in
space and in time by taking turns. The unity of society was deeply felt
only at the time of the seasonal festivals, in the stressed periods of the
rhythm of peasant life: when male work was to follow from female,
or vice versa, men and women gathered together in the Holy Place and,
having taken up position in opposing ranks and sung by turns, joined
together in a deep sense of harmony and in great hopes of fruitfulness.
In the same way, *yin* and *yang* were appointed to meet in the spring
and the autumn; then they were face to face; depending on the season,
one called and the other replied;* then, to make the world fertile and
form its harmony, they came together sexually; their splendid union
was manifested in the rainbow. Separated after the nuptials, they took
it in turn to labour: *yin*, like women, was active in winter, and its
activity, inward in its nature,[25] could be conducted only in withdrawn,
dark, and closed off places; *yang*, like men, was at work during the
summer, in the full light of day, lavish in its output. *Yin* had the meaning
of shaded, north of the mountain, south of the river; *yang* meant
sunlight, south of the mountain, north of the river. The names of the

* The terms used by the Chinese are the very same as those which designate
the alternate challenges sung by girls and boys, the calls and answering calls of
pairs of birds, and the call of the betrothed and the reply of his fiancée. According
to Chinese authors, girls submitted to the ascendancy of *yang* and boys in the
spring; in the autumn the situation was reversed.

two principles are explained by the appearance of the Holy Place, and they are a reminder of the sunny or shaded slopes where the opposing choruses of girls and boys took up position. Thus these two principles for organizing thought were conceived during the seasonal festivals whose ordering made the principles of the organization of society perceptible to everybody. But not only did the two directive ideas draw all the elements of which they were made up from the arrangement of the Festivals: it was also to their sacred origins that they owed the religious prestige which gave them their prosperity and the dominating role they kept, during the whole course of Chinese history, within the totality of dogmatic and scientific thinking.

Closely binding together ideas of human and natural fertility, the representations formed during the ancient festivals were not simply at the origin of the work of reflection which attained the conception of the two great cosmogonic entities; they were also the elements of the beliefs which, from the time of peasant society, became sufficiently specific to serve as the basis of distinct systems of ideas and religious practices.

The Holy Place was first the origin of all fertility. The most important act in the Festivals, especially in the spring, was the crossing of the stream. When the young people crossed the ford, before their first unions, they were moved by an enormous hope of creation. They imagined that their dances and their songs, their movements, their calls, and the scent of the plucked flowers drew the principles of fruitfulness to them. Shuddering at contact with the running water, the women felt as though they had been penetrated by the souls floating on the sacred springs; these then gushed, and it seemed that the coming of spring had freed their waters from the underground prison where the dead season had enclosed them. From these images and feelings was born the idea that the souls of the dead, seeking a new life in the time of spring, broke loose along the vernal streams from the subterranean retreat in which death had shut them up. And the belief came to be held that the dead lived under the earth* in a deep abode, the winter refuge of the waters, called the *Yellow Springs*. The Yellow Springs to begin with appeared to be very close to the peasants' native land; people thought they could almost reach the Springs and open up for the souls an easy path to the land of the dead by digging grave pits. But death dictated a change of orientation: while the living opened their dwellings to the South and faced in that direction, the dead were buried to the North with their heads to the North. When the Chinese thought of their land on a vaster scale and wanted to give a common dwelling-place to the dead of the whole of China, they put it at the very edge of their

* In China, earth is yellow (loess) in reality and in theory (the colour yellow is attributed to the element earth).

country, to the North; and since to them the North was Down, the Yellow Springs were sited in the depths of the North. The fate of men could not be separated from the fate of things; water, sacralized in winter, was female, *yin*; the residence to which it was forced to withdraw for the winter by the chants of the autumn festivals, subterranean pole upon which converged all the waters of the world, was also recognized as the residence of *yin*. The Yellow Springs, retreat of the souls aspiring to live again, were furthermore the prison where, overcome by *yin*, *yang*, on the lookout for the spring, awaited the moment when it could kick the earth to make the springs rise up and bring back life and fertilizing waters to the land. And it was thought that the Yellow Springs, retreat of the dead and reservoir of life, were the place from which there emanated the principle of the fecund humours which endowed human beings with creative power. In this way from an ancient moving rite there developed a belief which was soon put to use and made more precise by scholastic speculation. In popular thought the belief must always remain unclear and confused, hardly distinct from the images and emotions which had given it birth. The Yellow Springs were invoked only for the most solemn oaths, and were avoided in speech. Practices seem to have been connected with the Yellow Springs, but not a cult.

It was otherwise with the beliefs about Mother Earth and reincarnations. In the Festivals, in order to get into touch in any way they could with their Holy Place, the members of a rural community maintained among themselves a sense of belonging to the soil which was and has remained the most powerful of all the sentiments their race has known. A saying expressed it forcefully: 'The dying fox turns its head towards its native hill.'[26] There was a kind of mutual belongingness between the country and its natives. The solidarity uniting the members of a local group was in essence territorial; it seemed to be founded upon the ties between each individual and the Earth common to all. In reality, the awareness of it appeared only when the collective marriages were celebrated upon the earth. By a transfer of emotion these sexual communions in touch with the earth were communions with Earth. A complex and powerful sentiment caused the Holy Place to be venerated as the origin of all fertility and all matrimonial alliance—a total fertility whose manifestations did not at all call forth the definite idea of creation, an alliance in the widest sense and superior to the specific idea of kinship. The power with which the Holy Place was invested remained indeterminate in nature; it bestowed upon the totality of beings every kind of fertilizing force (the seeds of spring and of new life) without having the special attributes of a creative power; it bestowed upon the collectivity of neighbouring families a general sense of harmony and a common faith in the future of their Stock, without having the attributes proper to the originator of a family. The Holy Place was venerated in a neutral form, and rather as a supreme Chieftain and with the attributes of a Regulating Power. Thus it was in no way the site of domestic festivals, but that of the federal festivals of initiation and marriage.

The beliefs attached to the idea of the Holy Place dominated the conceptions formed of the Earth; but these conceptions took on a more precise shape under the influence of images conceived in another setting and of emotions aroused at other times. The opposition of the sexes, kept up even in the round of domestic life, preserved all the value of an act of communion to the sexual encounters all husbands and wives (ever of different name and essence). These sexual communions, likewise made in contact with the earth, entailed the idea of a communion with Earth, but with domestic Earth. They took place in the dark corner of the house which served as granary and where the seed was stored. Now, the house first belonged to the wife, who received into it her husband come from another hamlet, and from the time that the ties of kinship no longer appeared solely in the form of village consubstantiality, from the time when the basis of family organization was not merely group kinship, and the notion of filiation, taking on importance, began to appear to be its foundation, it was the women who transmitted the name, real emblem of domestic consubstantiality;[27] from that time on, the wives—if I may so put it—were mothers when their husbands were still only sons-in-law. By the contagious effect of emotions of communion there were created a veritable confusion and an interchange of attributes among the mothers of families, the female originators of the stock, the stored seed, and domestic Earth. Life was enclosed within seed as it was within women; stored near the conjugal sleeping-place, the grain fertilized the women; guardians of the seed, the women conferred upon it the power of germination. The seed nourished; the women nursed. Earth was a Mother, a Nurse. Sowed with seed it spent ten cycles of the moon in gestation, and women followed its example. Within Earth[28] all life was contained; through It all life was developed; It took the dead into its bosom and alone fed infants during their first three days. It was a maternal, a nurturing, a lifegiving Power. The stock was born of It and drew from It its substance. Contact with It was necessary at decisive moments of life: upon entering the world and quitting it. The first act of attention was to place the dying and the newborn upon the ground.[29] As the supreme domestic power, only Earth could tell men whether a birth or a death was valid. Only It could withdraw or give the right to live within the family group.

When, after three days of fasting upon the domestic earth, the infant, nourished by Mother Earth, had shown by its loud cries the power of life it drew from her, its mother could carry it following the example of the earth. She could feed it, and the child itself would later be able to eat grain. It had entered into the group of the living. When the dying man placed upon the ground could no longer revive, despite the wailing of all the family, three days after his death, now finally cast out from the group of the living, his body was put into the earth. There was a double ceremony of burial. In historical times, the second interment was carried out outside the towns and villages, and the family graveyard was then forbidden ground to all who were not of the family. In ancient times the burial was within the domestic compound. The first interment was always in that compound and in the house itself; it lasted the time it took for the flesh to rot. The stuff of the dead entered the domestic Soil. It shook off its flesh near the dark corner where people kept the seed that germinated when placed in the ground. And in that same corner the conjugal sleeping-place was situated where the women conceived new lives. They imagined then that their conception was the work of fecund Powers emanating from the domestic Soil, that the Soil itself had germinated the life they felt grow within them, and finally that the child they got had taken its substance from the very substance of the ancestors. The belief became established that life principles floated in the dark corner where the ancestors had become discarnate: every birth seemed to be the reincarnation of a forbear. Since women conceived in their natal homes, reincarnation must be in the uterine line: a newborn child was none other than an ancestor who, after a stay in Mother Earth, the stuff common to maternal forbears, took on individual life again and reappeared within the living section of the family.

At the same time as the idea of Mother Earth was elaborated—basis of kinship in a family attached to a plot of land of its own and organized according to the system of descent through women—the belief was formed, in the family groups fixed to domestic Soil and confident in their perennity, that the family substance was as eternal in the same way as was their Soil and like it ever unchanging. It was neither diminished by a death nor augumented by a birth: but every member of the group passed by birth or death into a different form of existence. The family was divided into two parts: one was of the living, strongly united but endowed with the peculiarities inherent in each individual life; the other, that of the dead, formed an indistinct mass. It would suffice, when another form of kinship organization emerged, that well-marked individuals endowed with personal authority appear within the group of the living for the solidary group of the dead to seem to be composed of individualized souls to whom worship would be addressed: that was to be the cult of the Ancestors. It was in the process of being formed from the moment when people believed that they could sense the souls of the dead floating confusedly in the dark corner of the house.

A cult of the family dead and a cult of the domestic Earth were founded upon beliefs that developed in parallel. In the South-West corner of the house there lived a blurred mass of familial spirits, manes, penates, and lares. But the idea of Mother Earth was indebted for its first elements to notions formed in the festivals of the Holy Places, which were celebrated on land withdrawn from cultivation; in every dwelling a private cult rendered to the natural Earth was added to the worship of the cultivated and appropriated Earth; the lar to which the cult was properly addressed was placed in the middle of the house, at the spot where under the opening in the roof all the productive forces of Nature managed, along with the fertilizing rains, to pierce to the very centre of the domestic Earth. On the other hand, bound from the beginning to the agrarian cults, the worship of the Ancestors always kept the appearance of a seasonal cult whose chief ceremonies were performed in the spring and autumn, just as the gatherings were held in spring and autumn in which the idea of reincarnation was sketched in. These gatherings were federal festivals: the cult of the Ancestors succeeded only very late (and perhaps it never completely succeeded) in taking on the appearance of a purely private cult. If family solidarity beyond death was manifest in the incorporation of a mass of ancestors into the domestic Earth, and if the discarnate souls awaited a new life around the conjugal bed, the solidarity of local groups required also that the many collectivities of ancestors in the land be brought together at the Yellow Springs, and so that reincarnation might take place in the flow of the sacred founts. On the one side, the Holy Place was a grouping of Ancestral Centres, each of which was necessary to make up the sanctity of the whole. Just as the ceremonies of ancestor worship always required public participation in their performance, so too the common interest always demanded that no family cult be allowed to escheat: the integrity of society would have been attacked. Furthermore, the upkeep of these cults associated from the beginning with those of the cultivated Earth was indispensable for achieving the prosperity of agricultural work. And that is why, while the private cult of the appropriated Earth was rounded off in each house by that of the natural Earth, and while the worship of Ancestors seemed to be a matter of public interest, there was associated with the public worship of the common Earth a cult of the tilled fields: the public cult of grain, the cult of millet.

In this way the linked development of agrarian and ancestor cults, of public and private cults, is explained.[30]

Popular mythology and folklore

One might imagine that at the time when the cults destined to a long fortune were born and in a period when the religious festivals aroused so much poetic feeling, a powerful effort of mythological creation was carried out. Yet, if we set aside the myths of belated and quite artificial invention, China's poverty of myth and divine figures seems extreme, and it contrasts with the richness shown in this field by the Mediterranean and Indian worlds. Does the reason for that poverty lie in the Chinese language? It is true that that language, in which no differentiation so to speak is made among verbs, substantives, and adjectives, is ill-adapted to the play of epithets which appears to be one of the primary conditions of mythic invention. Furthermore, in ancient Chinese the verb was thoroughly impersonal; nothing predisposed people to conceive of active forces in the form of individualized agents. Why should they have personified them? Actually, the earliest religious beliefs were scarcely differentiated from the confused emotions, from the complex images whence they sprang. No sacred force appeared in an individual form; neither the Holy Places nor even the Ancestors were thought of as distinct substances endowed with personal attributes. As soon as people conceived the idea of individualized powers they easily enough found the means of designating them in their language:[31] many myths owed their existence if not to a play upon epithets, then at least to a play upon words. The majority of them were attached to the local cults which perished when feudal society was destroyed; as creations of vanished settings, these myths, deprived of support in the system of worship, likewise disappeared from memory and with them a number of legends from which they had drawn their substance. The same fate probably befell many remaining peasant legends which the literati in their disdain would not collect. The only myths from the earliest times whose memory has been preserved are those in which the feelings characteristic of the ancient festivals were directly recorded, and their conservation is due to the fact that those emotions answering to everlasting ideals, something of the festivals survived in the popular calendar.

Such is the case with the myth of the Heavenly Weaving Maiden. It is a stellar myth; along with the fact that bright Heaven and the Dawn were perhaps already for the peasants divinities invoked in oaths, it is the only indication we have of a rural cult of the stars. But the elaboration of a calendar by people for whom it was a deep conviction that nothing human could be without resonance in the whole of nature, could not be carried out without all the habits of men being lent to the constellations and meteors: we have already seen it happening with the rainbow, the resplendent nuptials of Nature. The legend of the Weaving Maiden was born of a like transposition. Emblem of young peasant women in times gone by, the Weaving Maiden is a constellation which all through the year leads a life of lonely work; not far from it but also alone, another constellation, the Cowherd, labours in the heavenly fields: it was

necessary everywhere for the sexes to remain apart and for their tasks to
be apportioned. Between them, as a sacred frontier, flows the river
known as the Milky Way. Once a year, work stops and the constellations are reunited: at that point, to celebrate her annual nuptials, the
heavenly Maiden fords the holy river of Heaven. As on earth, birds
take part in the wedding festivals; magpies form an escort at the wedding
ceremony: if their heads are bare of plumage, it is because, having
gathered over deep waters, they have formed a bridge for the procession
to cross. By her fidelity to ancient usages, the Weaving Maiden deserved
to become and to remain the patron of women's work and of conjugal
life: on the night of the heavenly nuptials, Chinese women, in order to
promote pregnancy, float little figures of children on the water, and
in order to become skilful, they thread their needles by the light cast by
the holy Constellation. But if in the whole course of Chinese history,
the Weaving Maiden has had offerings of fruit and flowers set before
her, if her graven image is to be found on the walls of funerary chambers,
and if she has come to the aid of filial piety in difficulty, it is because the
calendar has given her a place and because, even in times when and
places where women remained always shut up, there were gardens
made up of water, rocks, and venerable trees between the walls of
noble residences recalling the ritual landscape of the Holy Places.
There the memory of the ancient Festivals could be preserved by
carrying out some of the seasonal rites which originated from them.
Still innocent and very close to its deep sources, sufficiently alive to
extend all over Japan, young enough constantly to enrich itself with new
elements, the legend of the Weaving Maiden has kept a poetic prestige
which has allowed it to cross the centuries and to come to bear witness
before us to an ancient religious past. It had been fated in days gone
by not to find favour with theologians; they did not speak of it, and they
neither knew how nor wished to adapt it to the myths to which they
strove to give an apologetic twist; saved from religious pedantry, the
Heavenly Maiden has kept the grace that makes her for ever a power
in men's hearts.

The Weaving Maiden has been preserved from oblivion by an old
ideal, ever young, of feminine purity and diligent and fruitful domestic
life. Despite much contamination and roundabout use, the myth of
Dragons survived, as did the festivals in their honour. Rain is the first
need of an agricultural people. Among other purposes, the crossing of
the stream in the ancient festivals procured rain in season: the crossing
was made by opposed choruses of girls and boys. When women were
denied the right to take part in the public festivals, two choruses were
still used to sing and dance face to face in the holy stream in order
to cause the rain to fall: one of the choruses had to be made up of
young men barely out of their mothers' houses and still completely

imbued with feminine influence. From that moment it was thought that the rhythmic movements of the opposed choruses were governed by the desire to imitate the movements of dragons leaving their winter refuge in order to mount up to heaven and cause the rain to fall from it: by imitating the customary actions of the divine monsters, people urged them, they forced them, to comply with their customs. But it was thought that the rain was the result of the struggle and coupling of two dragons of opposite sex, one *yin*, the other *yang*: a simple transposition into the sacred world of the seasonal marriages and contests in the water. These contests were conducted in many different ways, and sometimes in the form of boat-races: a place in the calendar was given to these nautical competitions; preserved in the custom of dragon-boat races, the myth of the Dragon masters of the rain still forms part of Chinese beliefs.

Two powerful mythic themes were born of a single aspect of the festivals at the Holy Place. How many sacred legends must have emerged from the many and stirring practices of those festivals, the gathering of flowers, the climbing of hills, encounters with springs, stones, and divine trees? Sometimes the mythological datum has served as matter for dogmatic speculation, which has reduced its elements to scholastic entities: that is what happened to *yin* and *yang*, to the rainbow, and to the Yellow Springs. Sometimes the theologians of feudal religion collected the mythic elements (we shall see later of what the genealogical legends and the recitals of miraculous conceptions were made up): incorporated into a body of official dogmas, quickly stripped of their charm and their emotive power, they fell into the oblivion that comes sooner or later to all dogma. Other legends, probably the majority of the themes relating to animals, have had by the erosion of time to fall to pieces by themselves; they have formed the foundation of Chinese folklore: there the new religions came to take what could be used to make a semblance of national and popular religions. But how are we today to find our way in this mass of hybrid products? What role has the popular imagination played, what role Taoist invention, what the Buddhist or other share contributed to the legends of the sun raven, of the hare, the frog, the old man, and the cassia-tree that inhabit the moon, of the phoenix, the unicorn, the dragons themselves, the Isles of the Blessed, the Queen-Mother of the West's marvellous garden of peachtrees, the flood, the turtle whose severed feet hold up the world, the mulberry tree from which the sun emerges, the cranes ridden by Immortals, the pheasants changing into oysters, the playful and helpful foxes, the tigers for whom the souls of their victims serve as spies, and the hedgehog which seeks safety by waiting in a rut for the carts to go by?[32]

Chapter Two

Feudal Religion

The life of the nobles

We have no means of knowing when the towns of China were established, but we are able to say what constituted a town in principle: it was the seat of a lord and his vassals. There was no lord without a town; there was no town without a lord; whoever lived in a town was a vassal of the lord; whoever went to live there put himself under his control. A lord could possess several towns; any of them in which he did not reside he put into the keeping of one of his vassals, who became its immediate lord and who lived there with his private court. The town where the lord had his seat was the very centre of his domain. The towns were differentiated by the rank of the fief and the dignity of the lord: there was a royal town which was that of the suzerain lord; there were towns of lords proper and towns of high officials who were also lords but with precarious title and, at least in theory, on life tenure. The vassals inhabiting the towns were nobles: they led a special way of life which qualified them for that title;[33] they looked down upon 'the people of the fields, the rustics—living only to eat and drink;— but they, all the nobles, they, all the vassals—form a group and are the Virtue of the Chief'.[34]

That Virtue shone out from the ordering of the domanial city. It had been founded by an Ancestor. From the top of a ridge he had first of all observed the sunlit and shady slopes (the *yang* and the *yin* of the landscape), the river courses, and the position of the mountains; he had chosen the site which was generally on a height, as was the case with villages. The Ancestor had then observed the shadows and determined the correct orientation of the city. Finally, the lots having been cast at the beginning of winter when the constellation Ting culminates at dusk,[35] people set to work, starting with the ramparts. They were of rammed earth or stone, according to the standing of the

lord and the town; they formed a square enclosure, pierced by a gate
at each of the four Directions. Then temples, the palace, and houses
were put up; their walls were compact, their sturdy frames made of
cypress or pine; the edges of the roofs curved back like the wings of a
pheasant in flight; the pillars were very high: the main court perfectly
smooth; there were large and deep rooms for rest, others bright and
gay opening due South. The lordly residence, centre of the town, was
the heart of the domain. The main access was on the line drawn from
the south gate; it led to the audience chamber where the Chieftain
faced South. There the life of the nobles and the lordly city were
inaugurated by a communion banquet: 'Gathering his people to
attain Glory . . . ,—he will take a pig to the sacrifice,—he pours wine
into the gourds,—he gives them to eat and drink:—Lord of vassals,
Head of the kin group!'³⁶

Far from contact with the rustics, enclosed within the ramparts of
the city, which was holy to them, grouped around the lord of whom
they were the Glory, whose Virtue they formed, the nobles lived in
great dwellings populated by a huge group of kinsmen. All the houses
were surrounded by walls; there was no land common to the different
buildings. A noble residence was a vast compound formed of walled
courts. At the end of each of them there was a building facing South,
of one storey but raised above the ground. Access to it was gained by
two flights of steps, one to the East, the other to the West. At the rear
there were small closed rooms entered by a narrow door; in front, taking
up nearly the whole width, was a hall completely open to the South:
two independent pillars supported the central beam. Inside his walled
court, the occupant of a set of buildings was as though he were a lord;
he climbed to the hall by the steps to the East and faced the South.
In the middle of the noble residence, like the town in the centre of the
domain, was the building reserved to the Head of the family: the hall
in which he faced South was on the axis of the great entrance gate
but it had no view towards the south gate of the town.

All those who, descended through males from the same grandfather, held their movable property in common, must live in the family
residence, at least in theory: that was the elementary family grouping.
The family embraced a great number of such groups; for kinship
extended to all those who shared the same great-great-grandfather. The
head of the great family was the representative of the direct line
traced from the great-great-grandfather: around him were the lesser
heads descended by primogeniture from the great-grandfather or
grandfather. Every oldest son was at the death of his father head of a
small family; among all his sons he singled out one, the continuator of
the principal line descended from himself, and that man was the
principal son; the others, secondary sons, eventual founders of second-

ary lines, he merged with his nephews, the sons of younger brothers. At the death of his father, a younger son did not become the head of the family; within the group formed by his own sons and nephews he made no distinction. His sons, on the other hand, gave him first place; for them he was superior to the oldest uncle, head of the small family. While their father was alive they were the subordinates of that head through him. Once the father was dead they formed a small group placed under the leadership of the firstborn; but the grandfather, or if he was dead, the oldest uncle, his successor, was the real head of all the small families; he was the authority to which, directly or indirectly, all the cousins submitted. In every household, authority vested in the husband, not in the father-in-law. The noble family was an agnatic family, which was not an undivided family nor yet in the precise meaning of the term a patriarchal family. Kinship did not flow from the relationship of father to son (and still less from natural filiation); it flowed from a relation of enfeoffment tying groups of collaterals to the head representing a more or less ancient principal line. In this essentially hierarchical organization paternal authority sprang derivatively from a lordly kind of authority belonging to the head of a family residence and which that head held from the overall head of the kin group, heir by primogeniture of the common great-great-grandfather.

Organized differently from the peasant family, the noble family was, like it, a group in which solidarity, if not homogeneity, was extreme. All agnatic kinsmen bore the same name, passed down indefinitely through males. When kinship with the head of the oldest branch came to an end, that is to say, when a collateral branch had as its point of origin an ancestor further back than the great-great-grandfather of that head, that branch could assume a special name which was a *cognomen* and not a family name: the obligation of mourning ceased among the lines of one family so internally differentiated, but the obligation remained not to marry within it. In the *segmented agnatic family* of feudal China, mourning was the sign of kinship in the strict sense, the prohibition of marriage was the sign of the deeper kinship of which the common name was the symbol and whose basis was the consciousness of some consubstantiality. This was maintained by communion feasts; these meals were more or less frequent according to the degree of collateral nearness: kinship appeared subject to degree and susceptible of progressive attenuation. The feasts still brought together, at least in principle but at very long intervals, all the family branches of a distinct *cognomen* which preserved the memory of common descent and bore the same family name. Although kinsmen were distinguished by degree, kin relationship continued to be a community tie. Men were kin by virtue of a specific and definite identity, capable of being specified in certain ways. In the peasant family the specification was by individual age and seniority of generation. In the noble family, it was according to the privilege given to direct lines: it resulted from a hierarchical organization of family groups, itself subordinate to the establishment of the principle of primogeniture. The adoption of that principle signalled the advent of a domestic authority, a lordly authority, which, being essentially individual, could be transmitted only from individual to individual. Between father and son there was in the first place a community of substance, which followed from their incorporation in the same group. Between father and oldest son there was, besides, a special tie *resulting from a contingent fact*, namely, either the transmission of a portion of domestic authority when the father was himself the oldest son (with an increase of that authority in all cases where the father was not the direct heir of the great-great-grandfather) or the setting up of authority when the father was not the oldest son. Always limited as such by the existence of higher authority, paternal authority was moreover limited in every case by the eminent rights of the domestic community. A father could adopt only if he was the oldest son; he could adopt only from a younger branch; he had to adopt his closest nephew; the adopted son had to belong to the same family branch; if it became absolutely necessary, one could adopt someone of the same name; it was strictly forbidden to bring into the family somebody who did not already bear its name. The name, the virtue characteristic of a domestic community, and the specific identity created by communion feasts were essentially religious and incommunicable.[37]

The noble family as segmented familial community was just as much a closed group as the undivided community of the peasants. In both cases, and for symmetrical reasons, marriages were contracted between members of different families: they broke down their exclusiveness, periodically introduced into each group a basis of union with the others, and marked out to all their mutual dependence. That dependence was less absolute than within rural communities, for it was limited by a dependence of another kind and of a higher order: noble families depended principally upon the authority of a lord or of the suzerain. The quota of matrimonial exchanges was regulated by protocol in conformity with the political hierarchy; at each marriage a noble family had a right to two girls, a family of high officials to three, a lordly family to nine, and the king to twelve. Because a pattern of authority had emerged within the family, the bevy of wives[38] was not divided up but was allocated as a whole to one husband; group marriage gave way to the practice of polygyny. A noble married two sisters. A high official received two sisters, plus one of their nieces who had to be the daughter of their oldest brother and was a pledge given by the future head of the affinal family; that was a result of the rule of primogeniture. A lord and a king had a right, respectively, to three and four bevies of wives: as a consequence of the specific identity maintained among the family branches of one *cognomen*, when one of them contracted a matrimonial alliance, two other branches, obliged to take part in the alliance, had themselves to add to the first bevy of wives two analogous bevies of attendants. The practice of polygamy, rounded off by the custom of marrying sons into the kin groups of their mothers, conferred a rare homogeneity upon the female part of the noble family. It was organized in the same way as the male part: the womenfolk were subjected to a hierarchy of matresfamilias with a right to that title partly because they were the wives of firstborn sons, and partly because, at least in principle, they were themselves oldest daughters. The authority of the mothers of the family (the term must not be taken in its physical sense) was exercised in a fashion parallel to that of the fathers of the family, and, at least in part, surpassed marital authority. The women formed a group apart, and, at least in theory, lived more together than each did with her husband. They inhabited the remoter parts of the house; there they were carefully shut in and watched. When they went out they had to be veiled. Nothing that happened in the women's quarters was to be known outside. When the women were young they each had attached to them a duenna who monitored their behaviour, their speech, and their work, and who was responsible for them. When widowed, they had more authority than a paterfamilias. In ordinary times they had the strength of all the prestige that might be vested in their natal families. Contracted without the future spouses having seen each other or their having been consulted, marriage was the result of negotiations carried out by a middleman and in protracted overtures: as was also the case with repudiation, marriage was a quasi-diplomatic rite, so great was the distance between the two families of different names, so important the bringing together produced by matrimonial alliance.[39]

The habitual antagonism and basic solidarity of the different family groups were asserted on occasions other than marriage. The ceremony of majority, which for the men had become quite distinct from that of marriage, appears at first sight to have been a private ceremony: it seems to have been intended first of all to remove the young man from the influence of maternal authority, and then to create between his father and him the agnatic affiliation[40] by which he assumed his rank in the kinship group: it remained essentially a ceremony of initiation into social life. It had to be in public, and the initiative for the ritual acts lay with the representatives of friendly families whose presence and supervision appeared necessary. The same was true of mourning observances whose final result was the endowment of the family with an Ancestor; only the collaboration of neighbouring groups could render them effective. During the funeral rites, these groups formed a chorus antithetical to the family chorus. By their bringing a double obligatory tribute of gifts and condolences, they bore witness to the interest taken by the whole society in preventing each of the private groups from feeling itself diminished in its potency and prestige. The integrity of substance of each group was thus in turn affirmed by an exchange of prestations material and moral.

All these prestations (as we have seen in the case of matrimonial exchanges) were subject to rules of protocol: family groups depended on one another, but they were also dependent on their lord. Society, like the family, was hierarchically organized. The alternating prestations kept up among family groups the feeling of solidarity that corresponded on the domestic plane to the feeling of consubstantiality created among kinsmen by the practice of communion feasts. Just as the domestic community remained the foundation of kinship ties, so the local community persisted as the core of social ties. But the advent of domestic authority was accompanied by the establishment of public authority. If family communism still strongly limited the exercise of paternal authority, then lordly authority decidedly prevailed in the organization of society over direct inter-family solidarity: their interdependence appeared to the different vassal families in the main indirectly and as consequence of their common enfeoffment to their lord. Their relationships were governed by protocol because henceforth they seemed to be dominated by the nature of their ties with the lord's court: these ties involved feelings of equality, inferiority, or superiority. The humblest vassal families were involved in lesser alternating prestations and felt themselves more distant because they were more distant from their lord. Collateral groups thus understood the distance separating them by being aware of the distance separating them from the direct line; they gained this feeling by taking part less frequently in the family communions to which they were invited by the head of the large family. Similarly, the heads of vassal families knew their rank, their obligations towards the lord, and the duties among their many family groups, from the degree of intimacy established between them and the chieftain of the country by the proportioned intensity of their relationship of communion with the domanial court. In urban life, human relations, both private and public, but especially public, were no longer egalitarian relationships among groups, as in rural life, but hierarchical relationships as between chieftains.

The whole of religious life was to be dominated by that basic fact—and by another: instead of being rare and periodic, as among the peasants, urban relations were on the contrary permanent. In domestic life husbands and wives were daily in touch with each other. The village was only a winter haven; the peasant house was entirely the woman's:

the noble residence was inhabited permanently by both sexes. They each of course still lived their separate lives, differently occupied: the separation of the sexes, with the consequent need for their collaboration, remained a cardinal rule of society. A paterfamilias required a mater-familias; a lady was necessary to a lord; and if the patresfamilias formed a court of vassals to a lord, the matresfamilias formed a court of vassals about the lady. Women were not completely shut out from either public or religious life. But the sexes no longer formed two cor-porations taking turns at work, two groupings of equal importance. In general, the women remained closed in, busy with the same homely tasks as the peasant women; at birth they were given a terra cotta spindle as a toy; boys were given a jade sceptre, for they would spend their lives at court and take part in the pomp of the ceremonies forming the glory of their lord. Within every man there was a small part of the public power, something sacred. By contrast, women seemed to be of an inferior essence and as though charged with malign power: while amid the fields the betrothed peasant women cooperated in the annual renewal of the springtime, the noble fiancée, after three months of strict confinement, was conveyed veiled and at dusk to the husband's harem, where she was shut up for another three months. The separation of men and women preserved to sexual union its mysterious character; it was not linked to the unusual emotions of times of festivals and harmony; it became domestic and secret, surrounded by ceremonies stressing the inferiority of wives and enabling the husband to avoid sullying the august within him. In urban life with permanent ties, in noble life, the man became the chieftain, the woman a servant; sexual union retained only a maleficent efficacy; it lost all religious virtue.

Only the union of the Lord and his Lady possessed Virtue. King and Queen had to come together on the nights of the full moon. The royal couple were matched in conformity with Nature's orders and to establish the natural Order. In effect, the Lord permanently held all the powers acquired by the Holy Place from being the witness of the seasonal assemblies because he presided over the gatherings at his court; there in the heart of his domain, the vassals shared in his power, manifested his Glory, established his Virtue. The feudal Chieftain was endowed with a religious Majesty kept up by daily rites, that is, the homage of his followers: he fed upon the tribute of their offerings, a religious form of tax, assimilating through them the totality of sacred forces emanating from his domain; and he was thus filled with the essence characteristic of his domain. As to any god, one gave to the lord only in order to receive: by eating the remains of his food, the followers procured a small part of the Power realized by their common effort. That Power had immediate effects: it worked unmediated, from mind to mind, upon all things animate and inanimate: 'the thought of

the Chieftain is without bounds: he thinks of horses and they are
strong! . . .—the thought of the Chieftain is wholly correct! . . .—he
thinks of horses and they run straight!'[41] Like god, like followers: here,
the followers are the whole country. The princely Virtue imbued and
vivified it as the dew the plants in the fields: through that Virtue the
land was strong; through it the waters flowed; through it the reeds
grew and the grasshoppers bred; through it the arrows flew straight to
the mark; through it the hearts of men went undeviatingly along the
path of duty. It shone upon the vassals who, endowed with power
delegated from their lord, governed towns as lords, if they were enfeoffed, and as plain nobles, domestic groups: in the domestic dwelling
the father of the family held a Sovereign Majesty maintained by the
homage of the kinsmen; he received tribute from his kinsmen; the
food prepared in the house nourished within him the Virtues specific
to his Line, and his Virtues passed to those who ate his leavings. Like
paterfamilias, like kinsmen: paternal power radiated in the same
fashion and by the same processes as the lordly authority from which it
derived.

By a parallel development, private and public cults in the town were
based upon paternal and lordly authority: the cults centred upon a
permanent chieftain; they had a priest and faithful (should we say
faithful and a god?); they were not the cults of homogeneous groups;
no more were they total cults. In the ongoing social life of noble
cities the power of the chieftains was always exercised over everything,
but by specialized acts. Doubtless, vassals, and kinsmen even more,
formed groups in which all were filled with the same Virtue and everyone was capable of doing everything, but in these groups there was
after all hierarchy, a particularization of relationships, and a tendency
to specialization. The permanence of life in common was advantageous
to the sharing out of work, to the classification of activities and ideas.
Feudal religion embraced a totality of cults and beliefs that were still
poorly distinguished from one another, but in the end so distinguished.
A process of abstraction was about to begin from which religious
life was to emerge better ordered but impoverished. Feudal religion
already had the features of an official religion: definite dogma and
ritualized practices took precedence of faith.

The cult of Heaven

At least in theory, the chief place in feudal religion was given to the
Sovereign On High-August Heaven, *Huang* (or *Hao*) *T'ien Shang Ti*.
The four words making up that redundant expression could be used
by separating the two parts in apposition; one could say the Sovereign

On High, August Heaven; or one could dispense with one of the terms, saying for short Heaven, Sovereign; one could even say (the power of) On High, and the word *Hao*, which means August, is found without its being affixed to Heaven, just preceded by the word indicating lordly possession: the Master (of) August (regions). In this way the different elements of the redundant expression could replace one another; they appear indifferently alone or grouped in twos or fours in the same hymn or strophe: it is clear that all of them, whether taken as a whole or in isolation, refer to the same sacred Power and that that Power was at one and the same time single and complex. The Sovereign On High-August Heaven had a variety of attributes.

In the first place he was the Regulator of the seasons; in that respect his cult was akin to the agrarian cults. Heaven was sacrificed to to beg for a good Year: Year meant harvest. The harvest depended upon seasonable rains: they were asked of Heaven; it seemed to command the weather: from that immediately beneficial aspect, from that concrete manifestation of its Power, directly sprang for the main the veneration that Power inspired. Yet it was of a deeper and, in some ways, a more abstract nature: Heaven was the supreme Regulator of the natural Order; it was the originator not only of seasons but of time, not entirely of pure duration but certainly of the continuity of the facts of nature. It was a divine projection, a realization of the calendric Order: in this regard it appeared as a sovereign Power and unique in its essence. Its cult could be ensured only by a person vested with an authority of like order; it was ensured, in the name of all, by the unique man to whom the Chinese Confederation entrusted the care of the Calendar, that is to say, the suzerain. The feudal suzerain bore the title of King, *Wang*: he might be also called *T'ien Wang*, which may be translated as King by the grace of Heaven. The expression exactly signifies that the King who promulgated the Calendar on earth, great law of an agricultural people, was the human collaborator of Heaven in the regulation of the natural order. But a divine power could work only through its followers; these reciprocally participated closely in divinity: the king bore the title of *T'ien Tzu*, Son of Heaven. We shall see that to give that title its fullest value, priestly speculation was able to create genealogical myths that connected the royal line to a true son of Heaven. The basic idea was that the King was one whom Heaven treated as a son, that is to say, one to whom it delegated its power.

That power the Son of Heaven actively exercised; it was not enough for him to publish a calendar showing the inhabitants of all the domains how to conform to the natural course of things; he must realize the human Order and the natural Order together and in order to bring them into harmony. By virtue of their common participation in the categories of *yin* and *yang*, there existed an absolute tie between space and time. It sufficed that the actions of the Son of Heaven be carried out in sequence and in a fixed order, at the different points of space, for the orderly succession of Time to be effected and (as a normal consequence of the Virtue constituting royal authority) the adjustment of human actions to the heavenly Order would follow automatically from the adaptation of the king's actions to each direction.

If we are to believe the old historical legends, when all the vassals were gathered together in plenary session the suzerain went to receive them at the four gates: the chieftains of the four mountains were the first among them; below them were the nine shepherds; it is said that at that time China was divided into nine provinces; it is also said that it was divided into twelve. In the same era, the vocation of the Son of Heaven consisted in processing through the kingdom, 'bringing the seasons and the months into harmony, rectifying the days' in such a way as to be in the East in the month in which the spring equinox falls, in the South for the summer solstice, in the West for the autumn equinox, and in the North for the winter solstice. These kingly perambulations worked the cycle of the seasons. They took place only every five years, but the influence of the supreme Chieftain was exerted every year and at the due times and places through delegates. One of them, the second Hsi brother, living in the East Valley, controlled sunrise and the spring equinox, and promulgated 'the beginnings of the East': the people then went to their work in the fields and the animals bred their young. The second delegate, the third Hsi brother, in the Elevated Shining Residence, controlled the summer solstice and promulgated 'the occupations of the South'; that is, for people to continue to live in the fields, and for creatures to shed their coats or plumage. The third, the second Ho brother, in the West Valley, controlled the sunset and the autumn equinox and promulgated the 'completions of the West': people then lived peacefully and creatures resumed their coats and plumage. The fourth, the last of the Ho, living in the Elevated Dark Residence, controlled the winter solstice and promulgated the 'change of Winter': in consequence, people shut themselves up deep in their houses; creatures thickened their plumages and coats. The Hsi and the Ho second and third brothers, respectively governing the *yin* and *yang* Seasons-Directions under the leadership of their eldest brothers, who were watchful observers of August Heaven, men and animals managed to make their way properly through the whole cycle of the seasons, and they did so under the impulsion of the royal Virtue exercised by the four regional delegates: that Virtue was thus constituted by the homage of the vassals gathered about the suzerain, entering by the four gates, led by the four group chieftains.[42]

The Son of Heaven could perfectly well carry out the celestial Work of Time without either using regional delegates or circulating through the regions. A suitably constructed building could suffice to make the Sovereign Influence shine upon the whole country. It was supposed to be surrounded by a circular pool and covered with a round roof, since the cyclical Work of the calendar was supposed to be consummated there (Heaven is round); but it was to have four oriented sides around which the vassals were grouped, not in a square, admittedly, nor according to region. Within the enclosure of the Ming T'ang[43] (the Hall of Distinction) the vassals were to be placed according to noble rank with none of them to the North, for in that holy place the suzerain alone could face the South. But outside the enclosure, the barbarians of the four frontiers (they could not but be there if the royal Virtue had its full efficacy), and the barbarians of the four seas, each at his own Direction, would form a square. The building was thus to be square (Earth was square) and to be divided into nine square rooms (China had nine provinces), but nevertheless in such a way that they might be used as though they were twelve (China had twelve provinces; the year had twelve months—or roughly so). In order to promulgate the calendar, in the months in the middle of each season, the months of the solstices and equinoxes, the king would stand in the central rooms facing due East, South, West, North, as the two Hsi and the two Ho stood at the four Directions. The four corner rooms each faced in two Directions; the suzerain would take up position in each of them during two months, the months of transition between the seasons, and in this way the eight outer rooms of the square would serve to make up the twelve months. Twelve lunar months did not fill the 360 days of the year, but had not the kingdom a centre, the year a pivot, and the Ming T'ang a central room?

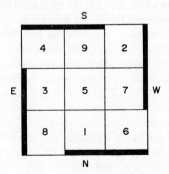

At the end of the summer—a critical period when the transition was made from the *yang* seasons to the *yin* seasons—it was from the central room that the Sovereign Influence would be exercised. Thus the annual cycle would be completed by the royal tour of the square mansion of the Calendar: in fact, that square was magic in the proper sense of the term. Each hall bore a numerical symbol. In every direction the numbers added up to 15. Was not the year divided into 24 periods of fifteen days, each of which had a seasonal saying as its emblem? The base number was five: each of the 24 periods was divided into periods of five days, similarly marked by a saying. Five was the middle number; the numbers congruous with five were distributed in pairs on each side of the square: each pair signified a direction: 1—6 = N; 3—8 = E, and (as a result of a reversal explained by other numerical speculations) 2—7 = S; 4—9 = W.[44] It would be easy to use the symbolic value of the Numbers, of that magic cross oriented in time and space, to procure an exact rotation of the seasons: to each numerical pair there corresponded a pair of cyclic signs marking the days, a note on the musical scale, an animal species, a part of the house, a part of the body, a taste, a smell, a colour, a sacrificial animal, a cereal, an element. For the year to turn along with the symbolic cross, it was necessary and sufficient that the king, by his clothes, his food, and so on, dazzlingly manifest his being in conformity with the system of the universe. Winter was brought about when, dressed in black, with black stones at his belt, using black horses, a dark carriage, a black standard, the king took up position at the NW corner of the Ming T'ang and ate millet and pork. Did he eat mutton and wheat? Did he wear green with green stones? Was his flag green? Did he give pride of place to sour taste, rank smell, the spleen of victims, the number 8, the note *chio*? Did he put himself in the NE corner of the Ming T'ang? Spring was coming.

When the royal Virtue was perfect, and as a true Son of Heaven the Sovereign knew how to identify his life with the Order of the Universe, when he was at all points a legitimate sovereign, at once, by the side of the Ming T'ang a tree grew which in the first half of the month was every day decked with a new leaf, and which every day lost one when the month was on the wane: Time was regulated. But if the seasonal rules were not applied, the seasons ran ahead or lagged behind, rain and hail fell untimely, it was cold when it ought to have been hot, Time was thrown off course and the order of Space no less; the sun and the moon failed in their duties and 'lost their way', there was an eclipse: immense disaster! 'Flashes of lightning and claps of thunder one after the other—there is peace no more and no more rest—all the swollen rivers overflow—from the tops of mountains rocks crumble—the heights are made valleys—vales turn into mountains!'[45] It was because '*in the domains of the four regions* there has been a deficiency in governmental action'; the king was at fault, and he had to restore order. He himself struck the great drum; he put all his people on a war footing:

all the vassals present, those of the East dressed in green with green standards and two-pronged lances, those of the South dressed in red with red standards and hooked lances, those of the West dressed in white with crossbows and white standards, those of the North dressed in black with shields and black flags, all, around the suzerain and the retainers in the capital dressed in yellow, all the *vassals of the four regions* formed a square: Space was reconstituted, Time resumed its course, the moon and the sun found their proper way and correctly followed their road: the royal Virtue had been restored in its strength. Activated by that Virtue, the arrows shot by the trusty hands of the vassals in order to come to the aid of the darkened star, went straight to their mark. As soon as social Order was shown in perfect shape, the Order of Nature was reestablished.[46]

The sovereign action which, thanks to the help of the followers of the four regions, radiated from the capital to the nine provinces of the Chinese Confederation, was performed by the king as a colleague of Heaven, in whose name he promulgated the Calendar. Heaven was itself a Sovereign whose elevated residence (the chieftain stood High, in the North, and he was the Centre) was at the very top of the nine celestial spheres, right at the far North, and in the middle of the four peripheral Regions. On earth, all investitures were received in the suzerain's town; the suzerain obtained his own investiture from the Sovereign On High and the power that passed down to him from his forbears. He called that power a heavenly mandate, treated Heaven as father (literally, father and mother: the title always given to a hierarchical superior), associated the first of his dynastic Ancestors in the homage he rendered to that higher Power, made of that Ancestor a true son of Heaven and the mediator of his Line to Heaven, and made no distinction between the Court of the Sovereign On High and the Assembly of the souls of his forbears and their immediate followers. From that point of view, the dynastic cult of Heaven was a sublimation of the cult of the royal Ancestors, and in that regard it was connected with the agrarian cults in a new fashion. If Heaven caused the rain to fall, it was so that the millet might grow and provide for the sacrifices and libations from which the ancestors drew life. Essentially charged with the maintenance of Natural Order and calendric Regularity, the kings of the Chou family, feudal sovereigns of an agricultural people, were specifically appointed to be in hereditary control of the harvest (literally, of millet). They called their Ancestor the Harvest Prince (literally, Prince Millet) and sacrificing together to the 'August Sovereign August Prince' and to the 'August Ancestor Harvest Prince', his incarnation, they cried out in time of drought: 'The Harvest Prince no longer has power—the Sovereign On High is no longer benevolent!' 'Ancient princes, ancient chieftains—there is none of them will help me!—My father, my mother, my dead forbears—how can they take no pity!' 'August Sovereign-Heaven On High—will not let me survive! —How could we not all tremble? My Ancestors will be destroyed!'[47] Originator of dynastic power as of royal power, Heaven appeared as the Providence of the suzerain family. It established the kings in their capitals, provided them with wise counsellors, furnished them with virtuous wives, watched over their conduct, admonished them for their faults: thus giving them all the means not to dishonour their Ancestors and not to allow them to perish by perishing along with them.

As dynastic Providence, Heaven was an all-seeing and justice-meting power. It was the god of oaths. One swore by the light of the day and of the dawn; one called to witness the blue sky, the azure heaven, 'the Heaven which on high shines, shines'! All the epithets applied to Heaven—and they were the same as those applied to the Ancestors— were to show a luminous nature and a power of radiance which were the proof of an August Intelligence: that word August expresses the value placed upon the cult of Heaven as on the cult of the Ancestors, the epithets implying an idea of light. Heaven was as the abode of moral powers giving force to imprecations: 'I shall seize those slanderers —I shall throw them to the wolves and the tigers (animals of the North)! —If the wolves and tigers do not eat them,—I shall throw them to the Masters of the North!—If the Masters of the North do not seize them,—I shall throw them to the Masters of August (Heaven)!'[48] Witness to contracts, avenger, helper, protector of just princes, brought close to men by its nearness to the Ancestors, Heaven was thought of as having the features of a sovereign with a noble and human face: people said of a beautiful and wise princess that she seemed to be the younger sister of Heaven, or they even cried out: 'Is she not truly Heaven?— is she not the Sovereign!'[49]

Heavenly Providence showed itself in human guise in dreams in which an envoy of Heaven, who was at the same time an Ancestor, often brought warnings or gifts. Thus there were diviners appointed for dreams and traditional rules for interpreting them. In exceptional circumstances and, for example, during fasting, it was also possible to enter into communication with the mind of Heaven. Moreover, without waiting for the actions of Nature to portend the judgment of the Sovereign On High, it was still possible to know it by divination. For that purpose the tortoise or milfoil was used; the tortoise could tell the more for it lived long: besides, care was taken to sacrifice the animal before using its shell, and to preserve its virtue by anointing it with blood every year. 'Wise and bearing characters upon its shell', which was round as Heaven, the tortoise responded immediately. It sufficed to inspect the cracks induced by passing the shell through fire; they showed whether Heaven replied 'auspicious' or 'inauspicious' to the question put to it. The milfoil did not give the advice of Heaven at once: a plant with a strong smell which induces sneezing, its virtue was revealed only after a long preparation. People took 50 sticks* of milfoil but used only 49 of them. By means of successive sortings a hexagram was designated. There were 64 hexagrams, resulting from the combination 2 by 2 of the eight basic trigrams, *pa kua*. These latter, made up of the combinations of three broken or unbroken lines, were arranged in an octagon oriented in time and space, a sort of compass-card and cosmic wheel whose every element (each trigram) corresponded to a constituent principle of the Universe. The comparison of the lower and upper trigrams making up the hexagram so obtained indicated a change, a mutation, which by recourse to a reference table (the Book of Changes, *I Ching*) allowed people to see whether Heaven, interrogated in its deep structure and fathomed in its inmost intentions, replied 'auspicious' or 'inauspicious'.

When the tortoise and the milfoil persisted in replying 'inauspicious' to the prince's questions, then it meant that Heaven rejected him. At the same time the whole of nature, and especially the stars, signified the heavenly judgment: for the evils of government had a repercussion in the first place upon the world of the constellations. They resounded precisely in the heavenly region corresponding to the area of the land where their effects were manifested. Heaven had its regions, its provinces, and groups of constellations which were as though an astronomical projection of the different lordly states. When the suzerain to whom Heaven had entrusted 'the Mandate', that is to say, 'the Numbers of the heavenly Calendar', wished to verify whether, his Virtue being perfect, a proper order was maintained in the feudal hierarchy, he had only to inspect the map of Heaven. If, for example, three planets appeared together in one mansion, then the domain which was its earthly pendant suffered bereavements and internal and external wars: there was a change of lord. If four planets met there, wars and bereavements swooped down together; superior men were struck, and the common people reduced to vagrancy. Did five planets reveal themselves there? There was a complete change: he who had Virtue obtained Fortune; a new great man took power; to him fell the possession of the four cardinal points; his descendants teemed and prospered. Thus informed, the suzerain had accordingly only to reform his Virtue: in order to govern in the name of Heaven, a team of astronomers was of

---

* 50 is the product of 5×10; $49 = 7^2$; 7 is the classifier of things divinatory. 7 is moreover the approximate value of the diagonal of a square with a side of 5: $5^2 + 5^2 = 49 + 1 = 50$. There is a relation among, first, the magic square in which the number 5 played a basic role; second, the *pa kua* which played a part in the divination by milfoil; and third, the assignment of the classificatory number 7 to the divining operations.

greater help to him than the cleverest corps of diplomats. Like any diplomatic technique, astronomy had its dangers. At the end of the feudal period the lords made use of that art to their advantage; cosmological theories were constructed to show how dynastic Virtue irremediably waned in the end and in order to justify a revolution in the governmental order by the revolutions of the heavens.

But if everybody could make use of Heaven's foreknowledge, if Heaven was the object of general veneration, as was implied by the common use of divination and even more by the ancient practice of swearing oaths by the light of the day, there was as a true cult of Heaven only a royal cult. Heaven was the patron of the suzerain family: the royal Ancestors and their close followers alone participated in a sort of Elysian life, while the lords and their vassals continued to meet at the Yellow Springs; only the suzerain, as long as he retained a shadow of power, disposed of the Numbers of the Calendar. In the royal court, in a quasi-sacerdotal setting of diviners, astronomers, and annalists, Heaven appeared as a sovereign Power, basically unique and omnipotent; it was endowed with the essential attributes of a supreme God. In that, there was a sketch of monotheistic beliefs: but apart from the fact that these beliefs were still highly indistinct and very closely related to the beliefs about the Ancestors and agrarian Powers, they bore within them, to the extent that they corresponded to an idea of the supreme Order, a seed of abstraction predisposing them to become matter for philosophical speculation and a pretext for cultic inventions rather than a source of religious life and thought. In feudal religion, the cult of Heaven was only a dynastic and quite official cult, superimposed on the agrarian cults and the cults of Ancestors.

Agrarian cults

The Chinese say that Heaven is *one* and Earth *many*. That does not mean that they oppose the variety of the appearances of the earth to the unity of the blue sky. Their heaven, quite concrete, is a complex of heterogeneous entities, a composite of astronomical regions, climates, and seasons, and we shall see that the God of Heaven was scarcely conceived as a single person and that he was broken up into diverse hypostases. We shall even see that these hypostases took their respective attributes from the peculiarities of the earthly regions to which they were attached. If Heaven appeared one, in theory, it was because it was conceived as the source and the emblem of all authority. The king was Heaven; the lord was Heaven; the father was Heaven; the husband was Heaven. Heaven was a semi-concrete realization of the principle of order which then found expression in social organization through a hierarchy of group chieftains. Essentially, Heaven was one because it was the object of the suzerain's cult. Earth was many because there was no royal cult of the Earth to form a pendant to that of Heaven. That was so because the suzerain's power was ideal and did not correspond to a true territorial power: the suzerain ensured a sort of moral unity to confederated China by introducing a single calendar into all the domains; but every lord dated his Annals not by the reigns of the Sons of Heaven but from his own accession. A certain hierarchy among the diverse territorial powers (of which we shall find traces in the agrarian cults) was indeed established, but the fact remains (and it is the dominant fact) that because those powers antedated the conception of hierarchy itself, they continued after their being hierarchized to appear chiefly in their particular aspects. Although from feudal times Sovereign Earth was treated equally with August Heaven in being called to witness in oath-taking, Earth was not really conceived as a single power until the moment when, the Empire being established, it came into the possession of a single Master and became the object of an imperial cult parallel to that of Heaven.

But if Earth seemed many by nature it was not only because the regional agrarian cults each looked to a Power that had remained distinct; it was also because those cults were in themselves of varied kinds. The beliefs about agrarian deities preceded the existence of domains; alongside their urban deities of Earth, the nobles continued to venerate properly rural deities. And there was to be seen coexisting with an already abstract religion of earthly forces a more concrete agrarian religion deriving directly from the ancient beliefs centred on the Holy Places.

'Mountains, forests, rivers, valleys, hillocks, hillsides can produce clouds, make rain and wind, and cause wonders to appear; of all these things it is said that they are holy Powers.'[50] Every lord worshipped such of those Powers as resided in his territory. Every spring the lords of Lu caused dances and songs to be performed by two choruses of men and young people on the banks of the river *I*: they all bathed in the current and so thought to make the rain to fall. In Ch'en girls and boys sang and danced under the oaks of the *Yüan* mound, and the lord's consort hoped for children as a consequence of these practices. But mountains, woods, and rivers were not confined to yielding, along with children and rain, the universal fertility that allowed the lordly houses to perpetuate their Line and to feed their Ancestors with offerings; their benefits were wider: just as the Holy Places were the tutelary guardians of rural harmony, so the holy rivers, mounts, and woods were considered by the lords as the Ancestral Centres from which they drew the specific Virtue to provide them with the authority to govern their territories. They often bore the name of a mountain or a river; they thought that they had received from it, along with the name, their particular essence and (just as the Sons of Heaven saw in the Sovereign On High the origin of their Line and the originator of their Power) the feudatories imagined that they were truly descended from the divine places whose worship constituted their prestige and which seemed to them to be the externalized basis of their authority. While in the royal court celestial disturbances were taken as signs of the exhaustion of dynastic power, it was thought in all the territories that 'a domain must have the support of its Mounts and its Rivers. When the hills crumble, when the rivers dry up, there is presage of ruin': lordly Virtue was drying up, the power of the lord was crumbling. The prince's only recourse then was to renew his Virtue by a solemn consecration that reestablished a perfect communion between him and the source of his power. Thus it was that T'ang the Victorious, after a long drought ('The mountains and forests' were then 'exhausted! exhausted!'), offered his body as a victim to the Mulberry Forest: 'He cut his hair and clipped his nails' and probably secreted them in the earth (when people offered themselves to a river they cast their nail parings into the water).[51] T'ang's sacrifice was effective, and the rains fell; it was not the less total for its having been conducted by symbolic forms and committed the very person of the chief. A domain bordering on the Yellow River maintained contact with this local god by less striking but periodical sacrifices: it married to the waters of the river daughters of the lordly line.

Closely related to the dignitaries of the feudal hierarchy, mountains and rivers took their rank in that hierarchy: they had bestowed upon them the style of duke or count. And there came a time when it was fancied that, following the example of lords receiving investiture from the suzerain, they held their power by delegation from the Sovereign On High. Indeed, it was with these holy places as it was with lordly lines: their twin powers were local, autochthonous. Mountains and rivers were confederated under the authority of Heaven only when, under the authority of the Son of Heaven, the confederation of Chinese domains was formed. One can glimpse the reasons why rivers and especially mountains were looked upon as earthly and regional delegates of Heaven in the very moment when the local chieftains accepted to appear as vassals of the suzerain. Legend has it, we have seen, that the royal officials of the Calendar lived in the heights or valleys situated in the four directions. Legend further has it that the sovereign circuits which worked the cycle of the seasons were marked by four stations on the cardinal mountains. In the course of feudal history the lordly assemblies were by preference held on sites, both neutral and sacred, formed by the dependencies of a mountain or river. In the same way the rural communal assemblies took place outside appropriated lands, in the valleys, in the woods, on the hillsides which became Holy Places; there peasant harmony was created. In the lordly assemblies feudal harmony was created: then the suzerain received, along with the homage of the feudatories, the power which constituted him the supreme authority of the Confederation. He considered as a heavenly Mandate the right with which he was invested to promulgate a Calendar common to all. He obtained that right and exercised it actively in the Holy Places whose chief power was to ensure the natural and social orders together. At each of his stations on the holy mountains, surrounded by the vassals of the region, he set going a new season in its turn: all then imagined that the celestial labour which he thus began as Son of Heaven was duly completed by the mountains acting as permanent delegates of the seasons. They thought that while the Hsi and the Ho brothers represented in each direction the human collaborator of the Sovereign On High, the mountains on their side were none other than the immediate subordinates and earthly emissaries of August Heaven. Thus the chronicles affirm that when T'ang the Victorious, the Son of Heaven and founder of the Yin dynasty (second millennium before our era), sacrificed himself to the Mulberry Forest, he used the holy place as intermediary and only to cause his prayer to reach the heavenly Sovereign. Dispossessed in favour of Heaven (but de jure rather than de facto) of the regulative functions which, in both the natural and social order, they had been the first to be entitled to exercise as Holy Places, the cardinal Mountains were ready to offer a seat and particular attributes to the hypostases of the Sovereign On High. One of them, that of the East, T'ai Shan, benefiting by both its orientation and a richer legendary tradition, was to become the Supreme Power of life, and, uniting within itself Elysian Abode and Yellow Springs, was for long centuries to be the most important centre of pilgrimage and religious activity in the country.

All the Holy Places were not so fortunate: many remained what they had essentially been: local centres of pilgrimage. Their attributions changed little when later, as must often have been the case, some Buddhist or Taoist temple was joined to them. For the noble inhabitants of the towns they scarcely had more than the attraction of beauty-spots. Although for the lords the Holy Places of their territories were as external tokens of their power, the foundation of towns was, in general, a cause of decline for these religious centres. The cult of the Ancestors developed in the cities: from the beginning, that cult and the agrarian cults were one. The lord drew his power from them, and that power which was to be exercised permanently—social life in the town being continuous—needed to be not distanced from its source; in feudal organization the agrarian cults were centred in the towns. These towns, moreover, were holy places. Nothing allows us to assert that the towns were built near the Holy Places. But it is nonetheless certain that the peasant agrarian festivals bore the appearance of fairs and that the Holy Places were sites for the conduct of exchanges; now, the domanial towns were essentially markets: it was precisely in the markets (markets were, besides, places where peace was kept and blood vengeance normally forbidden) that, in the towns where some traces of peasant customs remained, there were held in the spring the assemblies of boys and girls who danced and sang. It was also in the section of the outskirts reserved to exchanges that there was celebrated in the capital the sacrifice to the Patron God of marriages, official substitute of the spring Festivals. In any case, a town was always established in accordance with the *yin* and the *yang* of the landscape, of its rivers, mountains, and woods: beautiful vegetation had to bear witness to the potency of the Earth. One author appears even to say that the siting of a capital was determined by the choice of the mound and the grove where the cult of the Ancestors and that of the Earth were to be conducted. The founder of the State of *Shao* is supposed to have exercised his power as the Great Go-between (a function long preserved at the royal court); he chiefly bestowed care upon the matching of couples and the making of marriage alliances which were the basis of civil harmony. We are told that he judged the sexual contests, that is to say, that he presided over the rivalrous rounds of love songs between boys and girls, under an ancient pear tree venerated by all his vassals: that was his Earth God.

Established in the town, under the influence of that principle of abstraction which, for every system of ideas, is formed by the permanence of an active social life, little by little the agrarian cults were stripped of their concrete richness, and distinctions began to be noticeable among them which in the beginning were barely perceptible. In the cities of the domains there existed a cult of the Earth in the strict sense and a cult of Harvests, but the two remained as one; there were there public and private agrarian cults, but they were bound together by a hierarchical link.

A lord raised two Earth altars, one to the South of his residence, in the same line as the ancestral temple but to the West; the other to the South of the town, in a field the grain from which was destined for the sacrifices; to each of them was joined a Harvest altar, and both were in close relationship with the cult of Ancestors. But the former was considered as the altar of the Earth God of the Domain and of the domanial town, and the latter as that of the Lord's Earth God.

A patrimonial cult, yet not purely private, was addressed to the Lord's Earth God and to his Harvest God. Its essential ceremony was the spring ploughing; the lord had in person to inaugurate the season's work. In the capital, the suzerain himself ploughed three furrows; the ministers followed him in ploughing five; then the feudatories present ploughed nine. Three is a totality; when he had three times ploughed, the sovereign had by himself done all. The ploughing which followed and which called for an increase in the number of furrows with a decrease in authority, had the effect of diffusing the initial effort through the whole extent of the country. The ceremony performed in the patrimonial field, but with the help of the vassals, served to desacralize in the whole domain the Earth forbidden to human labour during the dead season. By the cult thus rendered to them, the twin Gods of the patrimonial field made possible that form of the appropriation of land which consisted in the right to cultivate it and use its fruits. Only in this respect may we consider them to have been private Gods. But the produce of the field could be eaten only after the portion for the offerings due to these Gods had been deducted, and also when there had been removed the tribute imposed as homage to the patrimonial Gods of higher authorities, the first who laboured to desacralize the soil and the originators of the right of appropriation. Only a lord who held eminent right over the Land (and in the first place the suzerain of the Confederation) could proceed to the desacralization effected by the communal assembly in the festivals of the Holy Place, and in consequence, only he might raise patrimonial altars to the Gods of the Earth and Harvests. A high officer, whose title to lordship was precarious, could not do so, and even less so could mere nobles.

The Earth and Harvest Gods of the Domain and the domanial town were the object of a cult that made evident the public ties existing, not among landed estates, but among the hierarchized human groups making up feudal society. The altars to these Gods were raised, for the benefit of more or less extensive collectivities, by the Son of Heaven, the lords, the high officers, the Chieftains of districts, and the heads of families. The setting up of the altars was as an emblem of the enfeoffment of different local groups. The Earth God of the suzerain was a square formed on each side by land of appropriate colour, with yellow earth at the centre and at the top. At their investiture (it was a case of investiture *per glebam*) the lords received a clod of earth of a colour taken from the part of the royal altar corresponding to the position of their domain; the clod was covered with yellow earth to show the pre-eminence of the head of the Confederation. With that clod each made the Earth God for his domain: it legitimated as Earth Altar the square of earth he raised to the south of his residence and the tablet surmounting it. In theory, four regional Earth altars needed to be raised in the centre of the four great divisions of confederated China: they were of the colour agreeable to their direction and were topped by a tree whose essence was characteristic of the spring and the East (thuya), of the summer and the South (catalpa), of the West and the autumn (chestnut), of the North and the winter (acacia). The Earth God of the domain was placed in the centre of the domanial city; a part of his Virtue was incorporated in the four town gates. Similarly, the central lar of the house was properly the Earth God of the family group; but the four lares theoretically arranged in a square around it shared in its essence. The power of the central lar did not radiate beyond the domestic compound: the Earth God placed in the centre of the domanial Town was the Earth God of the whole Domain. The chief sanction for a crime entailing the suppression of a family or a domain was the destruction of the Earth altars or lares: the house was razed, the site turned into a quagmire, the altar's lands dispersed. A change of dynasty brought with it not the disappearance of the altar but its imprisonment. The immured altar then served as a screen for the temple of the Ancestors: it became a second Earth God of evil power and had attributed to it the negative qualities proper to the agrarian divinities. This God of interdiction sent delegates into all the domains. To the South of every lordly residence there were to the West an Earth God, beneficent power although severe, and to the East, close to the Ancestors, another Earth God who was a God of death—both flanked by their acolytes, the Harvest Gods.

The possession of these agrarian Gods was the sign of an authority exercised by means of positive and negative sanctions on a human group attached to a territory, an authority at one and the same time territorial and personal in character. From that fact flows the complexity of the attributes assigned to these Gods. The power extended in the first place to the things of Nature. Just as the central lar was, in the beginning, placed under the opening in the roof, so the altars of the Earth and the Harvests had to be open to the sky. To kill them and to make of them powers of death it was enough to wall them up; and yet they were left with an opening to the North through which they received the influx of destructive forces emanating from the dark north. The living God of the Earth at all times received sun, rain, dew, and hoar-frost, incorporated within itself all the active principles of Nature, and became the originator of the fertility of the fields.

It was propitiated in spring, thanked in autumn: but it is clear as we read the hymns sung at these seasonal festivals, that the honours that the Earth God then received it owed principally to its equality of status with the Harvest God and to the alliance which, through the latter, brought it close to the temple of the Ancestors: 'Behold our ploughs sharpened!—First to the work in the fields of the South— Let us sow the grain of all seedbeds—Within them there is life! . . .— Let us therefore in crowds get in the harvest, in crowds!—How great the abundance at the harvest!—Thousands, thousands of millions, and quadrillions!—Let us make wine! Let us make must!—They will be offerings to the ancestors—to perform the rites!—How delectable is this odour!—It is the glory of the region!—How piquant is this perfume!—It is the comfort of the old!—It is not just here that things are as they are here!—It is not just today that things are as today!—Among our most ancient forefathers it was so!'[52] The veneration in which the native held his land bursts from this song, but it is noticeable that piety went first to the Powers that fertilized the grain. Positioned by the cult and the beliefs which depended on it, and in some measure in opposition to the Ancestors and Heaven, Earth by comparison appeared as a divinity of the second rank. Although it was seen chiefly as Soil appropriated or enfeoffed and as such was given a masculine appearance, people still felt a feminine nature in it which made it akin to the *yin* principle; now, *yin* and women were thought of as inferior to men and *yang*. As power of Nature, the Earth God was far from having kept the prestige enjoyed by the Holy Place and Mother Earth. A sacred wood is far removed from the square of earth around which the urban ceremonies were performed.

The association was all to the benefit of the God of Harvests, and the Earth God showed his own power in the ceremonies in which he appeared as the centre of feudal grouping. When an eclipse made manifest a disorder in Nature and the decay of the social bonds which were its cause, it was around the God of enfeoffment that the vassals gathered, each in his place, in order to restore the order that had been disturbed. Their warlike hubbub had to appear at a given moment to be a demonstration of constraint upon the God; it was he who was held responsible, as a realization of *yin*, for the defeat of the principle of light, and they fancied that they were attacking him when they grouped themselves around him in military array. But actually, men then gathered about the Earth God because, the origin of all investiture being there, all the great feudal assemblies had to be conducted in that place. And indeed the Earth altar was the starting point of all parades of lordly power. From it began hunting expeditions and expeditions of war. There men presented themselves upon their return. They sacrificed to it the game they took; prisoners (at least one of them) fed the Earth God with their blood. Human sacrifices are rarely noted by Chinese authors—they are rather unwonted in a religion remarkable for the gentleness of its rites—but the fact of those sacrifices is nonetheless certain. It is true that in the sixth century B.C. the victim was immolated to the fallen and walled-up Earth God; but a century earlier the sacrifice was performed to the reigning Earth God. Every vanquished man, besides, had to appear before his conqueror in the symbolic attire of a victim. The sacrifice was justified by the idea that war was a form of penal sanction and every opponent a rebel: it was conceived as a punishment. Wicked vassals as well as enemies were subject to disciplinary measures. The feudal army took with it its Earth God, or at any rate the tablet that could serve as its double. The oldest military proclamation we possess (it is probably more than three thousand years old) ends with the words: 'Those who will not obey my orders I shall put to death before the Earth God!'

It was before the Ancestors that rewards were made; at their side, the Earth God appeared as a stern Power:[53] it is true that it was the God of punishments only because it was the God of feudal fealty and only because through it investiture was acquired. But, by its character as heir of the Holy Place, it was perhaps inclined to demand human sacrifices. Have we not seen that the chieftain to whom its cult fell thought himself obliged to sacrifice his body to the deity when the latter seemed to lose its potency and that its energy had to be renewed? In feudal religion the Earth God was the only one to feed solely on raw meat and to will that its tablet be anointed with blood. Despite its cruel aspects, its cult made everybody experience the strong cohesion of the feudal group: the raw meat served for communions through which—a positive blessing—the vassals felt united among themselves and with their chieftain by a common sharing in the Genius of their country. The association of the Earth God with the Harvest God had allowed the idea of Mother Earth to remain potent: it was in this way that the Earth God had been able to preserve its character of agrarian divinity, although in feudal society and urban life it had appeared chiefly as a deity who presided at the enfeoffment of a group of vassals to a lord. The sentiment of attachment to the chieftain did not prevail over that of attachment to the native Soil. A distinction was made between dying for one's lord and dying for the altars of Earth and Harvests: in Chinese these last words do not evoke the devotion owed to a master but the veneration which the fatherland merits. That fatherland was something quite different from native soil; the feudal hierarchy reacted on the organization of agrarian cults: the worshipped Earth stretched beyond one's native land, and the veneration for it was made up of less concrete sentiments.

The cult of the Ancestors

In every peasant house, not far from the central lar, exposed to the influence of all the powers of Nature, there was a dark corner where beside a pile of seed awaiting the time of its germination, the Ancestors lived confusedly around the domestic bed. In the domanial town the ancestral temple was built beside the uncovered altar of the Earth and Harvest Gods. In the temple of the lordly family as in the temples of vassal families the ancestors did not lead an indistinct life; the piety of kinsmen was not addressed to a sort of collective tutelary spirit, to an undifferentiated group of protective powers: it was addressed to distinct Ancestors each of whom preserved his personality and who each was the patron of one of the kin groups of the segmented family.

In the city as in the family residences, there were chieftains upon whom the possession of authority conferred a powerful personality. That personality was constituted by the prestige accruing from the rank occupied in the feudal hierarchy, the extent of the subordinate family group, and the luxury of the style of life; all that was expressed in a sort of increase in the substance making up the individual. The nobleman nourished himself in such a way as to possess a vigorous soul as much in the moral as in the physical sense. The greater his nobility, the more numerous and the more magnificent the sacrifices in which he took part: he partook more often of the repasts at the end of the sacrifices; he ate more of them; he ate the better parts of them; he ate the offerings of greater variety and greater importance; as he ate he communicated more directly with higher authorities, divine and human. He assimilated great quantities of essences. From his enriched substance his soul drew a quality of duration which, first, enabled it to live long within his body, and, second, assured it a long survival. The souls of men and women of the common people, if they died before their time, remained active for a while. The soul of a nobleman in any event possessed a certain durable potency whose strength, as well as its persistence, was in proportion to the nobility of the dead man. It retained its personality, its independent life, its capacity for action to a degree and for a time defined for each individual according to his social position.

Just as it fixed social rank, protocol determined the survival of souls as personal forces. The Chinese of feudal times doubtless did not have a consciousness whose activity was organized in a unitary fashion. They did not have a unified soul, but different and many souls, as numerous as the vital functions. They divided these souls into two groups, into the categories of *yin* and *yang*: they spoke of having two souls. One, the *yin* soul, was called *P'o* during life, when it was joined to the other, and *Kuei*, after death, when they were divorced. That was the lower soul, the group of souls on which the animal functions depended; the *P'o* was the soul of the body and especially of the blood: it existed by the fact of conception alone. The soul of the *yang* class was called *Hun* during life and *Shen* after death; as the higher soul and more ideal in essence, it was the first to depart and the last to arrive; it was a breath-soul which manifested itself in the voice, was called back at its departure by the cries of the kinsmen, and whose arrival was signalled by the first wailing of the infant; it corresponded to the highest parts of the personality and to the personal name by which each individual held a position in the family group; it was that which constituted individuality. When that individuality was strong the soul did not at once perish. When they died, the common people could be only indistinct *Kuei*. The *Shen* of nobles of the second class survived for a generation, after which the Ancestors entered into the vague group of *Kuei*. The nobles of the first class remained *Shen* for two generations; but it was only in the fifth generation that they entered for ever into the mass of the *Kuei*; during the two intermediate generations they were ordinarily *Kuei* and at special times *Shen*. Let us say, in short, that a high officer lasted as *Shen* for three generations, that he was not finally *Kuei* until the fifth generation, that only the founder of his family was *Shen* for ever, and that the lords and the suzerain were *Shen* for four generations, except for their first Ancestors who were *Shen* in perpetuity. Such was the official status of the dead.*

Personal survival, if I may so put it, was a public privilege granted to the vassals by lordly authority. The right to survive for a fixed period as a distinct Ancestor, or conversely, the right to conduct a special cult for a fixed number of Ancestors, was a consequence of the character of the investiture by which enfeoffment to the chief had been effected. Nobility did not come from antiquity of Line but by the lord attributing a certain number of 'quarters'—I mean, by the assignment of a sort of genealogical tree made up of a collection of tablets each representing an Ancestor entitled to receive periodic honours. The lord gave the right to build an Ancestral temple, to keep a fixed number of tablets there in a fixed number of sanctuaries; he gave, in quantities regulated by protocol, the *imagines majorum*—he gave Ancestors; he could take them away; he could degrade and reduce the ancestral line in status; he could withdraw investiture, destroy the temple, and suppress the Ancestors. The advent of the feudal regime threw into relief the authority of group heads and the importance of personality; it created conditions favourable to the establishment of a cult of the Ancestors: hence the cult of the Ancestors closely depended in its organization upon the order established by the feudal system.

Filial piety was expressed by that cult; that piety was not addressed only to the dead: it was composed of all the homage that a person should receive during his life on earth, at the moment of his death, and in the course of his ancestral life. Filial piety constituted, from the time he was alive, the Majesty of the Ancestor to be; it effected the

* It is necessary to add that the powers of the *Shen* were diverse and also depended on protocol: each *Shen*, according to its rank, received a fixed number of sacrifices a year. The substance of the different *Shen* was fed in proportion to their nobility.

difficult transition from life to death; and finally it nourished the substance of the Ancestors.

A son dared not use the flight of steps reserved for his father; he touched neither his clothes nor his bed-coverings, nor his mat, nor his pillow, nor the stool upon which he rested; 'he especially respects his staff and his shoes and he does not allow himself to draw too near to them; he does not allow himself to use his bowl, his cup, his water-jar . . . ; he must (in his presence) walk gravely . . . , refrain from belch-ing, sneezing, coughing, yawning . . . , from standing on one leg . . . , from donning an outer garment, even if it is cold . . . , from scratching himself even if he itches . . . , from allowing the lining of his clothes to show . . .' On the other hand, 'he must wipe away his father's spittle or mucus . . . , prepare him a bath every five days . . . and, in the interval, if his face (or feet) are dirty, prepare rice water for him . . .' At dawn he must do him homage in ceremonial costume, offer him dainties, massage him, scratch him, serve him his pap and put vege-tables and condiments into his dishes to make muscle; then he ate and drank the leavings. In the evening he once more paid homage and brought dainties.[54] By all these attentions he gave his father the vigour of body and soul appropriate to a Chieftain, he procured him long life and the means with which to survive death, and, finally, he communed with him in order to be able to succeed him and to preside at his worship.

When the father died, the son withdrew to a hut made of branches; he slept without bed and bedding and used a clod of earth as pillow, 'for his father is in the earth';[55] he wore clothes of very loosely woven cloth and at first remained barefoot; for some time he fasted and ate only when ordered to do so by neighbours or his lord; he washed only when there were ceremonies; he kept silent and abstained from music; he weakened himself to the point of not being able to get up without the aid of a staff; he lived alone, without his wife, beside his brothers and kinsmen, but without communicating with them; he fostered within him a state of stupefaction and prostration. By these means which made him share in the mortuary state and which grew milder as the mourning diminished, he hoped to extricate the dead man from the impurity into which death had plunged him. Helped by all his kin and the neighbouring families, he proceeded at regulated times to the ceremonies which marked the stages of the dead man on his road to his destiny as an Ancestor. By his cries and his rhythmic leaps he actively showed his grief; he rested on the corpse breast to breast: the supreme contact of communion. The public display of filial sentiments, the condolences, and the gifts from friends formed a veritable consecration of the dead man.[56] When he had shed his flesh, having first been buried in the earth inside the house, the body would be gathered to the bodies of the Ancestors in the family grave-yard. It was shut up for good in the earth and, by means of the appropriate rites, its *Hun* was brought back to the house; it was fixed to a tablet associated with that of the dead man's grandfather. At that point, under the patronage of the latter, there began for the dead man a sort of apprenticeship to the ancestral life; little by little he made his way into the group of the *Shen*, the Ancestors who were entitled to personal survival. When the mourning was over, the Ancestor was constituted; his worship began.

It consisted in seasonal sacrifices taking place in the autumn and spring, at the times when the peasant communities celebrated the death or the renewal of the year: 'When the hoar-frost fell, the cultivated man, crushing it underfoot, felt sadness in his heart; in the spring, when the dew moistened the earth, while treading it underfoot he had in his heart a feeling made up of respect, as though he was about to discern his dead Ancestors'.[57] Such was the time of ordinary offerings: it goes without saying that the noblest souls, whose substance was richer and activity more continuous, were entitled to more frequent sacrifices. They were monthly for the souls of lords when they were in the first stage of their survival. When it had reached the furthest limit of its ancestral career, a sovereign's soul was still entitled to offerings; these were entirely of raw meat, for it was about to sink into Mother Earth. Ordinary offerings consisted essentially of cooked meats, cereals, and spirits. To suit the Ancestors, all the offerings had to come from the domestic fields and be prepared by the family. The victims had to be perfect, the dishes and the drinks prepared according to the rules, the stands and vessels placed in proper order to bear witness to the sincerity of the descendants. Purity was demanded; before being sacrificed the victims were subjected to a sort of quarantine analogous to the fast kept by the sacrificers. All the objects used in the offerings were sacred: they were called only by ritual terms; water was blackish liquor; fermented liquor, pure drink; rice, excellent potherb; leek, abundant root; ox, animal with broad feet; sheep, (animal with) soft hair; pig, (animal with) stiff silk; fish, stiff offering; hare, the clear-sighted.[58] The utensils were of set form, decorated in traditional designs and with inscriptions rich in auspicious characters. The sacrificer cut off a little hair near the victim's ears, then cut it into pieces with a knife the handle of which ended in a bell. The sacrifice began with a libation prepared from black millet: 'it went down to the deepest springs' and there sought out the *yin* soul, the blood soul. Then the fat of the victim, mixed with wormwood, was burned, and the odorous smoke, passing through the roof, went towards Heaven in search of the *yang* soul, the breath-soul. All this was as though the Ancestor returned both from Heaven and the Yellow Springs. 'The

Hun and the P'o were joined' as at a birth: the Ancestor was present.

The pious son gained the feeling of this sacred presence in preparing himself for the sacrifice by a retreat of ten days in which the most rigorous observances fell in the last three days (10 and 3 are characteristics of totality). He lived as in the mourning period, shut up, alone, deprived of his wife, without company, without social intercourse, without music, and he fasted, allowing himself to take 'neither fermented liquor nor vegetable of sour taste'. At the end of the seclusion he washed and put on new clothes: he was another man ready to enter into communication with a sacred Power. Indispensable for meriting the presence of any Authority, fasting, when it preceded sacrifice, brought about a glorious result: 'Purifying oneself by retreat is unifying and concentrating one who is not so . . . , it is protecting oneself against all dispersion . . . and turning aside useless thoughts (personal inclinations or desires) . . . , all movement of feet and hands is then avoided . . . (and one succeeds in) bringing one's Virtue to its highest point of enlightenment . . . Having thus fixed one's thoughts and one's feelings and gained a perfect *enlightenment* it is possible to communicate with the *refulgent Shen*' of the Ancestor. By thinking only of the way in which the dead 'behaved, joked, conversed, thought, felt, and rejoiced, one could see the Ancestor for whom one fasted appear'.[59]

Communication with the Ancestor, achieved through the enlightenment produced by the ascetic observances of the retreat, was rounded off by the communion effected by a repast served to the Ancestor by the pious son, which the former consumed and of which the son ate the leavings. All this was conducted in a most realistic fashion. The dead man had a representative who ate and drank for him: he was identified with the dead man to such a point that within the enclosure around the sacrifice a lord himself showed the most absolute respect for this representative who was after all only a vassal. Of course, retreat and purification were required of the man who represented an Ancestor, as they were of the sacrificer and the victim. Just as the victim had to come from the family fields, so the representative had to be drawn from among the kin. He must even obligatorily be a grandson of the dead man or, failing that, a kinsman of the dead man belonging to the generation of his grandsons. That is to be explained by the history of the Chinese family. Kinship and name were transmitted through women before they were transmitted through men.[60] In the ancient uterine organization everyone was the kinsman of the father of his father and not the kinsman of his own father.[61] In the agnatic organization which followed, the grandfather remained the most important of one's kinsmen; the father was rather a chieftain, agnatic filiation resulting from an affiliation of the son to the father analogous to the enfeoffment of the vassal to his lord.[62] During the sacrifice to the Ancestor, the father, a veritable lord, served his own son,[63] offered him food to eat, bowed down before him. The latter, sometimes very young and carried in the arms of a kinsman who acted for him, was treated as a lord by his own father because he was then like a reapparition and an incarnation of the dead and discarnate lord of that father. The words the ancestor pronounced reached the sacrificer only through a chanter authorized for oral communication with holy Powers. The words were taken as coming from the very mouth of the grandfather, whose soul and voice then animated the grandson. The words were the sanction of the sacrifice; they were a formula of investiture. By their Virtue the pious son, head of the family, was invested with the family Fortune and received Happiness in its three forms: a long line of descendants, feudal honours, longevity. Thus the transmission of the *sacra* was effected *from father to son, but through the grandson.* The effect of sacrifice was twofold: on the one hand, the pious son drew from it the authority constituting the head of the family and which the practice of filial piety, by creating agnatic affiliation, caused to pass from the lord (father) to the chief vassal (son); on the other hand, the continuity of domestic ties was established by practices whose effect was to bring it about that, at each seasonal ceremony, the grandson was possessed by the soul of the grandfather.

That process of transmission of domestic ties appeared in the custom that governed the choice of name taken by a family branch when it was detached from the common trunk: the name was by preference that of the grandfather. The ordering of the ancestral temple was similarly determined by the principle by which there existed an essential opposition between two kinsmen belonging to two consecutive generations and, in contrast, a solidary group was formed by kinsmen belonging to alternate generations. We have seen that every dead man, once he had shed his flesh in the domestic Earth, completed a probationary phase before becoming a *Shen* and receiving personal sacrifices: the apprenticeship had to be undergone to the grandfather, and nobody was born into ancestral life without feeding upon the offerings intended in the first place for his grandfather. Only a family head, once that initiation had been ended, received sacrifices in his own name; the dead younger brothers were still only commensals; but even among kinsmen, one ate only with people of one's own rank; in a lordly temple, a younger son, not being a lord, would not be able to eat with his grandfather who was a lord; he would take his share of the offerings in association with his grandfather's brother; and if the grandfather had no brother, the association would be made with a brother of the great-great-grandfather. In the same way, a wife of inferior rank would eat only with a wife of inferior rank; if the grandfather had no secondary wife, the dead woman would eat with the wife of the great-great-grandfather: she could in no case share in the offerings of a wife, principal or secondary, of her father-in-law or of her husband's great-grandfather. In the ancestral temple the tablets were arranged right and left by alternate generations: there was no communication possible between the left group and the right group;[64] on the other hand, each group was undivided. The noble family was separated into two parts because domestic solidarity rested upon two principles: the enfeoffment of the son to the father and the kinship between son and grandfather.[65] Kinship involved an identity of substance: grandsons, grandfathers, and great-great-grandfathers formed a homogeneous group. The temple of a lord embraced four sanctuaries in two lines (the solidarity of mourning extended to all the collaterals springing from the same great-great-grandfather).[66] The temple of a noble of the first rank—who represented the basic class within the feudal hierarchy—embraced only two sanctuaries (economic community existed only among descendants of the same grandfather), but that was enough for each section of the ancestral family to receive, through a representative preserving his personality, the share of the cult to which it was entitled.

From this organization of the family and of the ancestral cult derived the chief obligations of religious morality. And in the first place there was the obligation to marry. A head of family must have a wife, who was an indispensable adjunct in the service of the ancestor cult. If he was wifeless, he was obliged to remarry, unless he had a married son and was seventy years old, the age of retirement; his son in that case replaced him, but that created an abnormal situation. If the family head remarried, his new wife did not provide him with a perfect collaborator and indeed, second marriages were forbidden to lords, heads of ancestor cults whose importance was greater. The prohibition would be inexplicable if conjugal collaboration was made necessary simply because the husband was charged with making the offerings to the Ancestors and his wife similarly charged in respect of their wives. In fact, the distribution of tablets in the ancestral temple took no account of the opposition of the sexes; it was governed only by the alternation of generations. The head of a cult was charged with the whole service of the temple; but he was personally qualified only for the cult of his grandfather and great-great-grandfather, who belonged along with him to the same family moiety. We have seen that the fact was a consequence of the principle, anciently recognized, of descent through women. The son of the head of the cult would later be qualified to preside at the sacrifices to the other half of the family. His mother was already so qualified; she was so if she had been chosen as wife in a family associated by a tradition of intermarriage and taken from a generation corresponding to that of her husband.[67] That is why it would have

been a great crime to marry a woman whom the equivalence set up
between the generations marked out to be the wife of one's father or
son (this rule still plays the greatest role in Chinese incest laws).
Again, that is why it was appropriate to get married at a fixed age, the
men at thirty, the women at twenty, and, so to say, among members
of the same age-set.[68] That rule was absolutely adhered to in peasant
unions: performed in a collective ceremony, marriage coincided with
initiation. Noble marriage indeed retained something of this collective
marriage, and from that followed the possibility for a husband of
pretty well certainly having with him in the cult the female collaborator
he needed; if, in conformity with the practice of sororal polygyny, he
married, at the desired time and in the appropriate generation, two
wives who were sisters or cousins, when the principal wife, the elder
of them, died, he was not a widower: the younger one was a perfect
substitute for the dead woman. The ancestral temple would continue
to possess the conjugal pair necessary to meet the needs of the cult of
two groups of dead.

We see the reason why, in the texts which speak of ceremonies of
worship, the son often figured by the side of his mother. We see
further why the obligation to have descendants was strict: to have a
son was the first duty of filial piety. Every man was supposed to give
his father, a revered lord, a grandson to be his continuator and who,
being of exactly the same essence, would be first his incarnation, at
least in the cult, and then later, having become head of the cult, specially
qualified to make offerings to that kin moiety of which grandson and
grandfather were together members. He who did not procreate might
adopt. Anyone without descendants did not count in the family, and,
once dead, received only lesser offerings, unless he had a rank in the
feudal hierarchy; but in that case, in order to eat the sacrifices to which
he was entitled, he had first to have a posthumous successor instituted
for him.

It was not enough to have male offspring; they had to be fit for the
cult. Confucius's father had a lame son; we are told that he remarried
when he was more than seventy, and Confucius was born of that union
contracted in despite of custom, so great was the obligation to leave
behind someone who might be head of the cult. The sense of that
obligation served to justify minute rules the observance of which was
imposed upon pregnant women; their actions, their comportment,
their speech, the music they had to hear, the food they needed to eat,
the scents they must breathe, all was ordered so that well set up boys
might be brought to birth. The most rigorous of the practices of filial
piety was connected with the same ideas: a pious son had to preserve
his body intact. 'He does not bind himself to death by a bond of
friendship'; 'he avoids climbing to great heights, he avoids going

near precipices, he avoids cursing or laughing incautiously; he avoids moving in the darkness; he avoids climbing up steep slopes: he fears to dishonour his parents!'[69] A sage who hurt his foot remained sad even when he was cured; this is the reason why: 'what makes up a man is given to him by his parents in a state of perfect wholeness: if he gives it back to them in the same state, one can say that he is a pious son . . . A good son does not move a foot, does not say a word without heeding the duties of filial piety; he takes the main roads and never the byways: he goes by boat and never swims; he has not the boldness to expose to danger the body he has received from his parents.'[70]

The body (like the soul), nourished by family communions, was a portion of a substance that was the indivisible property of kin; everybody held only a precarious title to his body: it was held in trust, and the holder at the end of his term would have to restore it intact to the stock. Whence the importance attached to mutilation in public and private penal law. To eat the gall of an enemy or put his body in pickle, to quarter a rebel or reduce him to ashes, to cut off the ear of the vanquished, to amputate a rival, to castrate a criminal, was above all to strike in his family honour the man upon whom one avenged oneself: it was to reduce the capital stock of substance belonging to a family. For the family, as for the individual, mutilation was graver than death. The same sentiments explain the penal solidarity existing among kinsmen and the treatment of hostages. It was of no great moment to hit directly at the guilty man or enemy; it was enough to strike at one of his kinsmen; the entire family group was affected and together with the others, just as much as the victim replacing him and no more so, the individual responsible. Alongside the feeling of family unity there acted the sentiment of domestic hierarchy: to hold one of his kinsmen as hostage was to gain a hold over somebody; but when pledges were exchanged, care was taken to weigh their value. The greatest advantage would be to seize a rival's father or mother: to dare to demand them as hostages was a form of insolence that in itself brought shame. Conversely, positive sanctions honoured the whole group of kin: they honoured the individual they were meant to affect even more when they were first applied to the family head. A faithful vassal was better recompensed when it was his father or his mother who ate the leavings of the offerings made by the lord. In the same way, an increment of prestige accrued from the retrospective ennoblement of the Ancestors. A vassal unhesitatingly sacrificed his body, or the bodies of his children, for his master because that master, who had invested him with the right to have Ancestors honoured by a personal cult, disposed of a power sufficient to restore to the family's patrimony, in the shape of substantial honours, more than the sacrifice of one of its members had caused it to lose.

Besides, if in order to preserve his body intact, a noble had hesitated to fulfil his feudal obligations, the lord would have had the power to suppress him, his whole family, his cult of the Ancestors; but such sanctions, dangerous for the domain, were in normal times rare. If individuals were obliged to watch over their bodies and to keep intact the trust received from their Ancestors, the preservation of every family unit was not a less basic necessity for society: there were numerous examples of families destroyed by a blow from lordly authority and soon after reinstated completely in their power and their cult. Not only did reigning dynasties take care to perpetuate the ancestor cults of the dynasties which they had supplanted—just as they kept their Earth Gods; they felt, besides, the obligation to feed offerings to the dead deprived of descendants and sacrifices. The cult of the Ancestors centred upon the family, but the head of the family held its priesthood only by virtue of the authority which he received from lordly investiture. If the family disappeared, the obligations incumbent upon men in regard to their dead fell to the charge of the local power. The cult of the Ancestors was always a matter of public interest; the cult of the dead who were no longer Ancestors was essentially a public cult: as much as the cult of the Earth, it bore upon the prosperity of the country. Solidarity persisted between lord and vassals after death: brought together in hazy dwelling-places adjoining the domain, their souls jointly exercised the functions of a tutelary Power that was the Fortune of the fief.

Mythology

However frequent they were, the ceremonies of the great cults in the domanial towns did not exhaust religious activity. Even if we ignore a multitude of ritual acts performed in honour of deities of place and occasion[71]—those performed in passing through a door, getting into a chariot, eating vegetables in season—we can say that the daily life of a noble was spent wholly in religious exercises: such were the exercises imposed by filial piety or the fealty of vassals, for father and lord possessed a Majesty nurtured by continuous homage. The relations among heads of different families or even among ordinary nobles—contacts among personalities more or less rich in sacred power but always of a different essence—never belonged to profane life: there was a ritual of visiting and a ritual of gift-giving. In the home, husbands and wives observed the ritual of conjugal life. There were rites for sitting down, for drinking, for eating. Every moment of the day, so to say, was spent, at least by chieftains, in some religious practice.

Continually taken up with practices great and small, that life tended to the refinement of ceremonial technique and to the analysis of ritual mechanisms: in this fashion the reign of religious formalism was prepared for the future. Propitious to the technical development of religion, urban life was much less favourable to mythic invention: that, work of a priestly milieu, was so shaped that its creations were artificial in nature. They sprang not from imagination and faith but from a voluntary effort of abstract thought: they were articles of dogma and speculations aimed at protecting a religious system, a political system.

The myths of feudal religion owed their existence to a priestly poetry which inspired a large part of the pieces in the *Shih Ching*. All the urban ceremonies were accompanied by dances, music, and song. Every lord, according to his rank, possessed several groups of mummers and masters of music. Every domain had its own songs which were thought to express its special genius. Many of these songs were simply composed with the aid of popular themes: sung in the lordly courts, they took on a symbolic value brought into harmony with the senti-ments of this new setting. Other songs, inspired by the same poetic technique but invented in princely conservatoires, were intended to be performed during the great sacrifices. They were inspired by a desire for dynastic glorification and were sung in festivals where, to make the sacrificial communions effective through the sacred Powers, these latter were represented by a man, member of the family group or the group of vassals, depending on whether he represented a divinity of the Earth or an ancestral god. Besides, cults of nature and cults of the ancestors were very close and were scarcely to be distinguished. Whence a tendency to euhemerism.[72] To the extent that they were conceived under a personal aspect, all the venerable forces appeared as dynastic Patrons, as Founder Heroes. Priestly poetry, which had bor-rowed its forms and its stock of images from peasant poetry, also drew from rural legends elements of the panegyrics composed to the glory of dynastic Heroes. It made use of them in order to create genealogical themes.

Composed upon that uniform model with the aid of hardly varying elements, the greater part of the divine legends go back to the tale of a miraculous conception or birth. The mother of Ch'i, second king of the Hsia dynasty, was a split stone. His father, Yü the Great, was wholly preoccupied with causing the flood-waters to drain away; his food had to be brought to him where he laboured; when he was hungry he summoned food by striking a drum; as soon as she heard the drum, his pregnant wife ran up bearing the meal. Now, in order to carry out his task Yü took the shape of a bear; his wife, seeing him in that form, and overcome by bashfulness, changed into a stone; but Yü, not wanting to be robbed of his child, demanded it, whereupon the stone split and Ch'i came into the world: indeed, Ch'i means *to open*.[73] Hsieh, founder of the Yin dynasty and ancestor of the princes of Sung, was born of a swallow's egg. Chien Ti his mother, accompanied by her two sisters, at the 'spring equinox, the day when the swallows return . . . , bathed in the stream of the Yüan mound; a swallow with an egg in its beak let it fall; it was of five colours and very beautiful; the women vied in seizing it . . . Chien Ti was the first in getting it; she swallowed it and conceived'.[74] Hsieh, her child, founded the Tzu family: among other things, Tzu means *egg*. The genealogists of the lords of Ch'in, whose power was of late date, did not put themselves out for their masters: by means of a common doublet,[75] they caused them to be descended from a forbear who was likewise born of an egg. The change of customs was marked by the fact that the princess-mother did not bathe in the open when she gulped down the miraculous egg; she spun hemp in the women's apartments.

The share of invention in these genealogical legends is slight: they were simple echoes of the festivals of the Holy Places where the peasants celebrated their marriages and which the lords made the basis of their power. We sense a more systematic thought in the legend of Hou Chi. Hou Chi was the ancestor of the Chou dynasty; his myth was shaped in the royal court; it contained richer and better ordered elements; the hymns devoted to him have great beauty of form; they take wing and bear an accent of piety; they are the work of poets skilled in their art and of vassals filled with the sense of loyalty.

Hou Chi, like Ch'i, was born of a stone. That stone was marked by a great footprint; his mother put her foot upon it as she performed a lustration; she wished to have a child; her wish was fulfilled. But the legend does not leave the matter there; the large footprint became that of a giant; and being born of it, Hou Chi derived from it first 'the strength of a mountain, consonant with the will of a giant'. That would have sufficed for the ancestor of lords who simply took their authority from a holy Mountain. But Hou Chi was the forbear of a royal house and it was necessary to show whence came to him the many attributes demanded of, in this case, a Founder Hero.

Hou Chi was the Great Ancestor of a line of Sons of Heaven who 'hereditarily perform the function of Harvest Princes'. He bore the name Prince of Harvests (Hou Chi); he was born with 'the virtue of helping Nature'; he was the true son of Heaven. In the time of the Chou kings, agnatic succession was the basis of all legitimate authority. The prince had a civilizing mission (the town-dwellers were 'civilized', the peasants 'rustics') which he received from his father and whose source was the First Prince, the First Civilizing Hero; that Hero was called Huang Ti. The Chou and Hou Chi had to be descended from him. So that it was known that Hou Chi was the son of Ti K'u (Kao Hsin), son of Chiao Chi, son of Hsüan Hsiao, son of Huang Ti. Descent was not everything; prestige was necessary. The prestige of a family branch came to it from its Great Ancestor who must have obtained glory and merit by manifesting his Virtue in governing a Province of Nature; Hou Chi, indeed, had been named Prince of Harvests. Every power of command resulted from an investiture by a sovereign and was gained at the same time as a fief; on the same occasion there was conferred a family name, sign of a specific Virtue: along with his office, Hou Chi was given the name Chi and the fief of T'ai by a qualified sovereign.

These human titles having been settled, the Celestial Mandate remained to be justified. It was all the more necessary to justify it in that, from an examination of the historical title, it emerged that Hou Chi was only a junior endowed with an apanage, the founder of a collateral branch (separated from the trunk, in conformity with the rule, in the fifth generation, including that in which the separation was effected), that he was in fine merely a vassal. It was acknowledged to begin with that he was the son of the principal wife and the first-born; in this fashion the Chou no longer appeared as usurpers; the accusation of being usurpers was transferred to the dynasties that had preceded them; Hou Chi was no longer de jure a vassal. It remained to explain his new name and his apanage: they were ascribed to him in his own right. To achieve that it was enough to make use of the right based upon uterine descent, agnatic right and descent having already been utilized. Hou Chi held his fief of T'ai direct from his mother, Chiang Yüan, Princess of T'ai. From her he also took his family name, which was Chi; *Chi* was allowed to be the equivalent of *Chi* which means footsteps. Walking upon a footprint, Chiang Yüan gave Hou Chi, along with his existence, the name that is the specific essence of every being. In order to add to that the Mandate of Heaven, nothing more needed to be done than to decide that the footprint was not that of a giant but that it came from the Sovereign On High; it was affirmed that it was the mark made by his big toe.

Little more needed to be done to make Hou Chi a worthy Ancestor of the Son of Heaven: all that remained was to suggest that his birth was the work of the Heavenly Sovereign and of Him alone. Chiang Yüan was married to Ti K'u (Kao Hsin); but the married state mattered little if the means could be found to establish the wife's purity. The hymns are careful to speak only of her, and they emphasize her labours of purification. She carried them out during her months of pregnancy: that was the rule. She had performed a lustration when she stepped into the footprint. Recounting these different acts, the priestly poetry was cunning enough to use the same word: it was an ambiguous term marking the practices performed for self-purification and those which could be carried out only when in a state of purity. The withdrawal during three months required before childbirth did not differ in nature from the retreat imposed upon maidens for three months before their marriage; the sanctuary devoted to Chiang Yüan was called the Temple of the Retreat; the word was taken from the set expression for designating the wise virgins in their period of retreat. When the poets sang 'In the retreat she had a son!' they could be taken to mean that she gave birth to him after a period of purification, but that suggested that, when she conceived, she was in a perfect state of purity. Thus the hymns celebrated the venerable Chiang Yüan 'whose virtue knew no lapse'. The commentators say in a more pedestrian way that she became a mother 'without the help of a man'.

Hou Chi was sired by Heaven: it was Heaven that had caused the seed of life to descend into his mother, or, according to another Chinese expression, that had caused the celestial breath or spirit to penetrate her. 'The Sovereign On High has come to rest upon her', said the hymns, and she had then felt 'a trembling' in her womb. Assuredly, the kings of Chou had the right to claim to have caused the Great Peace to reign in this world; they could bear the proud name of Sons of Heaven, they who were descended of Hou Chi, incarnation of Heaven within the body of an immaculate virgin. And Hou Chi was fully entitled to be associated by them with the cult of the Heavenly Sovereign and to be the Mediator of his Line to that supreme Power. That did not prevent their continuing to say (for historical claims certainly have their value) that the Son of Heaven was also a son of man; care was always taken to write: Huang Ti begot Hsüan Hsiao, Hsüan Hsiao begot Chiao Chi, Chiao Chi begot Ti K'u (Kao Hsin), and Ti K'u begot Hou Chi. Besides, it would have been a scandal for Chiang Yüan, virgin and mother of the God Hou Chi, not to have had a husband. In order that Heaven might favour her by visiting her with its breath, it was necessary for her to be pure; it was also necessary that she have a husband. A young girl does not go out into the countryside; morality forbids it. A wife may do so, at least when she accompanies her husband to the festival of the Patron of Marriages: it was deemed fit to recognize that Chiang Yüan, when she stepped into the divine footprint, was accompanying Ti K'u, her husband (the same was said of Chien Ti who conceived while following her husband to the Marriage Festival). Thus Hou Chi could have a father after the manner of men. Some traditions have it that Ti K'u raised difficulties before bowing before the divine miracle. He gave in, however, and the reward he obtained was to be looked upon as the patron of conjugal life: for Ti K'u is Kao Hsin, and *Kao* Hsin is none other than *Kao* Mei, he who is honoured in the spring festival of marriage. In French his title is translated by the expression *Entremetteur suprême*, but the meaning is that the husband of the holy mother of Hou Chi was sanctified in Chou theology as the being who matched couples and procured to them fertility.

'Give me wheat and barley' it was said in the prayer addressed to Hou Chi. To 'feed the people with their grain' it was not enough to be the Son of Heaven and of a virgin without stain: it was necessary to have passed severe tests. Hou Chi was spared some of them,* for in China religion and morality are mild. He knew at least the testing-time of birth, and that firstborn who was brought into the world 'without a break, without a crack, without hurt, without lesion', that divine infant who did not have to undergo all the defilement of common births and who was born 'like a lamb' of a ewe, had to spend his first days abandoned and lying upon the earth; but that abandonment which touches us when we think of his holy origins was in reality the promise of a destiny full of glory: thus the hymn that sings of him bursts out joyously like a Christmas carol: 'Now, in the lane abandoned —oxen and sheep have protected him!—Now, in the low wood abandoned—woodcutters have met there together!—Now, on the ice abandoned—by a bird was he brooded on!—and the bird, why then it flew off!—Hou Chi, why then he wailed!—How he can be heard from afar! How well he can be heard.—His cries fill the way!'[76] The placing of the child upon the Earth and the obligatory phase he must pass through of three days in touch with Mother Earth are the ritual elements from which the myth springs: but what a fine expression poetry has given it! The three days of abandonment become a three-fold exposure. Hou Chi made contact with the inhabited earth, the earth of the woods, and the frozen waters; domestic and wild animals lent him help; humble woodcutters came to him and saved him; his spiritual strength burst out in loud wailing. Not only must he be gathered up as a son, and it was by a judgment of Heaven that he emerged victorious from the test, but in addition, he had acquired, by contact with Mother Earth, 'the Virtue of helping Heaven', gained the title of Harvest Prince, and earned the right to be associated in the royal cult of the Earth God.[77]

The abandoning of Hou Chi upon the Earth is the central feature of his myth: his first name was Ch'i, 'The Abandoned'; in addition, his character of agrarian God was the chief of his attributes. He was, further, a civilizing Genius who 'extends his Law over the whole of China'; he was a Founding Ancestor, an Eponymous Hero and the Associate of Heaven. His legend touched all the great feudal cults; it made use of ritual facts and popular beliefs; in it genealogical invention and dynastic poetry worked together. The myth was well ordered, cleverly constructed, expressed in fine verse. It did not live. The Chou had hardly disappeared when Hou Chi interested only the learned who

---

* Hou Chi did not experience the persecution of the newborn by the wicked king: that mythic theme is scarcely sketched in his legend. We find it developed in a legend of another child, a girl, who was also born of a virgin mother.

were in search of historical facts. Hou Chi spent twenty centuries in neglect and the missionaries who first took him up now abandon him to his fate. The first propagators of Christianity in China, in their apostolic kindliness towards the natives, thought they could see in the legend of Hou Chi the sign of a pre-revelation favouring the Chinese. Later, it was thought that that legend could be brought to the service of Christian preaching. It was finally appreciated that it was dead and evoked no sentiment of faith. Such was to be the fate of a myth completely saturated with apologetic intent. The ladies and fairies of popular belief, such as the Weaving Maiden, remain young. The divine hypostases invented by a learned theology sometimes have their day of success, and then live on only in books.

Chapter Three

The Official Religion

The literati

Feudal religion already bore the character of an administrative religion: from it emerged what one may call the official religion of the Chinese. Unlike the former, it was not reserved to one social class: it was, in a sense, a national religion, in the first place because it was instituted for the benefit of the whole nation, but also because the influence of its principles permeated the religious life of all its members: in this context the problem is raised of the spread of beliefs and their movement from one social class to all the other classes. The official religion dates from the foundation of the Chinese Empire: it was the imperial religion. A second aspect of the problem is how a State religion could become established. That religion owed its existence to the activity of a defined corporation; it invoked the authority of Confucius who became the patron of the corporation. Why did the *literati* build up a religious system? Why did the Empire adopt it? Whence came the force that first made its success and then afterwards allowed it to resist victoriously the attacks of rival religions? What were the literati? Why was Confucius their patron? These are the essential questions.

At the decline of the feudal system, those who claimed to be followers of Confucius and to be the guardians of his teaching were specifically called *literati*. Even in this special usage, the word *literati* was employed concurrently with a word whose primary meaning was quite other— namely, the word by which the bottom class of the nobility and the body of the nobles were designated. The literati were those members of the nobility who codified the principles of noble life, presented them as rules valid for all, and finally, who assumed as their vocation the mission of spreading those rules and making them obligatory.

In the domanial courts the life of the nobles was spent in practices of a noticeably religious character, but which—given the ordering by protocol that came to them from a social organization founded upon the idea of hierarchy—above all allowed their symbolic and properly moral character to appear. It was precisely that which made apprenticeship and the observance of those practices difficult. The place to occupy in a gathering, the act to perform, the word to say, the moment to speak or act, the least detail of costume and deportment, the tone of voice, gait, all had a ritual value: the smallest error would have been a religious fault. It would have annulled the ceremony or even have made it disastrous. Every noble entitled to the name had to have the competence of an irreproachable master of ceremonies: he had to know the rites in detail and the general spirit of the ritual. That was the first duty of a vassal: if he had not acquired that competence he would have been incapable of fulfilling his chief obligation, namely, to advise his lord at his court assemblies. Reading the feudal chronicles, one perceives the importance of that role of counsellor. A minor lord is visiting a powerful one; the latter dies; the ministers want to force the guest to dress the corpse: that is to dishonour him, to treat him as a vassal. If he obeys, he gives up his sovereign independence; and how could he not obey? His own vassals first try to refuse, then find an answer: their lord proceeds to the dressing, but he brings a sorcerer with him; it was thus that a prince acted in his own estates when he paid a visit of condolence to a vassal. In that way, the situation is completely transformed: the humiliation rebounds upon the presumptuous domain.

In public life all was religious: the political use that could be made of ritual language imposed upon everyone the need to learn it thoroughly and to know its spirit. That was the field in which a noble was trained from an early age: he served his apprenticeship under the guidance of a learned master. The tradition of that teaching led to the establishment of rituals which were handed down in the first place by word of mouth along with the commentaries of the ablest masters: the rituals taught the practice and the commentaries the spirit. In this fashion there was formed a corps of technicians expert in religious matters. Their importance grew at the end of the feudal system. The lords then began to engage in struggles of influence, formed leagues, and frequently assembled. The anecdote I cited shows what benefit there was for a prince in having among his followers counsellors imbued with ritual knowledge. Diplomacy was carried out less by means of material than of moral forces: everything was a matter of Prestige; Prestige was a Virtue, a religious value kept up by the practice of rites, and that practice was the result of good counsel. Furthermore, 'as the prince, so the vassals' was a principle of religious law; the wisdom of the counsellors was taken as an effect of the Sovereign Influence of the master. Simply being surrounded by renowned counsellors was a sign of Virtue:

prestige and success resulted from that fact at once. Schools were formed that were no longer attached to particular domains: they were no longer formed by young vassals during their apprenticeship but by people wanting to specialize in the profession of State counsellor. They were composed of a master and disciples who learned from him the wisdom of the rites and the art of making use of them for political ends: they formed a sort of government personnel grouped around a chieftain and placed themselves at the disposal of ambitious princes. Some of them were sedentary; they grew more and more mobile as the instability of the political system increased. From the class of vassals subject to a lord, from the urban nobility, had emerged a corporation of people exercising their art for the benefit of any governmental power.

The journeyings of these schools and the spreading of their fame had without doubt the effect of beginning the unification of moral ideas; nevertheless, what was most marked in the first place was a specialization in techniques. Religious life dominated everything; the vassals and then the wandering counsellors were jacks of all trades; but the growing sharpness of feudal struggles and the formation of great States quite quickly gave a positive turn to politics: material forces showed their importance. Thus there were technicians in the military arts, in political economy, in legislation, in astrology (the stars represented a practical force as soon as it was known how to capture their influence), and in sophistry. It was above all these last whose role was considerable. In order to be able to destroy the antiquated feudal order so that it might be rebuilt to their profit, the lords laying claim to hegemony needed to procure the ruin of the ancient system of beliefs and ideas upon which the old organization rested. The sophists worked conscientiously at the revision of received ideas. If the language had not been recalcitrant to it, they would doubtless have succeeded in creating a Chinese logic.[78] We shall see that their speculations on black and white, the opposition and resolution of contradictions, were not without effect upon the development of religion in China. The chief result of their influence was to reinforce a trend to moral positivism. That tendency had already taken on great strength since reflection upon ritual technique had brought people to be aware of the symbolic character and moral value of religious practices.

The different schools of technicians kept in mind the memory of a time disturbed and made bloody by great feudal quarrels. All of them were held responsible for the disorders and rebellions: it is true that they had been employed for the benefit of private interests. One of them perhaps would have deserved to escape that reproach. It was a school whose centre was a small domain in Shantung, the country of Lu. The domain of Lu was very weak: it played only a secondary role in the quarrels of the warring kingdoms. It derived all its glory from the kinship of its princes with the kings of the Chou dynasty. Its founder was reckoned to be one of the great sages of China. Lu thought of itself as the guardian of ancient traditions, and its inhabitants were famed for their knowledge of the rites. Nowhere was formalism more powerful. But the masters of the school of Lu, Mencius (372–289) especially and Confucius (551–479) himself, had figured as pedlars of political advice. When the Empire was established by Ch'in Shih Huang-ti (246–209), the monarch and his grand counsellor Li Szu methodically prosecuted the destruction of all that might have helped in the founding of rival powers or in arousing a spirit of local particularism. With rare exceptions, all books were condemned to the flames: the proscription was especially harsh in respect of what were looked upon as products of the school of Lu. The traditionalist spirit of that school was then the chief cause of its temporary ruin.

Ch'in Shih Huang-ti's dynasty did not last long, but the Empire persisted, taken up by the Han; the Han sought to oppose themselves in all matters to the Ch'in whose heirs they were. For a time they even kept up the appearances of a feudal system. The reigns of the first Han emperors were a period of reconstruction in which tradition was honoured. In religious matters these emperors especially followed the advice of counsellors from Shantung or affiliated to the traditionalist school of Lu. Ch'in Shih Huang-ti had been able to destroy the books, not the oral tradition. The country of Lu was little touched by the troubles that followed the fall of the Ch'in. The prestige of the school had grown under persecution; that which in fact rid it of competition from rival schools seems to have been directed especially against it. While the products of all the other schools, when by chance they were recovered, appeared as heterodox works, inspired by the baneful spirit of rebellious times, all the books inspired by the school of Lu were carefully reconstituted. They were attributed either to Confucius or to his disciples, or even to the august founders of the Chou family. They became classics and formed a canon. It was in the tradition recovered in Shantung that wisdom was to be sought: all those who made of it their study, wishing to take part in affairs of State, were called *literati*. The literati formed the administrative personnel and were considered to be disciples of Confucius.

Who was Confucius and what was his teaching? If it is true that fortune favoured his school, it does seem that Confucius held every claim to become the patron of the official religion. He was a Saint in the Chinese sense, but also in the strict sense of the word; admittedly we know his life only through hagiographic accounts. His family was of high lineage and his birth miraculous. He was tall and of imposing appearance. Being poor, he began by doing humble jobs, and then at one time hoped to become the chief adviser to his lord. During the short period he was influential there was no longer a single robber in Lu; throughout the country men took care to keep to the right of the roadway and women to the left. But as soon as Confucius became aware that his master lacked Virtue, he left him and went in search of a lord worthy of that name; none had the wisdom to employ him. Untiringly he travelled through China; he returned to his own country only in order to die there. He endured trials and sometimes found himself in danger. His disciples accompanied him and loved him; he lived on terms of familiarity with them. In their presence he allowed himself displays of emotion which astonished them: when he was moved by the sight of a sincere grief, he participated in somebody else's mourning more deeply than usage allowed. All happenings along the road served for his teaching. The master exercised close supervision over his disciples, moderating or exciting their zeal, knowing the character of each. His *Analects*, which allow us to know him, reveal that he taught with timeliness, that he had authority, a lively imagination, great self-mastery, and the sturdiest faith in his mission. He believed in the original goodness of man, in the effectiveness of virtuous governments, in the excellence of tradition; he did not claim to bring new ideas; he always kept in mind the thought of the ancient sages, and he seemed to commune with them. He said that he could do nothing by himself: for Virtue is efficacious only in a prince; therefore he offered his services; yet he was without personal ambition. He did not doubt the value of his doctrine, but he thought that it came from conformity with the providential Order of the Universe: 'If it is spread, then Heaven will have willed it so!' In danger he remained impassive: 'Since Heaven has entrusted to me (the wisdom formerly possessed by King Wen), no man can do anything against me.' At the moment of his death he thought of his unfinished work, experienced a moment of anguish, and sang out: 'See T'ai Shan crumbling—the main beam is failing —and the sage departs like a faded flower.'[79]

His basic idea was that of an Order superior to human will, but which was not independent of it: 'The *ancients (kings) who wished to cause their Virtue to shine in the kingdom* first regulated the government of their States; wishing to regulate the government of their States, they first put their families in order; wishing to put their families in order, they first regulated their own personal conduct; wishing to regulate their own personal conduct, first *they made their sentiments conform to the rules*; wishing to make their sentiments conform to the rules, first they *made their desires completely sincere*; wishing to make their desires completely sincere, they first pushed their knowledge to the highest point. To push one's knowledge to the highest point is to *penetrate the nature of things*. Having penetrated the nature of things, their knowledge had been pushed to the highest point; their knowledge being pushed to the highest point, their desires had then been made perfectly sincere; their desires being made perfectly sincere, then their sentiments had been made to conform to the rules; their sentiments being made to conform to the rules, then their own persons had been regulated in their conduct; their own persons being regulated in their conduct, their families had then been put in order; their families being put in order, their States then had regulated government; their States having regulated government, then *the Empire enjoyed (Great) Peace.*＊ *From the Son of Heaven to the common people, in the same way, everyone must take as first principle: regulate one's conduct.'*[80] In this development, the very form of which is characteristic, the idea is expressed of a circulation through every domain, natural, social, and moral, of a Principle of order, effectively realized as soon as a total awareness of it is gained. That idea is in the first place connected with ancient Chinese beliefs according to which natural Order and human Order were thought of as being one. The ancient religious conception of Sovereign Power is also to be found in it. The prince is charged with a civilizing mission whose effects extend over things as over men: his collaboration is necessary to create the harmony of the world. In this double aspect, Confucian thought, completely imbued with a spirit of loyalist tradition and with a will to conform, was worthy of inspiring the founders of a State religion and an imperial religion with universalist aims. In another aspect, that thought had elements within it which could provide the official religion with devoted followers and defenders. The analysis of ritual mechanisms embodied in the tradition that generations of masters of ceremonies had bequeathed to Confucius, had brought to the fore the idea that the efficacy of a ceremonial act depended on the perfect performance of the ritual acts that made it up, and that perfection in detail was possible only when the humblest performers carried out even the smallest of those acts in full awareness of their value and meaning. Pursuing this analysis and formulating it in moral terms, Confucius had the incomparable merit of making men feel the role remaining to faith and to the inner life in the practice of a religious, political, and moral conformity, and in the obedience to traditional rules. The great Confucian virtue is *Sincerity*, that is, a total commitment that the soul makes to the accomplishment of the conventional acts by which the individual collaborates with universal order. That commitment can be absolute only when the individual is endowed with a personal cultivation such that it is sufficient to penetrate *the nature of things*. The loyalism and traditionalism of Confucius left a major role to the democratic spirit and even to the critical spirit. There is a sociological sense and a practical spirit in his teaching which inspired

＊ The Great Peace extends over things as well as men.

his disciples in the defence of national institutions. It is doubtless thanks to them that Chinese civilization and the Chinese empire were not ruined by Buddhism, while Christianity was ruining the Graeco-Roman world. The Chinese literati were able to save the State because, at their Master's invitation, they had penetrated the nature of the links which in their country tied men together in society and had become aware of the interdependence of human society and natural conditions. The practice of Confucianism demanded a labour of inner cultivation that in the course of Chinese history inspired innumerable acts of courage in the followers of Confucius when they saw that the government was turning away from the principles consistent with natural Order. The obligation to make an effort of personal criticism which, in forms laid down by protocol, is rendered as vigorous censure, has remained a national tradition: we have seen how Confucian analysis combined it with orthodox practice. But there is more to it than that. From the deep conviction he had of the solidarity of all things and of a general law of interaction, Confucius drew the principle of propriety. *Propriety* is the second Confucian virtue; it requires the penetration of the nature of things in such a way as to make every action accord with the given circumstances of the context. In that way the general traditionalism of the doctrine was made specific. It is not the Master's fault if on this point he was less well followed by the body of his disciples: the literati in general were less successful in combining opportunism with orthodoxy than they were in combining the latter with the critical spirit. If they were in general obstinately conservative, the fault must be laid not at Confucius's door but at that of the system of teaching adopted after his time.

Teaching is the Sage's prime duty: Confucius conceived of it as a heavenly mission and his life was an apostolate. Teaching consisted first in the education of the Prince. All the works inspired by the spirit of the Master were so directed. But if the Prince's Virtue as of right created that of the counsellors, in practice it existed only through the counsellors' Virtue. Whence a second aspect of teaching: it was addressed to the man who would become *honnête homme*. I so translate a term whose value the French words render approximately; but it is significant that the word *prince* enters as a component into the Chinese term. The *Chün-tzu*, the gentleman, is he who within his domain is capable of acting with the Virtue constituting a princely authority. Princely Virtue, a realization of Universal Order, is spread through wider and wider circles and penetrates every individual, even if he be a *man of the common people*; it then returns to the Son of Heaven as though reflected by that great collective looking-glass which is the nation. The Confucian idea, laden with concrete representations inspired by the nature of feudal power which was essentially religious, bore a democratic principle within it: the emperor taught the people and the people taught the emperor. It also bore within it a principle of religious organization. The teaching that formed the gentleman proceeded by moral contagion from a central Power which appeared as a supreme source of religious Efficacy. Any cult practice had value only if it was carried out by the emperor or in his name and by a delegation of his spiritual authority. There lay the basis of the official religion. The emperor was the supreme religious head; the cult was ensured by the emperor or his administrative delegates. The administrative cults had value only as reflexions of the imperial cult; in principle, the latter sufficed for the empire. If the official religion was inspired by Confucian doctrine, it was because it furnished excellent qualifications to a monarchical organization of religious life. Moreover, it provided the administrative personnel with essential qualifications; the imperial officials, in the exercise of local power, in which they replaced the lords and the nobles of the feudal system, needed to be endowed with qualities equivalent to those of their predecessors. These last had received the ritual education that produced nobility; the imperial officials, by the cultivation of the virtues peculiar to the Confucian gentleman, formed a *haute bourgeoisie* within the nation—the practices in the canonical books constituting a preparation necessary and sufficient for the exercise of the religious attributes apportioned to every administrator. In this way there was created within the whole country a quasi-sacerdotal class the members of which received the name of *literati*. The spread of the use of the term corresponded to a diffusion of noble morality. The diffusion was helped by the turmoil marking the end of the feudal system: destruction of families, removal of population, and above all the emergence of an urban population composed of artisans and traders. The foreign policy of the empire, a relative peace within it, the unity of the country's administration, caused the beginnings of a powerful commercial life. In the urban milieux, riches encouraged one to become a gentleman and Confucian teaching recruited new followers to the official religion. Only, the towns were no longer religious centres where the continuous practice of sacred things allowed the acquisition of a direct sense of their symbolic value and moral efficacy. Teaching from the book and by the examples of the past replaced oral teaching by a master commenting upon contemporary facts with an immediately sensed interest. The more it spread, the more Confucian teaching became formal and routine. For the effort of personal cultivation required by the Master as the basis of conformity was substituted in the bourgeois mass a formalist subjection to traditional practices. But, at least, religious life remained dominated by a certain practical spirit which on the whole and despite some accidents protected China from mystical adventures. [81]

Orthodox metaphysics and morality

The official religion owed to the Confucian classics its possession of a basis of dogma governing its development. On its moral side, it was on the whole strikingly homogeneous and derived from the teaching of the literati. The metaphysical side was made up of more disparate elements. Official doctrines were the result of the coming together of two competing influences: of the thinkers of the Confucian school and of those of the Taoist school. It would be idle to wish to determine in detail the roles of these two influences. Several of the elements were doubtless Taoist in origin; the ordering and the spirit of the system were Confucian. [82]

The orthodox metaphysics did not remain unchanged in the course of the centuries. It is almost impossible to give an exact idea of its basic principles: Chinese notions are concrete and complex, and the words of European languages have too precise a meaning. It is doubtless almost true to say that the metaphysics was idealist in spirit and dualist in tendency: it is at least by those characters that it appears opposed to Taoism, whose thinkers seemed to incline further towards realism and monism. In the personal thought of Confucius the idea of Universal Order was at once a central and a concrete notion; it corresponded to a properly religious belief. Confucius had faith in a Regulating Power the image of which was furnished by princely Virtue; he had transports of devotion for a heavenly Providence from which he believed he held his civilizing mission, and he felt that he communed with its thought. However, in the Master's system, Universal Order was already revealed as a half-ideal and almost abstract principle. It corresponded to a conception of the mind gained by analysis: the thinker represented to himself the Order of the world on the model of the principle of organization extracted by intelligence when it distinguished, for example, the bond that unites the different elements of a ceremonial act. The disciples did not inherit the Master's faith: the idea of order existed for them much less as a concrete notion than as a general principle of explanation. What occupied their consciousness was no longer the vision of a Sovereign Regulating Virtue of which men felt themselves to be vassals. They were officials; the idea of the State took on greater strength in them than the idea of the Prince. Order in the universe, as in the Empire, appeared to them as an abstract ideal. The trend to monotheism disappeared in proportion as the Empire created a State administration, in proportion as there disappeared the feudal idea of a direct sharing by the followers in the Holy Power of the chieftain.

In a similar trend the secondary notions of *yin* and *yang* [83] became

HCP

scholastic entities used by speculation for the ordering of facts. *Yin* and *yang* ceased to be concrete principles; yet the dualist orientation they had given to thought had become an established fact. Neither *yin* nor *yang* was itself to become a religious reality, but a prejudice in favour of bipartite classification would continue to dominate the world of things sacred: the soul was to remain dual, a cult of the Earth would be organized to confront that of Heaven.

It was the theories of the Five Elements which played the basic role in orthodox thought. Below *yin* and *yang* the Five Elements served as secondary categories in ancient classifications. They corresponded to the Four Seasons-Directions and to the Centre (which was at once a spatial and temporal reality). Space and Time were seen as the result of the interaction among these concrete categories. Their play was explained by different laws. These were simply the transposition on to the intellectual plane of the different modes of divinatory technique. There were three procedures for enumerating the Elements. The first of the procedures seems to have derived from the lay-out of the *templum*; the Elements (which were Directions) were arranged in a cross, the N–S branch being drawn first and begun from the bottom (North), the horizontal branch E–W drawn second, being started from the left (East). That produced the following numbering and order: 1 (=6 =North) Water; 2 (=7 = South) Fire; 3 (=8 = East) Wood; 4 (=9 = West) Metal; 5 (Centre) Earth. The second procedure appears to derive from the Calendar's order of movement round the square mansion; the Elements were in the following sequence: Wood (= Spring, beginning of the year); Fire (= Summer); Earth (= Centre-pivot of the year); Metal (=Autumn); Water (=Winter). The Elements being enumerated in the order of the sequence of the Seasons they symbolized, theory had it that the order must be that of a *regular succession* in a cyclical form. According to this theory, called the mutual production of the elements, Wood (the Virtue of Wood) engendered Fire (the Virtue of Fire), Fire engendered Earth . . . , Water engendered Wood. A third arrangement opposed the Elements direction by direction in the order W–E N–S Centre = Metal, Wood, Water, Fire, Earth. The corresponding theory was that the elements *conquer* one another in the opposite order to that in which they are enumerated: Metal (the Virtue of Metal) conquers Wood (the Virtue of Wood), Wood Water . . . , Earth Metal.[84] We do not know how divinatory, astrological, and astronomical techniques governed the development of these theories. It is certain that they assumed a great importance in religious politics (it was the essence of politics) in the time of the great feudal rivalries. A dynasty was defined by an Element and ruled by its Virtue. He who claimed to replace it must put himself under the patronage of a properly qualified Element as successor to or victor over the Element previously used. The Ch'in had reigned by virtue of Water; the Han reigned by virtue of Fire. Their founder acquired the prestige demanded of an emperor from the fact that he had been born to his mother by a red dragon (= Fire) and that he himself had killed a white dragon. The historians who arranged the traditions about national antiquities in an ordered sequence took care to recount the succession of dynasties in conformity with the principle either of the conquest or of the mutual production of the Five Elements. In this way the consistency of the historical and natural orders was made clear. We see straight away that the development of the theories of the Five Elements tended to a conception of Universal Order less as heavenly Providence than as determinism. Under the influence of those theories and as a consequence of the political role they played, Heaven, almost stripped of all religious reality, tended to lose its individuality and broke up into five hypostases, which were the Black, White, Red, Green, and Yellow Heavenly Sovereigns. [85]

The metaphysical speculations of the literati were practised upon the realities furnished to them by ancient religious beliefs and classifications; they transformed them into abstractions. The same rationalist spirit is found in the speculations upon morality. The literati reduced religious life to a collection of symbolic practices which, in their mind, were intended to govern social relationships in a manner consistent with the common demands of tradition and reason.

In the domain of sentiments and action, the tendency to dualism was marked by the opposition of rites and music. Rites were opposed to music rather as negative to positive sanctions or, more exactly, as a principle of constraint to one of emulation. Music which 'ensures the harmony of voices' also established 'the conformity of sentiments'. When it was perfect, 'there is no discontent'; it was the principle of 'mutual affection'. 'It is the flower of Virtue.' 'It imitates the harmony of Heaven and Earth', but 'it has its source in Heaven'. Heaven exercised its beneficent help by means of the twelve months and the Five Elements; music aroused happiness, joy, and produced harmony by means of the twelve pitchpipes and the five basic notes. Each pipe expressed the Nature of a month, each note had the Virtue of a season. The degree of perfection in a song allowed the estimation of the value of a man and, by inference, that of the government; for the latter was responsible for the behaviour of all. 'When the prince's spirits are not high, the songs are fast and short; the people's thoughts are sad. When the prince is generous, compliant, indulgent, easy, the songs are bright and simple, the people are quiet and content . . . When the prince is licentious, evil, depraved, dissolute, the songs are long, fast, and vague from beginning to end; the people live in licence and disorder.' Man is born good; he remains good, if the government is virtuous, by the effect of music which is also good. All ceremonies included a share of music because their end was to create *Goodness, Humanity*.[86]

They were also made up of regulated acts, the rites. They served to 'direct wills'. They engendered respect for others. Their effect was Courtesy. They did not have the virtue of producing union among men. 'If the rites prevailed over music, there would be no harmony.' But if music prevailed, 'each man followed the flow of the current'. In contrast, rites allowed the distinction that must exist among the rights of different people. They brought the result 'that desires are not applied to things immoderately and that things are not exhausted by desires'. They imported to men that state of dependence in which they stand to one another. Music aroused feelings and rites quietened them. They moderated the expression of joy or grief so that individual passions might not trouble the common peace. The rites were the expression of Civilization. 'To give free rein to one's feelings is to imitate the barbarians . . . (who) in happiness sing, swaying as they sing, gesticulating as they sway.' The civilized man, the gentleman, showed his emotions only by conforming to the conventional rules for their expression. The expression of sentiments was regulated; the sentiments themselves were stripped of the turbulence and violence contained in passion. They developed in a measured, ordered, and rhythmic manner, and the soul regained its balance for the greater benefit of the individual and of those about him. The rites appeared as a collection of therapeutic practices the observance of which was aimed at the good hygiene of society. Negative rites were prescribed because of their homeopathic virtues. The obligatory sharing of the kinsmen in the state of the dead man does not seem to have been a simple consequence of the tie of belonging between the dead and the living of the same domestic group. The ascetic exercises of mourning appear to have been no more for the benefit of the departed, but only in the interests of the survivors. 'At the death of a father, one has *injured* kidneys, *withered* liver, *burnt* lungs; one does not carry *water* or *broth* to one's lips.'[87] Similarly, positive rites were not governed by the need to put an end to the impurity sullying both kinsmen and the dead. There was less thought for the efficacy of the ceremonies transforming him whose 'corpse inspired horror' into an Ancestor, than for the benefit resulting from it for kith and kin. If 'one bares the left arm and if one leaps, it is to calm the heart and to dampen excitement by moving one's limbs'. The ceremonies in which the mourning group publicly paraded its grief, made a spectacle resulting in a purging of the passions salutary to family and society. They were inspired by a practical spirit; they preserved the obligatory character and efficacy characteristic of religious exercises, but it was not sought to base them upon beliefs about the hereafter. Philosophers treated the question of the survival of souls and that of the consciousness of manes as pure matters of fact of concern only to knowledge. They did not at all feel the need to take sides and their discussions were mainly scholastic exercises. The solution mattered little: what was the good of busying oneself with the question of the nature of the dead? The rites performed for them were amply justified by their moral utility. The literati did not bother to formulate dogmas serving to prop up practices of worship. The idea of order and the sense of the value of conformity were enough for them. Their thought remained free and practical; their religious feeling was very lively, but it associated itself with no trend to mysticism.

Formalism took on a growing importance explained by the new conditions of religious life among the bourgeoisie of the towns. The great ceremonies were rare, and very few were the people who actively took part in them. Only in theory did music keep its role as a principle of emulation. Musical practice became for gentlemen, for those at least who had a genuine care for inner cultivation, the best means to regulate feelings. By fingering a lute a sage verified the harmony of his soul with Universal Order; chamber music was for him a religious exercise. It was an entirely personal exercise. Music lost the function, which came down to it from the religious gatherings, of bringing voices and hearts into unison. There was no longer a counterweight to the virtue recognized in rites of moderating feelings and avoiding the clash of personalities. These last, in the style of life in the new cities, remained apart: the custom of living in close proximity could never become established there. The chief rule of life—the prime religious virtue—seemed to be a sort of neutrality of souls: it was achieved by a practice of the golden mean which could scarcely be defined except in opposition to *excess*. Excess was already for peasants as for nobles the gravest of moral faults, the most serious crime against religion. 'Let us love joy without folly:—a worthy man is circumspect!' says a song of the rural festivals of autumn. 'Out of Pride comes Evil' was a principle of noble morality. The ideal set before the bourgeoisie of the Empire by the literati was never to exceed the limit, never to go beyond, never to remain on the other side: 'To keep in the unvarying middle! Oh, that is the highest perfection!' Unvarying middle has the meaning of exact harmony. In this fashion the religious life of the Chinese was definitively given direction. It forbade ambitious beliefs, excesses of faith, and all that is inhuman in the religions in which the conception of divine Powers has something realist and immoderate about it. On that point the literati were ruthless guardians and censors. However rude the life of the 'rustics' of the countryside might be, their religious customs were gentle: admittedly we know the festivals of peasant harmony only from the themes of love songs. Their idyllic features have been preserved. Did they have cruel aspects? There is no indication that barbaric rites were practised in those festivals of initiation; there was nothing bloody in the myths emerging from them. On the contrary, we find traces of cruel rites in feudal religion: that last knew powerful gods and, at their side, lords who were their priests and also war chieftains. These masters, divine or human, could demand the greatest sacrifices. If the agrarian gods quickly abandoned all right to human sacrifices, if such sacrifices could not be established to the benefit of the chieftain, even in the times of the greatest feudal ambitions and when dynastic prestige demanded to be richly nourished, that was due to the action of the ritualists who were the forbears of the literati. We see them going so far as to prevent the marriage of girls to the Yellow River. We see them struggling against the tendency to have the chieftains followed into their tombs by servants, men or women. They reduced the share of the Gods, and Chinese religion became humane. It remained so thanks to the literati: they made religious practices depend solely upon abstract principles. The Chinese had no longer to support anything but the weight of a completely formal conformism and a ritual symbolism with practical aims. They were no longer conscious of the weight of the Gods.

Cults and beliefs

The official religion was a State religion; it found its followers among the town bourgeoisie; it had the literati as guardians. Whence the divisions in cult organization: there were administrative cults that were chiefly feudal cults adapted to the Empire; private cults resulting from the extension of noble usages to the urban bourgeoisie; finally, a corporate cult in honour of Confucius whom the literati had taken as their patron. These cults are interesting only by reason of a feature common to them: the piety they served to express resembled idolatry as little as possible, and the benefits the faithful thought to draw from them were in no degree personal benefits.

The history of the administrative cults, instructive in detail, cannot be told as a whole; it consisted in the creation of a host of cults and divine figures whose success was in general shortlived. Innovations were especially numerous at the beginning of dynasties and during important reigns. They sanctified the religious prestige of the Emperors. They also marked the momentary victory of the Taoist or Confucian spirit. The latter usually triumphed in the end, and, taken as a whole, the dynastic rituals were remarkable for their increasing traditionalism. The dynastic cult of the imperial Ancestors always kept its leading place. Innovations were frequent in agrarian and astronomical cults, the fate of the Gods depending upon a decree by a sovereign. It had been so from antiquity in the case of the Heroes linked to the cult of a holy Power. Under the Empire, the Gods themselves were promoted, demoted, or cashiered; they were merely the officials of a State religion whose true deity was the Emperor. His will alone endowed all the other gods with being.

The ancient agrarian gods whose cult had been suspended by feudal anarchy were officially restored by the Han. The tradition was re-established of raising a mound of Earth in the capital: up to the seventh century A.D. its soil was used for conferring investiture upon lords in receipt of apanages. The apanages were not true fiefs; the God of the Imperial Earth was similarly only a survival. The officials, to whom real power had been delegated, were not invested with it *per glebam*. Nevertheless, they held from their appointment by the Emperor a religious authority that gave them the right to desacralize the earth every year, for the benefit of those they administered. They carried out the desacralization by means of a very ancient rite. They sent away the Cold out of their towns in the shape of an earthen ox; the ox was whipped with willow branches, and the Spring along with him. That official whipping excited the forces of Spring and allowed work to be done in the fields. The imperial ploughing remained the indispensable inaugural act, and the Year would not have been good without the sacrifice by which the head of the State propitiated it. Thus the Gods of the Earth and Harvests could lose all religious reality when the feudal system of the appropriation of the land by hierarchized groups had disappeared; the chief of the imperial functions remained that of the feudal suzerains: the emperors were in the first place religious officials responsible for the Harvests. Yet they conceived of their rights over the Chinese soil in a new way; they possessed it in its entirety and directly; for them it was one; they raised an altar to the Sovereign Earth. This last, first honoured in Fen-yin, was then honoured (31 B.C.) in the Northern outskirts of the capital. The cult of the Imperial Earth was from then on opposed to the imperial cult of Heaven whose ceremonies were performed in the Southern outskirts; in this fashion the dualist spirit was satisfied. Opposed to Heaven, Earth recovered its feminine attributes which the custom of male tenure of land had made less apparent during the feudal period. Nevertheless, during that period, Earth, by which people swore, was richer in religious reality than it was once the Empire had endowed it with an administrative cult.

The Emperor remained the chieftain of the Calendar through which the Virtues proper to the dynasty were expressed. The determination of a beginning of the year consistent with these Virtues greatly preoccupied the Han sovereigns. We may say that the labours of the administrative commissions charged with establishing, along with the Calendar, all the standard Numbers of the new dynasty, led to the religious revival that characterized the period. Time was conceived as a complex of heterogeneous units; every imperial house required a Calendar proper to it. The same idea led to the grouping of years in periods each singled out by a name that recalled a significant event and symbolically expressed the special values of that moment in history; quite late, these periods coincided with reigns. It was then that Time was constituted, essentially, by the sequence of dynastic Virtues and, secondarily, by the sequence of Virtues proper to each imperial person. These facts show how little the individuality of Heaven was felt. To the idea of a heavenly multiplicity in the order of duration, there corresponded the idea of a spatial multiplicity. The dismemberment of the Sovereign On High had begun in the time of the feudal struggles. Its cult was reserved to the suzerain. The suzerain was without effective power. The most powerful lords marked their ambition and sought to increase their prestige by creating regional cults serving hypostasized Heavens. In the domain of Ch'in which succeeded in providing China with its first emperors, different Holy Places were inaugurated where there were sacrifices to the Green Sovereign (creation of Duke Hsüan, 675–664 B.C.), then to the Yellow and Red Sovereigns (Duke Ling, 424–415), and finally to the White Sovereign (Duke Hsien, 384–362). The Han completed the series, in conformity with the theory of the Five Elements, by instituting the cult of the Black Sovereign.

Becoming diversified, Heaven took on no more religious reality than Earth gained by becoming unified. But the creation of hypostases of the Sovereign On High allowed the heavenly Powers to regain some strength from contact with the Holy Places rich in the prestige of the agrarian gods. The five heavenly hypostases were brought closer to the five Holy Mountains where tradition had it that the ancient sovereigns had called together their vassals from all directions. Every mountain possessed, in addition to the lustre given to all of them by their being the representatives of concrete categories, a special right to veneration. That of the Centre had as its lot the split stone that was the wife of Yü the Great.[88] That of the East, T'ai Shan, drew its glory from having been venerated by the people of Shantung and from being frequently mentioned in the classics. The ascent of it made by Ch'in Shih Huang-ti, founder of imperial unity, added to its renown. Finally, it was in the East of the Empire. Associated with the Green Sovereign, divinity of the East who presided over Spring, it was chosen to be the place where the Emperors would announce to Heaven and to all their subjects the complete success of their dynasties. For that, on the summit of T'ai Shan they had sealed (feng) a prayer addressed to the Sovereign On High in a series of coffers. The ceremony was completed by a second sacrifice to Heaven (feng) and a sacrifice to Earth (shan), carried out at the foot of the mountain. The first of the feng and shan ceremonies was carried out by the Emperor Wu of Han in 110 B.C., and repeated by him in 106, 102, 98, and 93. The eastern Han celebrated it in A.D. 56, the T'ang in 666 and 725, the Sung in 1008. The Empress Wu Tzu-t'ien celebrated it in 695 on the peak of the Centre. She had prepared herself for this glory, unheard of for a woman, by succeeding in taking part in the ceremony held in 666: basing her argument on the sex of the Earth, she got herself entrusted with the task of making the secondary offering to that divinity. Scandal notwithstanding, Wu Tzu-t'ien drew from it the religious qualifications required for reigning in her turn as a true sovereign and for carrying out the feng rite in person. This well shows the nature of the rite, which is to manifest the legitimacy of dynastic power in confirming the harmony of the Sovereign with Heaven. Thus it was acknowledged that it could not be celebrated when the slightest indication revealed a disturbance in Nature. Another end was also pursued: it was that of turning away Evil from the person of the sacrificer. Under pressure from the literati, this personal preoccupation disappeared. Hsüan-tsung in 725 decided that he would make no secret prayer. The one he sealed up finished thus: 'The four seas enjoy rest;—I thus make the feng sacrifice on the T'ai peak—to thank Heaven for my success.—May my descendants have all the Prosperities;—may the people receive happiness.' As early as 167 B.C. the Emperor Wen had abolished the office of reciter of secret prayer. In theory, if not always in fact, the imperial cult sought the happiness of the Empire and not individual advantages for the sovereign. On the other hand, the divinities he addressed kept an impersonal character, and the principle was to avoid idolatry. At Fen-yin, Earth was represented by a female statue; in the capital, the centre of the ceremonies was a square mound. From the T'ang on, T'ai Shan received many noble titles. All were abolished in 1370. The imperial cult asked only impersonal favours of the abstract forces.[89]

The private cults were no different. The changes undergone by the Chinese family at the fall of the feudal system must have been quite rapid. A bourgeoisie composed of officials replaced the nobility. No longer did an authority borrowed from the lord need to be passed down from father to oldest son. The privilege of primogeniture lost its raison d'être; only the obligation to respect elder brothers survived; younger brothers recognized the duty of leaving to them the supreme conduct of common affairs. The family became an agnatic group in which some power was entrusted to the oldest, thus coming close, at first sight, to the peasant family. Yet it differed from it essentially. In urban life the solidarity of the agnatic group was more theoretical than real; it was supported neither by community of living nor by community of interests. The brothers lived each apart. The authority acquired by the father in feudal times profited by this relaxation of domestic communism. It was no longer limited either by the existence of higher family authorities or by the rights given to the sons, at least to the oldest son, by the fact of their being true successors of their grandfather. One of the customs that disappeared in the course of the political revolution was that of the representative of the dead; the sons no longer formed a group of vassals subject to the father but belonging to another part of the kin group. Properly speaking, there was no longer enfeoffment and agnatic affiliation; between father and son there was direct kinship which seemed based upon filiation and which gave to the father the most extensive rights over his children.[90] In practice, these rights were not exercised without coming under the control of the kinship group. That control being assigned to an undivided group and no longer to authorities to which paternal authority appeared subordinate, it became less effective. It remained active enough for the Chinese family not to take on the monarchical aspect of the Roman family.[91] To this control was added, besides, that of the maternal uncles, for the sentiments inherited from the ancient uterine organization retained more strength among the bourgeoisie than they had had among the nobility.[92] But if de facto paternal authority was never absolute, it appeared to be so de jure. The fealty of the vassal no longer competed with filial piety. That became the single principle of moral and religious life. Duties to the Emperor or his delegates, duties to masters, seemed simple aspects of that piety.

The cult of the Ancestors assumed a place such that it could seem to be the basis of Chinese religion. In the imperial towns it acquired a new character: it was a moral cult, completely symbolic, quite abstract. Along with the nobility disappeared the moving ceremonies in which, in the guise of their grandsons, the dead were seen to eat, in which their words were heard, in which they were communicated and communed with directly. The tablets upon which their names were inscribed became centres of the rites. The tablet was doubtless sacred and as though animated by a divine life from the time when a name was written upon the wood and it had been ceremonially dotted. Doubtless too there were pious sons who had images of their parents painted, who consulted their portraits before any undertaking, and who believed that they knew their feelings from the expression on their faces. But these cases of idolatry were exceptional. In fact, the rites practised in honour of the dead seemed to have no other virtue than that of a commemoration. They were the occasion of family reunions in which the memory of the dead was kept up by means of conventional acts; a promise was solemnly given to perpetuate their virtues and

not to dishonour their name. As for wishing to make their presence
real or to fancy that their substance fed on the savour of the offerings,
that could be the object of the vulgar cult. For all those who deserved
the name of *literati*, the basis of the cult of the Ancestors was completely
ideal. 'To treat the dead as dead, as if they no longer existed, to care
for them no longer and to forget them, would be inhuman; to treat
them as though they lived would be unreasonable.' 'To perpetuate the
ancestors, to carry out the rites that they themselves performed,
honour what they honoured, love what they loved, to serve them
after their death as they were served during their life, to serve them
once they are dead as during their lifetime, thus must act the perfectly pious son.'[93] 'That man is wise who fulfils all his duties and
honours the Ancestors keeping at a respectful distance.' A horror of
the mingling of the divine and the human, as well as a loathing for
magical practices, served as the basis for a sort of religious positivism.
Before all else, it was desired that nobody should dare to communicate
with his dead in a personal fashion. Prayers could consist only of
invariable formulae; they could ask only for the Happiness of the
family. Any transport of piety that was individual or selfish was not
tolerated.

It was a public obligation for every citizen to render worship to his
Ancestors; but the ordering of bourgeois life as well as orthodox
morality reduced that cult to simple private manifestations, except
in the case of imperial Ancestors. It was quite other with funerals,
whose pomp added to the family honour. On that point Confucius
had warned as much against ostentation as against meanness; for him,
luxury meant little as long as the respect for form was joined with
sincerity. The literati admired costly funerals. Tradition told of the
brother of Tzu-lu that he had the idea of selling his father's secondary
wives in order to find the wherewithal to pay for the burial of his
mother, the principal wife. Tzu-lu, disciple of Confucius, prevented
him out of a sense of justice. Later the Master's disciples could not
resist the sway of the public; the reason for it was, doubtless, that
funeral ceremonies were, in the order of the new life, the only moment
when filial piety, the basis of the society, could be publicly expressed.
No protocol, besides, defined the funerary luxury that each family
might allow itself, and all wished to vie in sumptuousness. From antiquity, the preparations for burial were started in the first years of old
age; the making of a coffin was the most important part of them; it
even seems that everyone cared for a tree that was intended to provide
the planks for his coffin. The coffin became for the town bourgeoisie
the chief object of domestic luxury and the centre of religious preoccupations. It was constructed with rare essences and lasting woods.
It seemed intended to perpetuate the body of the dead. That was a

new idea: the ancients thought of the impurity of the corpse; they enshrouded it, buried it in the house so that it might lose its flesh, joined it with the collection of the Ancestors in a family graveyard, then concerned themselves only with the soul. They aimed only at getting a regular disintegration of the substance of the Ancestors and not at an indefinite preservation of the corpses.

The coffins were kept in the house during the first period of mourning, and were then put in the tomb. Formerly the tombs remained as they had been made at the time of burial; they lasted as best they could. It was recognized that the ancients built them with such care that they would never have to repair them. The munificence of families was displayed in building high tumuli, in digging vast underground chambers, in building sumptuous funerary resting-places. Imperial authority gratified the best officials with the right to build their graves near the imperial tombs or to decorate them with special signs. Sculpture was used for decorating the funerary columns with tigers (= West) and dragons (= East), charged with conferring a suitable orientation upon the tomb. More veneration was given to the tomb, public monument of filial piety, and less to the tablet, abstract centre of a completely domestic cult. The cult of the Ancestors tended to become a cult of tombs. In that, it once more moved nearer to the agrarian cults. Situated in a favourable landscape, arranged in a fashion to capture the influx of the sacred forces of Nature, visited and propitiated at the time of spring, the tombs transmitted to the living the good influences that had just been concretized in the bodies of the Ancestors.[94] The Ancestral cult had only a symbolic and moral efficacy; as a result of the funerary practices, the idea was preserved that the dead led a subterranean life joined with the deities of the Earth and, in consequence, a realist element was maintained in the beliefs. The virtue of the graves and that of the bones were used for magic; magical practices for individual purposes were always to be utterly condemned. What piety asked of the Ancestral tombs was never private favours but protection extended to the whole family. The religion of tombs kept up more concrete sentiments than the tablets could; the faith manifesting itself in it never took a personal turn. No more did it take on an idolatrous character, despite the use of sculpture in funerary ornamentation. There was not to be found any representation of the dead on the engraved stonework of the funerary chambers. The decoration was made up principally of mythological or historical scenes illustrating different traditional virtues, and in addition representations of animals or objects of good omen. Its value was that of a symbolic commemoration of the religious qualifications held by the dead as by every gentleman and every good official. It signified that during his official career he manifested the Virtues proper to a literatus invested with a portion of sovereign authority. As the product of his administration, there were within his jurisdiction, subjects, servants, sons, wives, who were faithful, devoted unto death, pious or chaste to equal the most celebrated examples of antiquity; similarly, as in the time of the best princes, signs appeared manifesting the perfect accord of his conduct with Universal Order, such as the white tiger, the six-pawed animal, the sacred tripod, the calendar tree, the giant lotus, the red bear, the unicorn, the fish with paired eyes, the red-maned white horse.[95] What was expressed by sculpture by means of traditional themes was repeated by an inscription with the help of literary allusions: 'He had received from Heaven a fine Destiny . . . , he showed himself to be intelligent when he was at an age when his hand was still held to help him walk . . . , he observed the courtesies . . . , his filial piety was as intense as the pleasant wind . . . , he was the legs and arms of the sovereign . . . , he maintained great harmony . . . , all the people received his benefactions . . . , he made his forbears illustrious: the writers of history recount his merit . . . , his renown will be imperishable . . .'[96] So that we see that for a bourgeois family, concrete and beneficent Virtues emanated from the tomb, but the latter was principally a monument of glory, a source of official illustriousness, a testimony to orthodoxy.

The increased importance of funerary practices did not prevent the cult of the Ancestors from preserving above all a symbolic and moral value. But, in part under the influence of these novel usages, filial piety lost something of the moderation and 'exact harmony' which made of it an instrument of inner religious cultivation. Once they had been represented by sculpture in schematic features, the tales that served for religious teaching took on a stiff, intense, exaggerated aspect. No longer was it the time when Confucius expressed his piety by fingering the lute at the conclusion of mourning without allowing himself at once to draw perfect harmony from it. Here are the examples proposed for imitation by the moral imagery: Lao Lai-tzu,[97] at seventy, in order that his parents may be prevented from thinking of old age and death, dresses himself up as a child and plays with his long sleeves; Po Yü,[98] beaten by his mother, laments for her: she is old and lacks the strength to chastise him well enough. Li Shan[99] saves his master's son and carries him off into the mountain; he chews his food for him, gives him the breast and it produces milk. A mother likes fish; her son brings her some in mid-winter: he catches it by melting the ice by the warmth of his stomach. A young widow is courted; she takes her mirror and cuts off her nose: 'Dishonoured by mutilation, who will want me?'[100] A fire breaks out in the women's quarters: there is no duenna to chaperone the wife: she does not leave and allows herself to be burnt.[101] Paternal authority, and with it marital authority, was made stronger; feudal protocol having disappeared, the sense of moderation tended to be lost; funerals and the tomb took the chief place in religious life; to prevent widows sacrificing themselves at the death of their husbands with the support of Buddhism, it would be necessary for the influence of Confucius's disciples to be actively exercised.

Confucius, whose thought animated the official religion, deserved to receive honours of worship from it: was he not a saint ? His worship was nevertheless slow in taking on the character of a State cult; we shall see in the next chapter that it was the most lasting of the official cults. The veneration of the Sage was manifested at first by the quite personal respect the literati professed for him: they called their patron a 'King without a kingdom', so designating the sovereign mission held from Providence by the Master. The emperors accorded public recognition, in the first place by pilgrimages made to his tomb, then by the granting of titles of nobility to the head of the family charged with the patrimonial cult of Confucius. In 442, a temple to him was built in his town, then in 505 another in the capital: that was canonization. Thenceforth, honours multiplied. Confucius was named Supreme Master in 665, King in 739, Supreme Saint in 1013; he was given the imperial robe in 1048 and his Ancestors were ennobled in 1330. From 637 his image appeared in the Schools. The temples of Confucius (there was supposed to be one in every subprefecture) were first adorned with the statue of the Master wearing his royal or imperial insignia. The statues were replaced by tablets to avoid all idea of idolatry. Fortune, honours, or talent were not asked for from the tablet of Confucius, surrounded by those of his disciples and of all the great literati whose wisdom was officially recognized. The cult had no other purpose than to commemorate the memory of one who would be a *Master for ten thousand generations*. Now a State cult, that of Confucius kept the character of a professional cult. It was a feudal custom that on the first day of spring, marked by the cyclical character *ting*, the chief master of the music led his pupils to make a vegetarian offering to the Spirit of musicians: after which a mime was danced. On the first *ting* day of autumn another festival took place. Then the pupils played a musical air on wind instruments. It was to these two *ting* days that were assigned the ceremonies performed in honour of the patron of the literati and the schools: they consisted in a sacrifice rounded off by traditional dances and songs. It is fair to say that Confucius never ceased to be the object of the cult he had wanted: the faith which he had received from Heaven for his safekeeping was spread in conformity with the heavenly plan. The Chinese 'gentleman' was formed by the teaching of the Master. He learnt from him that the true religious spirit consists in accomplishing, according to the time-honoured rules of his nation, his duty as a citizen and in developing in himself a disinterested sense of Universal Order; he acquired the wisdom that causes men to turn away from mystical practices and theories, from magic and prayer, from doctrines of personal power or salvation: he was strong for the fight with Taoism and Buddhism.

Chapter Four

Religious Revivals

Taoism

Both the Taoist and the orthodox systems were formed upon a common base; when they were in competition they defined themselves by opposition. Their antagonism was longstanding: it showed itself, on one side, by the desire on the part of the literati schools to adorn their theories with a kind of official prestige; on the other side, among their adversaries, by a great intensity of sectarian spirit. Yet individuals were not at first either pure Taoists or pure Confucians. When the Empire was built up and it was necessary to give it a religion, the competition between the doctrines was more forcefully marked: it began to correspond to a classification of persons. Even then, there were frequent interchanges of ideas. It was less by the ideological base than by the direction taken by practical speculation that Taoism and orthodoxy were distinguished: they represented twin streams of doctrine springing from ancient national beliefs. If we leave aside the question of an Asian *sophia* elaborated in an age that history does not allow us to reach—and if we take no account of Indian secondary influences exerted at least from the second century of our era—we may define Taoism as a truly native movement of thought, oriented to mysticism.

Taoist doctrine served to justify the practices of certain sectarian milieux: religious revivals were inspired by it, and doubtless it emerged transformed from each of them. The history of those revivals, which has not been written,[102] would be the true history of Taoism: what we know a little of is the literature of Taoism. It is immense and very difficult of access. A great number of the works of the sect appear to be the product of revelation: questions of time and person having no importance for those who believe in direct communication with the divine, usually these works are simply placed under a sacred patronage, and are neither dated nor signed, unless they are falsely dated and falsely signed. Intended for initiates, the terminology is obscure in the extreme: let us add that the expressions employed having served the Buddhist translators, contaminations of ideas have occurred which it is practically impossible to uncover. These works, grouped under the rubric of Neo-Taoism, have at least the merit of informing us precisely of religious practices. The works customarily ascribed to ancient Taoism are taken as being strictly philosophical. The Tao Te Ching, attributed to Lao Tzu, has been translated some tens of times; sinologists complain of the excessive number of those translations: not one of them truly deserves that name. The teaching of the *Taoist philosophers* was completely esoteric. The masters kept silent in the presence of strangers; in regard to their disciples, they took into account their progress in wisdom. They taught by parables, by means of semi-historical anecdotes the comparison of which suggested a general idea. If they happened to formulate their ideas directly, then it was by lyrical procedures, by means of developments conducted by a musical and concrete thought, by means, finally, of terms used with values peculiar to a closed milieu. The works of Lao Tzu, of Chuang Tzu, and of Lieh Tzu (fourth and third centuries B.C.),[103] full of reticences and polemical intentions, can be understood only by relating their ideas to the concrete religious practices to which they correspond (and to do that it is necessary to postulate some continuity between ancient Taoism and Neo-Taoism), only, again, by clarifying their terminology by a comparison with the common beliefs contained in the words they use (and to do that it is necessary to postulate a certain homogeneity of Taoist thought). The national character and continuity of Taoist doctrine appear certain; but every effort of interpretation will not be without its danger as long as we do not know the history of the religious revivals in which that doctrine was defined, particularized, and transformed.

Tradition has it that Taoist doctrine was elaborated in a special setting, that of the domanial archivists. That corporation possessed the traditional secrets of rules of divination, of magical prayers, of astral, medical, and pharmaceutical science, and, in short, of all the processes of knowledge and of action that man has with regard to Nature. Tradition also has it that from feudal times there existed sages (Confucius must often have encountered some of them on the road) who lived in the countryside, refusing to take part in the ritual life of the towns and taking refuge in Nature. In fact, while among the nobility, and later in the body of the literati, a religious spirit was formed to which the speculations upon the essence of things mattered little, but only an effort of inner cultivation allowing the sincere practice of the conformism indispensable to social life, the Taoists marked themselves out by their scorn for social duties, by the care for technical disciplines, and by a predilection in favour of ontology. Let us add that the literati, out of traditionalism, hated the sophistry which fought against received ideas, and that the Taoists, sectarian polemicists, enemies of society, technicians and gatherers of ideas, made the greatest use of it.

Taoism would not be Chinese if the idea of the participation of man in Universal Order did not occupy the central place in it. Universal Order was, for the literati, an abstract, ideal, order, conceived upon the model of social order. We have seen that there was more realism in the personal thought of Confucius.

For the Taoists, Universal Order was a Reality, a concrete Principle, the First Principle—not a Reality furnished with moral attributes and appearing as Providence—but a Reality characterized by its logical necessity and considered under the aspect of *a Power of Realization*, prime, permanent, omnipresent. Dialectically, the idea of that Reality was obtained by the sophistical process of the resolution of contradictions. By analysis the Taoists determined a thesis and an antithesis which they realized as second principles, then logically postulated a synthesis which they realized as first principle.* The operation, repeated for each of the categories of thought, allowed them to obtain the many modes of the first and second Principles. There is no way of translating the names of those modes, Chinese categories not corresponding exactly to ours: besides, the categories were unstable and ill-defined; the diverse modes were in practice equivalent. Taoists considered the first Reality as a harmony of opposites. They refused to define it; it was essentially the Unnameable. They designated it by lyrical epithets when they realized it by contemplation, or, when they proceeded by dialectic, either by a negative expression marking it as logically prior to all particular existence (the Void, Nothingness), or by the name of that one of the two principal modes of the second Principles which corresponded to the thesis and, in relation to the other, enjoyed a sort of primacy. So it is that the first Principle is often called *Tao* (whence the name of the doctrine), the two most notable antithetical modes being the *Tao* and the *Te* (Tao Te Ching means Book of the *Tao* and the *Te*). If it would be idle to try to give equivalents to those words in the French philosophical vocabulary, it is not impossible to convey a sense of their value. The Taoists (like the Confucians) speculated upon ancient national beliefs. If it is true that their adoption by the sect brought an esoteric value to the words, it was not completely different from the ordinary value. In ordinary usage, the double term Tao-te was used to designate the power of Realization that characterized every religious force and in particular princely authority. Te was specially related to that Power when it was delegated, particularized, and exercised in detail. The wife of a lord and his vassals shared in the

---

* Hence a trinitarian aspect of Taoist conceptions that has misled some commentators.

Te and possessed specifications of it. Tao was reserved to the Prince; it corresponded to a Power prior to each of its manifestations (we see why Tao could in need designate the First Principle), but already containing within itself all the specifications that were to appear as soon as it was exercised. Tao-te was Efficacy, Virtue. Tao was Efficacy in some degree of concentration (*yang* was another, more material, aspect of it); Te was also Efficacy, but somewhat diluted (*yin* was a more material aspect of it). A text of Chuang Tzu[104] makes perceptible the transition from the ancient beliefs to Taoist speculations and the kinship of these last with Confucian theories. For it, the totality of beings is realized by a liberal and total expansion of the Heavenly Tao; the empire is united by means of an analogous expansion of the Imperial Tao; the Tao of the Saint similarly subjects the whole country to his influence. But while in Confucian thought Efficacy was moral, it was for the Taoists as indeterminate in its nature, or almost so, as in popular conceptions. Nevertheless, to oppose itself to the more or less idealist Providentialism of the Confucians, Taoism took on the appearance of a naturalist, if not materialist, monism: its central idea was that of a *Cosmic Continuum* the existence of which allowed action from mind to mind. The theory of it was formed chiefly by Lieh Tzu and, as was usual, by means of fables. The Continuum is there seen to be radically distinct from material contiguity, from contact. Success in hunting or fishing did not depend upon the tools employed; however bad they were, the hunter or the fisherman reached his prey directly by the effect of his personal prestige, if he had Efficacy. Cosmic Continuum was a setting suited to the propagation of a personal power of realization, for it was itself the efficient Principle of all Realization. Appropriately enough, it was music (being the highest expression of the personality) whose efficacious Continuum best propagated Virtue. When P'ao-pa played the zither, the birds danced, the fish leapt. When Shih-wen, in the spring, plucked the string giving the note Shang (=pitchpipe Nan-liu =autumn), the fruit ripened; in summer plucking the string Yü (=the Huang-chung pipe = winter), he caused the snow to fall and the rivers to freeze; realizing perfect harmony with the four strings, he caused the springs to spurt forth and the dew to appear.[105] The World was made up of a Virtue that was specified by the quasi-real action of semi-concrete categories, without losing anything of its Continuum, and which allowed every distinct being (making use at once of the Continuity retained by the Supreme Power of Realization and its own sharing in the prime Efficacy) to act upon any other specification of the Primordial Virtue without spatial or temporal limit, by means of the correspondences established among the diverse modes. Tao-te and the Supreme Principle were the mystical setting of magico-religious actions and interactions.

The dialectic allowed individuals to conceive the logical necessity of the Supreme Principle: it was a preparation for conversion. That was obtained by emptying the apprentice-Taoist's soul of all received ideas. Whence the polemical and sectarian aspect of the preaching; whence too the use made in it of sophistry. The master applied himself to showing the relativity of social conventions: the Chinese sumptuously bury their dead; there are peoples among whom pious sons begin by scraping off the flesh before burying the bones, and others among whom the dead are burnt. Good and evil cannot be distinguished; the literati act as supports of the princes; a lord is nothing but a usurper; by what right are thieves and brigands condemned? The goods of this world are unstable: the greater fortune is, the closer it is to misfortune. All values are artificial; there is neither noble nor common, neither just nor unjust, neither great nor small; a hair is worth a mountain, a still-born child is not young, a centenarian is not old; heaven, earth, and any being are of the same age. All opposites can be brought back to unity. Epochs are immense and none of them is truly great as soon as one thinks of a vaster duration. The world is immense: after one stretch of land there lies another and there is always one beyond it. One should not prize life: what is life? Can it be distinguished from death or dream? In my sleep I dreamed that I was a butterfly; when I awoke I was Chuang Tzu. Who am I? Chuang Tzu who dreamed that he was a butterfly? A butterfly who imagines he is Chuang Tzu?[106] One should not prize one's body: the man whose feet were cut off was wiser than a whole man; the legless man is happier since he does neither corvée nor military service. One should not prize honours: a turtle dragging its tail in the mud of the marshes finds more happiness in doing so than in lending its shell to three thousand years of divination. One should not prize one's friends, one's masters, one's kin: they are specifications of the All who appear and disappear; at their death a meditation on the vanity of things amply suffices, and if need be, three short lamentations in order not to shock the common people. It is better not to practise any rite and to abstain from reasoning. The best music is silent; the true master is dumb. Practice is of no importance; wisdom cannot be learnt. There is no efficacious practice and no true wisdom other than those which consist in emptying one's heart and mind of every particular idea and every particular sentiment. One must 'forget [all] in immobility'. The aim of religious life is the ecstasy that allows a direct apprehension of the Prime Virtue and identification with the All. Taoist ecstasy was achieved by procedures analogous to those of the purification preparatory to the sacrifices of Ancestor worship. The rhythm was the same. Retreat lasted for a complete period of time to which was assigned the coefficient 10; it was subdivided into periods marked by the numbers 3 and 7. It consisted in successively externalizing all distinct ideas and in concentrating the attention upon a single point. Then enlightenment was attained. It was thus that Po Liang-i at the end of three days could cast the external world out of himself; at the end of seven days, he could cast out of himself the notion of any individual essence; at the end of the exercise, on the ninth day, he was able to cast out of himself the very notion of existence. He then attained enlightenment and enjoyed direct contemplation of the Principle, outside time, beyond life and death and change. In that state of ecstasy identification with the Primordial Virtue was marked by the feeling of an indefinite power over all things, by a dissolution of the body and an integration of mental power, which corresponded to the disappearance of all weight and which allowed one to ride the wind. Faced with its realized object, faith was expressed in the hymn: 'O my Master! O my Master! thou who destroyest all beings and who art not cruel! thou who spreadest thy benefactions throughout the ages and who art not good! thou who art older than the highest antiquity and who art ageless! thou who, covering or bearing all as Heaven and Earth, art the author of all things and who art not industrious! Oh! there lies heavenly joy!'[107]

The God-like vision conferred, along with sanctity, a personal power by which the individual was superior to death and every limitation. The Supreme Power with which the Taoist was identified by enlightenment was superior to that of a divinity which might be endowed only with moral attributes, which might be simply compassionate, intelligent, and good; it was total and, if one prefers, cosmic. When an idea was got of it by dialectics it appeared characterized by necessity and in the guise of Fate. It followed that every individual shared in that Power through a Destiny that characterized him personally and which should be an exact measure of his individual power. In fact, however predetermined each man's Fate might be, it depended on him to increase that power indefinitely: it would be enough, if I may so put it, if he increased his sharing in the Prime Power of Realization. He could do it, in the first place, by ecstasy, supreme religious act by which one was incorporated in Universal Efficacy; but secondary practices allowed one to make of oneself a more perfect specification of the All, and, in consequence, to enrich one's Destiny in the present and for the future, up to the point of obtaining, in addition to immediate powers stretching to infinity, an at least relative immortality. Those were the practices which, along with ecstasy, formed the basis of the religion of the Taoist sects; it was they which were the basis of their success: it was they too which, when Taoism came to be finally classified as a heterodox doctrine, gave it the character of Magic. The totality of these practices derived from ancient techniques whose heritage the literati, solely preoccupied with morality, abandoned to

the Taoists. They constituted an ascetic discipline dominated by two
intertwined rules: not to wear out one's Destiny and to increase its
power. Not to wear out one's Destiny was a necessary condition: it
was fulfilled by a systematic inertia. The sage lived in retreat, he feared
the crowd, fled popularity, disdained success, sought to avoid being
noticed, bent before everything and allowed himself to drift with
the current, like the water which was his model, did not enter
into dispute with anyone, and mistrusted all special attachments. It
was not that he did not act: he acted by contagion, without special
intervention, in the manner of the First Principle. He controlled by
letting things go: he was like a holy tree, useless for any special purpose,
preserved indefinitely. His attitude involved a political morality,
completely different from feudal morality, and which advocated the
return to the golden age, to the state of nature in which individuals
lived side by side without knowing one another, being unaware even
of the neighbour whose cockcrow they heard, abstaining from rites,
politics, war, refraining from using up the fat on their legs and the
hair on their thighs in the service of a chief. Preserved by retreat and
impassivity, the sage endured and, by itself, Duration enriched him: old
age augmented his Efficacy. But, besides, he took care to perfect his
substance. He observed a diet. That diet was characteristic of an
asceticism directed towards an ideal of personal potency. The
Taoist sage abstained from cereals, for eaters of plants and fruits
were stupid; he made use of other common foods with discrimination. He
drank alcohol, for drunkenness was an approximation to ecstasy, and
besides, the ancient belief was that alcohol, reserved to the old, preserved life. He sought to eat hot or cold dishes in fitting quantities,
that is to say, releasing *yang* and *yin*. He sought especially to absorb
concretions of *yin* or *yang*. The former were found abundantly in
Nature: silver, jade, pearls and especially the dew that could be extracted
from the Moon (yin) with the help of a certain shell (yin). Fire (yang)
extracted from the Sun by means of a mirror, being no more immediately edible than gold (yang), one sought to win potable gold by nine
times nine (yang) days of heating; failing that one contented oneself
with cinnabar. The sage could, for the rest, absorb yin and yang by
means of spells and talismans or even by having Sun baths and Moon
baths. By means of massage he directed towards the organs of the
bodily microcosm the quintessences taken from the macrocosm.
Finally, he preserved, improved, and refined his yin soul and his
yang soul by the combined use of sexual hygiene (that hygiene is
poorly known: it was not based upon abstinence) and breathing exercises. These last, in which prolonged retention of air played the greatest role, were aimed at preparing for ecstasy. Later it was thought
that the airy soul, enlarged by assimilating the retained air, ended by

acquiring enough potency to be externalized at will, and even to carry on its existence outside the body. That theory allowed action at a distance to be explained to the common people in a more comprehensible fashion. It also allowed a kind of personal immortality to be promised to every follower.

The naturalist monism that lies at the foundation of Taoism was the basis of its fortune. Its sectarian mysticism as well as its techniques, creative of personal potency and of immortality, was the cause of its first successes at the expense of a religion which offered itself as an official doctrine, guardian of the established order, and which, moral and abstract, promised to individuals only the satisfactions of inner cultivation. Taoism seems to have begun by finding favour in aristocratic circles; the asceticism that characterized it was within reach only of the rich. It is significant that we find Taoists in the entourage of the founders of dynasties such as Ch'in Shih Huang-ti or the first Han emperor, and of the great monarchs such as the Emperor Wu, or of ambitious princes like Huai Nan Tzu. The attempts made to gain immortality, to associate with spirits, discover the Isles of the Blessed, or create potable gold, were costly and demanded an expensive personnel and material. Only powerful princes seeking still more power could provide them. But if Taoism first found credit with the great, avid for every sort of prestige, and if it gained new favour at almost every establishment of a dynasty, it was in general abandoned as soon as dynastic power was consolidated and it suffered several persecutions. That heterodox doctrine seemed propitious to the formation of sectarian movements whose leaders might take on political importance. Indeed, it was by sectarian movements that Taoism spread through the country and became a religion. The first Taoist communities appear to have been formed in Shantung and Szechuan. Unfortunately, the history of these religious revivals is very poorly known. The most famous was that of the Yellow Turbans from which began the disturbances that brought the second Han dynasty to ruin. Placed under the invocation of the Tao of the Great Peace, the sect was grouped around a wonder-worker who effected cures by means of holy water. The sick had first to fast, examine their consciences, and confess their sins; their confessions, in triplicate, were taken to a mountain, hidden in a ditch, immersed in a river, and so reached the spirits of the Heavens, the Earth, and the Waters. Abstinence and good works were imposed upon followers for the remission of their sins. All awaited a new era whose arrival was fixed, by diagrams and magical numbers, for A.D. 184. At the beginning of the third century there emerged from a sectarian movement centred in Szechuan the dynasty of Taoist popes (the title of Heavenly Master was borne throughout Chinese history by a member of the Chang family); these religious leaders levied a tithe upon their followers; their authority hardly extended beyond their territory. The formation of a Taoist clergy was nonetheless quite rapid; in the middle of the eighth century more than 1,600 temples were served, a third of them by nuns. Great progress was made under the T'ang dynasty, in the seventh, eighth, and ninth centuries, then under that of the Sung, in the eleventh and twelfth centuries. The pope was confirmed in his title by Ch'en-tsung in 1015; a hierarchy of Taoist prelates was established and recognized by the State in 1113; it hardly existed in reality: only local heads enjoyed prestige. In 1219 Chengiz Khan endeavoured to get a religious leader of Shantung to come to him, and wrote to him in these terms: 'I have acknowledged that you, O Taoist master Ch'iu, personify Truth. You plumb the depths and entirely fathom reason: in you the Tao is empty and the Te manifest . . . You observe the perfect practices of True and Superior Men; long have you lived among the peaks and ravines of the mountains, you have hidden your voice and disguised your body . . . , remaining seated you caused to come to you the teachers of the Tao who gathered like clouds . . .' Although it did not succeed in creating a definite religious organization and a disciplined clergy, Taoism had become a power that the Emperor had to treat with care.

Combining monist and naturalist theories with the practices of immortality, it had come to people the world with Immortals and to take on responsibility for cults of Nature as well as, in part, the cult of the dead. The Taoist Pantheon embraced, beside the innumerable hypostases of the Supreme Unity and mystical triads, a host of Blessed Ones who, through the merit of their harmony with the Prime Virtue, had mounted to the Heavens in apotheosis upon dragons and cranes, or who had vanished in the vicinity of a mountain or a chasm. They usually lived in retreats or in the stars. They sometimes emerged; they were always seen in strange poses or appearances, for example hopping or mounted on white asses that, at the day's end, they shut up in a kerchief case. Sometimes they reincarnated and were magicians who fought armies of demons with the aid of magic weapons and strange illusions. They exercised the most diverse functions: some were patrons of corporations, some were simple *indigetes*[108] put in charge of points in the life cycle or aspects of Nature; the majority, water-sprites or goblins, were divinities of grottoes, springs, abysses, peaks. It was through the Taoist clergy that the emperors, always responsible for the Natural Order, caused these powers of Nature to be propitiated. They had slips of silver or of gold (often of copper), rings or tablets of jade (often of hard stone) and dragon images thrown into the abysses: on all these objects a prayer was written.[109] The divinities were summoned by magnificent offerings to come to a great Mass preceded by a fast. The liturgy, very solemn, comprised speeches, requests, declarations, formulae, acts of confession, of contrition, and of adoration; the holy texts were censed; the officiator knelt, clicked his teeth three times or twelve[110]; the drum of the Law was made to sound twenty-four times; Hymns were intoned; the ceremony ended with a formula of exit and leave-taking. In cases of failure, they threw to the Gods, not this time gold and perfume, but a dead pig or women's shoes. Too abstract, too administrative, too urban, the official religion had to seek the help of the Taoist clergy whose Immortals had taken possession of every sacred corner of the Chinese Land.

By endeavouring to become an official religion, at least to lend its services to the State, the Taoist religion ended up by taking on administrative concerns in turn: it became moralized, and doubtless the influence of Buddhism had played a part in that. From the fourth century the theoreticians recognized that if good behaviour without the help of Taoist practices was not enough to procure immortality, it was at any rate a necessary condition. The task of the Supreme Unity could not be to be concerned with the doings of the living: an hypostasis was procured for him, the Governor of Destinies. He was charged with keeping the account of good and bad actions. To help him in this task he needed a whole body of administrators. Taoism, religion of Nature, very close to popular beliefs, had quickly taken over their elements: it appropriated local and domestic deities, arranged them in a hierarchy in the manner of imperial officials, and superimposed on human administration a divine administration in charge of souls. It was laid down that every individual possessed a collection of three tutelary spirits and that that triple guardian angel reported to the Governor every sixty days (on the 57th day of the sexagesimal cycle)—this, in order to preserve the idea of individual responsibility. But the chief official of morality was, appropriately, an ancient domestic Genius, that of the family hearth: he gave his report on the last day of every month. The local Gods, Genii of inhabited places, formed the intermediate echelon. The primary sanction placed at the disposal of these divinities was penal in character and the simplest possible: a curtailment of life. It was quite reasonable to acknowledge that the individual who could increase his Destiny by Taoist practices could also shorten it by his impiety; yet Fate was replaced by administrative control. That was exercised by an assembly of Gods who were old Earth divinities; these divinities from the most ancient times were in touch with the souls of the dead. The growing attention given to the tombs highlighted that closeness in a livelier way. The officials appointed to watch over life were conceived of as infernal functionaries. By contagion from the Buddhist idea of a posthumous retribution for human actions, Taoism elaborated at least from the seventh century a code of sins leading to hell, each sin, as well as compensatory good actions, being assigned a value with the utmost precision. It is a fact worth noting that the Taoist hells were placed in the provinces where the sect had known its first successes: in Szechuan, at Fung-tu, a fearsome cavern and an infernal well. But it was beneath the plain of Hao-li, at the foot of the T'ai Shan, that the chief country of the dead lay. The god of T'ai Shan, heavenly hypostasis, thus became the head of the hierarchy of underworld officials. In every town, the temple of the local genius, served by the Taoists, was also a temple of the Eastern Peak. The seventy-five courts of law ruling the world of the dead were represented there. But there was also to be seen there a female divinity who was the daughter and incarnation of T'ai Shan; it was to her that true piety was directed. She was called the Princess of the Coloured Clouds and seems to have borne the name of a goddess of the dawn; but her acolytes presided over the first days of infancy; she herself awarded births. T'ai Shan owed all its honours to the fact that it was a great agrarian divinity; its daughter was worthy of even more veneration because she was a personification of Mother Earth. In them Taoism was able to find divinities with power over men's hearts.

A flexible and tenacious religion, it drew gods both supreme and close from its monist realism. It had the places of pilgrimage that formed the strength of a faith. Upon those who served it it conferred the gift of spells, the art of talismans, all the magical and religious virtues. It enjoyed more freedom than it would have had if it had become the State religion. Its priests were able to occupy themselves with realizing the most individual of desires, even the most forbidden; they could enjoy that major prestige, the prestige of sorcerers. It seems that nothing was lacking in Taoism for it to be a prosperous religion. It was not. It lacked a knowledge of how to organize a clergy. It no more succeeded in furnishing itself with a regular organization than in becoming an official religion. On these two heads, it achieved only ephemeral successes. As a sectarian doctrine whose chief object was to pursue personal power, it was able to excite great movements of faith and to preside over religious revivals: its normal fate was to furnish practices for enlightenment to mystical souls and the help of magic to the common run of men.

Buddhism

The history of the introduction of Buddhism in China is doubtless destined to remain a mystery.[111] The official chroniclers have ventured to speak of it only in the period when it took on political importance. On the other hand, in the Buddhist writings, as in all religious literature, pious frauds have swarmed; in the case of some of them, and those the most important, scholars have hesitated, after the most minute researches, to date them within three centuries. They were the products of rival sects which often sought an increment of prestige by veritable forgeries. It has been established for example that a Buddhist community completely invented a history aimed at accrediting the idea that the introduction of its faith was due at one and the same time to a miracle and a government decision. In 65 A.D. the image of a deity with a sun halo was supposed to have appeared in a dream to the Emperor Ming of the second Han dynasty; the sovereign was said to have been able at once to send an ambassador to the right place with the order to bring back monks able to instruct him. The result of that invention has been that up to our day orthodox Chinese have cursed the memory of the Emperor Ming.[112] In fact, there is proof that, from before the alleged dream, Buddhist communities existed in China in the lower basin of the Yangtze, and there is the strongest reason to believe that some of them also existed in other regions. All the indications are that Buddhism did not enter China by a single route.

Several roads affording it access had been opened up to it when the Empire had adopted a foreign policy and sought aggrandizement of territory and influence. The armies and explorers of Emperor Wu of the Former Han, towards the end of the second century B.C., had reconnoitred the routes leading to Central Asia and Burma. Those roads were used from the first century of our era as well as the sea route to the Indian Ocean. The Chinese were by this means put in touch with the peoples practising Buddhism. It appears to have come into northern China in the form it had taken in the then Iranian population of Khotan; its extension into maritime China in the south, and then into Shantung, appears to have been achieved independently.

The foreign policy of the Empire produced important economic consequences; rich traders and great estates were then to be seen; it was a time of agrarian crisis. When the Later Han fell, a great number of well-to-do Chinese, fleeing from the disturbances, took refuge in Tonkin. Taoist mysticism had prepared many of them for welcoming with curiosity the Buddhist propaganda being spread in that country. Such was the case with a man named Mou, one of the first Chinese writers to take up the cause of the foreign faith. He composed a little work for 'the removal of doubts'[113] that his fellow-countrymen might entertain on Buddha and his doctrine. His mode of argument shows that he aimed at educated people, Taoists or literati, ill at ease with the lack of moderation and the characteristic flavour of things Indian. In his polemic he made clever use of Chinese anecdotes in which there also showed through that spirit of immoderation condemned by

Confucius and which, as we have seen, had none the less developed in bourgeois morality. In this way he managed to present Buddhist asceticism as an heroic practice whose high object provided authority for not following the ordinary rules of filial piety. He cited a sage who shaved his head, failing to preserve the integrity of his body, because he wished to give up to a brother his right of succession in conformity with his father's wishes. What the most heroic of pious sons did, a monk could do: the literati could say nothing against it. The failure to establish a family and to serve the State as a civil servant were things that could be justified by a like demonstration. The Taoists had insisted upon the vanity and impermanence of the things of this world. In the troubled state in which the Empire found itself, their arguments, taken up by the Buddhists, became more effective. A less measured conception of the Confucian rules of life and a weakening of public spirit allowed the Chinese bourgeoisie to tolerate the excess and narrow individualism of the monastic morality reaching them from barbarous lands.

The singular curiosity that cultivated Chinese have always had about intellectual novelties, combined with the idea that one can never have too many gods or effectual practices, might perhaps have sufficed for the translation of a few books or the tolerance of the vocation of a few monks. Buddhism would doubtless never have become powerful in China if the government of the Empire had not been fragmented and if foreign dynasties had never been established on Chinese Soil. The national civilization was firm and fortunately resisted; but official religion was often sore struck; under transitory dynasties the literati had not the time to recover their power. Despite favourable circumstances, the new faith took nearly five centuries to establish itself firmly in China. It was at the beginning of the fifth century that Chinese pilgrims began to leave for India; in the same period, in the region of Yün-kang, there appeared the first Buddhist monuments.

During the early centuries, the monks coming from all the regions of Buddhist Asia set to translating into Chinese the works of the different sects claiming adherence to Çakyamuni Buddha. One of the earliest translators was the 'Parthian' An Shih-kao, who settled in Loyang in the second century. The difficulties encountered in rendering Indian theories into Chinese were very great; at first much use was made of the Taoist terminology: little by little a special language was created, and innumerable works allowed educated Chinese to study the different doctrines of the Greater and Lesser Vehicles. The desire to seek the true faith at its very source and to learn the true rules of the discipline, a drive to make the pilgrimage to the Buddha's relics and the sanctuaries of the Holy Land, often also diplomatic missions, caused a long succession of eminent monks to leave for India. Fa-hsien set out in 399, and via Tun-huang, Khotan, Kashgar, and the Pamirs, having crossed the Indus on a rope bridge, reached Kashmir, then the holy land of the Buddha: there he could see the spot where Çakya-muni had sacrificed his flesh to save a dove, the places where he had given away his eyes and his head and where he had offered his body to a hungry tigress; he saw the stupa built by King Kanishka, Buddha's skull bone, his beggar's staff, and then the Bodhi tree under which the Master had attained enlightenment, the Gazelle Park where, beginning to preach, he had turned the wheel of the law, the site where he had come down from the Heaven of the thirty-three gods on precious flights of steps, and, finally, the townships where he announced his imminent end and entered into parinirvana.[114] He learnt Sanskrit, studied the monastic rules, and did not return to his own country until he had seen the Buddha's tooth in Ceylon. A century later, in 518, the Dowager Empress Hu of the Tungus dynasty of the Northern Wei sent the ambassador Sung Yün and a few monks to India. The Emperor Yang of the Sui (605–616) despatched several missions intended to prepare for a new extension of Chinese power. Hsüan-tsang, setting out by himself in 629, visited princes of all races, and established diplomatic relations. Several embassies were entrusted to Wang Hsüan-ts'o; one of them was perhaps decided on as a result of the reports made by Hsüan-tsang; resuming after the Sui the Han policy of expansion, the T'ang were able to make use for political ends of the faith that the barbarian dynasties had allowed to become established in China. The reverses they endured in the eighth century interrupted the journeys for a time. They once more became frequent during the glorious beginnings of the Sung dynasty (tenth century). The diplomatic services rendered by the sectaries of Buddha were one of the reasons why the religion was tolerated or favoured by the great Chinese dynasties. But the distant pilgrimages, which called for un-usual heroism, in addition to bringing lustre to the Buddhist faith, supplied it with precise images and immediate emotions.

As soon as Buddhism was established at court, Chinese high society found in the doctrine of one of its sects the elements of a special mysti-cism in whose favour it had been predisposed by its association with the Taoist philosophers. From the sixth century, contemplative Buddhism (dhyana) was introduced into China; after quite difficult beginnings, the sect enjoyed a very great vogue under the T'ang and especially under the Sung. It recognized that the aim of religious life was the pursuit of enlightenment, following the example of Çakyamuni who attained it by meditation. Tradition, doctrine, discipline, texts, all were without importance. Outside the inner life all was vain and impermanent. Bodhi, wisdom, was the result of an intuition of the heart: the condition for it was a state of peace and repose, necessary

for forgetting external illusions and mirages. The only sin was
not to live in the quietude that allowed the concentration of thought.
Once that thought itself could be apprehended, simple and utterly
pure, salvation was achieved, and from then there existed no longer
either life or death, or the endless chain of rebirth. The enlightened
one was a Buddha: for him time was no more, enlightenment was
permanence itself, real and subjective all at once. No method led to it;
it was not something to be taught, or rather, teaching prepared for it
only remotely and negatively, because it allowed illusions to be turned
aside. Wisdom had no external manifestation; there could be no
communication between master and disciple (nothing was more vain
than reasoning) save by interjections robbed of meaning which showed
thought in the state of being concretized and condensed. That mystical
subjectivism had the wherewithal for seducing people of distinction. It
inspired artists and men of letters. It was that which gave to a great
part of Far Eastern painting and poetry their special charm. The subject-
matter of a poem or of a picture, taken from an unreal and fleeting
world, was of no account; but the rhythm of the verses or the strokes
of the brush could express, outside time and yet concretely, a state of
personal intuition that was a special and also a permanent reality.
What gave some solidity to the worldly infatuation for Buddhism, and
prevented it from being in fashion only when it was of use to diplomats, was the sense of value that contemplative intuition held as a
source of artistic inspiration. Beautiful figures of monks in contemplation, adding to the prestige of the religion, encouraged chosen spirits
to give a Buddhist turn to their mystical exercises. The subjectively
oriented meditation advocated by the dhyanist sects did not differ in
nature from Taoist meditation. The aim of both was the creation of
personal power. One could barely discern, at the very bottom of
dhyanist preoccupations, the idea of salvation. But no small service
was rendered to Buddhism by the higher classes of Chinese society
being habituated to a new terminology.

As soon as it had won some claim to be tolerated, Buddhism succeeded in spreading its faith among the common people. The propaganda became fruitful as soon as the direct contact acquired by the
missionaries with things Indian had provided it with a powerful mode
of preaching. The best method was apparently the use of fables. The
story literature, which appears from the end of the Han, was enriched
in the third and fourth centuries; it came into full flower as soon as
Chinese monks became familiar with Sanskrit. The Indian Buddhists
had taken over the matter of the folktales of their country; to illustrate
the doctrine of Karma, they turned the theme of animal metamorphoses to good account. They began from the fact that souls do not
always inhabit a human form, but transmigrate at death and are then

incarnated anew in a man or an animal, in a demon or a god. They added that the law of this transmigration, by which one rose or descended on the ladder of beings, was a moral law: every life was the result of the sum of good and bad actions accomplished during previous existences; the endless succession of future existences depended in the same way upon each act of present life. The first effort to be made to prevent falling into evil being to recognize the vanity of all desire, preaching needed to begin with to deal with the impermanence of the things of this world and of life in particular. It found persuasive images in Indian poetry. For example, it quoted the words of a sage who formerly lived in a country where a single tree, with its fruits bigger than a jar and a taste as sweet as honey, sufficed to feed all the people, the officials, the wives of the king, and the king. There life was passed without serious illness and lasted not less than eighty thousand years, and maidens did not marry before they were five hundred years old. The sage himself owned incalculable riches and yet he said: 'Human life is to be compared to the dew which is left upon the grass in the morning and which drops off in a moment: such being human life, how could it last long? Human life is to be likened to the raindrops falling in the water; bubbles spring up and burst at once; faster than these bubbles, life passes. Human life is to be compared to the lightning that disappears in a flash; more quickly than lightning, life passes . . . Human life is to be likened to an ox dragged to the slaughterhouse; each step the ox takes brings it closer to the place of its death; every day is for man what every step is for the ox; shorter still than that is the duration of life. Human life is comparable to a torrent that rushes down a mountainside and which, day and night, sweeps on impetuously without ever stopping; still faster than that life flies away; day and night it goes towards death and nears it endlessly . . .'[115] And the sage continued his despairing litany until he had stilled all desire to live. Then came the stories of animals lured into the worst snares by their appetites or their passions, even by friendship: such as the monkey who trusted the faith of a tortoise. 'He gave himself up to no debauch with it' and confined himself to discussing good doctrines. Yet he only just avoided being drowned by it. The perfidy had been conceived by the wife of the tortoise, for nothing is more dangerous than the love for a woman.[116] By these tales the Chinese were urged to profit by the experience of souls fallen into animality. Often the teaching came from the Buddha himself, in the account of one of his adventures in the time when he existed in animal form. He was once a peacock, and committed the error of allowing himself to be seduced by a blue bird whom he wished to take to wife. The blue bird demanded dainty food; the peacock who sought it for her fell prey to a hunter; he then recognized his folly and learned to judge women as one should do: 'The enticements of women are like those of demons; it is from them that always come the ruin of kingdoms and the destruction of people; yet stupid people esteem them highly.'[117] Thus were the Chinese warned of the danger of all worldly attachments: at the same time they could become convinced of the reality of transmigrations. Their own folklore contained many stories from which they knew that the souls of the dead could return to Earth, changed into snakes or bears. There was nothing in animal metamorphoses that could surprise them. The novel idea that the tales served to insinuate was that these metamorphoses were the result of a moral law and that rebirth in an unpleasant form could be avoided by the practice of Buddhist virtues.

The virtues were those practised by Çakyamuni during his successive lives and which, in the end, turned him into the Buddha. The first of these 'paramita'[118] was charity: charity consisted in stripping oneself for the sake of somebody else of all the worldly vanities opposed to salvation. Innumerable Kalpas (huge periods of universal life) ago the Buddha was heir apparent of the kingdom of Çibi. He was called Prince Sudana.[119] Out of respect for his father, he agreed to marry and had two children. He then thought that he would like to behave according to the paramita of charity. He gave away all the riches of the paternal treasure 'in order to satisfy all the wishes of men and not to refuse any desire'. To a rival prince, 'moved by evil intentions', he gave up the White Elephant that walks upon lotus flowers: it was the best protector of the realm. The ministers complained, and Prince Sudana was banished. He did not leave before spending seven days in extending his liberality to all comers. His wife asked to share his exile; he took her and his two children with him. In succession he gave away, the first time they were asked for, his horse, his carriage, his clothes, and finally those of his wife. He reached a place of solitude and began to meditate, while the princess went far and wide gathering fruits to feed him. She was away when a Brahman with the face of a demon came to ask Sudana for his two children; he gave them saying, 'You came a long way just out of the desire to have my son and my daughter; how could I forbear to give them to you?' The children said: 'You will bid our mother goodbye for us . . . we regret not being able to take leave of her ourselves.' Their father bound them with a cord, at the request of the Brahman, who, to get them moving, struck the two little ones 'until the blood spurted and fell upon the ground'. Sudana was seated meditating when the mother returned. 'Tell me at once where my children are,' she said to him, 'and don't drive me out of my senses.' He let her repeat her words three times and then said: 'A Brahman came from the kingdom of Kuru; he asked me for the two children, and I gave them to him.' Yet he consoled her, reminding her that formerly she had promised never to stand in the way of his liberality; she knew that he had made up his mind 'not to resist any of the desires expressed to him, and that he would refrain only from giving his father and mother'. 'And so now I have just made a present of the children and here you are disturbing my excellent thoughts.' There then came another Brahman who also had the twelve kinds of ugliness: 'I have come here to ask you for your wife.' The heir apparent replied: 'I consent; it is very well; she is yours.' The princess avoided the shame of belonging to two men, for it happened that the ugly Brahman was a god in disguise; as soon as he recognized that Sudana 'had at that moment no feeling of regret', he desisted in his request. But the prince insisted that he withdraw his refusal. He praised his wife to him: 'In everything she does, she is diligent and industrious and she is fair to behold. Take her away now and my heart will be content.' 'Such is the manner in which the Bodhisattva practises the paramita of charity.'

A Bodhisattva is one who, after having amassed much merit during innumerable lives, has vowed to become a Buddha. Those who are too deeply committed to the chain of existence are not qualified for the renunciation commanded by that high ambition. They lack vocation; simple laymen, they remain in the world and practise the virtues of which they are capable. They first follow a catechism in which they are taught what the Buddha, the Law, and the Church are; then when they know how to bend the knee, raise their joined hands, and examine their consciences, they pronounce the vow that makes them lay adepts for life. They will not kill, in order not to be reborn maimed and come to a bad end; they will not steal or practise usury so they may not later be shorn like sheep, exploited like asses or camels; they will not commit adultery, on pain of transmigrating into ducks; they will not practise deceit, they will not lie or curse, if they wish to avoid returning to earth as cripples; they will not get drunk for fear of being demented in another life. Furthermore, they will never be able to refuse giving alms, in default of which they would in their turn become beggars. If they fulfil all these prescriptions they will be reborn as men, will enjoy a prosperous life, and will live to old age. But the man who feels called to a higher destiny must withdraw from the temptations of the world and submit to monastic discipline. When he wishes to enter the novitiate, he chooses a sponsor who shaves his head before the assembly of monks. Baring his right shoulder and arm, removing his shoes, bending the right knee, raising his joined hands, he announces three times that he puts his trust in the Buddha, in the Law, and in the Church, and that he abandons his family. Finally, he promises to obey the ten rules: not to kill, not to steal, not to fornicate, not to lie, not to drink wine (these first commandments also apply to laymen), not to adorn his head with flowers nor anoint his body with scent, not to sing or dance, not to sit upon a raised seat, not to eat after noon, and not to possess money. The novitiate over, having proved that he has the loincloth, the inner robe, the outer robe, and the bowl, he must declare before the assembly that he is not tainted by any of the disqualifying faults such as being heterodox, having a contagious disease, being a eunuch or hermaphrodite, having raped a nun or killed a monk, being in debt, etc. He promises not to expose himself to the four reasons for exclusion: he will keep chaste, will own nothing, will kill no living being, and will refrain from evil talk. Finally he vows to practise the four monastic commandments: he will not dress in other than cast-off cloth, will eat only food he has begged, will sleep only in a hovel, and will use only dung water as medicine. He is then authorized to work for his own happiness, to do honour to his Order, and to raise himself to the highest degree of wisdom. A woman becomes a nun after analogous ceremonies, probationary period, and vows; but she is not finally accepted until after she has appeared before an assembly of monks, and she must obey the four supplementary observances: to avoid all kinds of contact with men, never to be alone with a man, not to conceal the faults of her companions, and not to take the side of a monk who has been censured. A twice-monthly assembly allows a watch to be kept over discipline: it prescribes expulsion for the four grave sins, penitence for the thirteen venial sins. Penitence consists in a seclusion that lasts as many days as the sin was concealed, plus a retreat of six days. Ninety minor sins are remitted merely by public confession. A hundred small sins involve only inner repentance. For nuns there are laid down, in addition to the cases of expulsion, seventeen cases of penitence and one hundred and seventy-eight cases of lesser sins, of which some are rather odd.

Laymen gain some merit by giving alms to monks, and the monks, living on begged food, attain sanctity: admittedly, laymen profit by their sanctity. The guiltiest souls fall into the state of starving demons, pretas. Buddhism recognizes that individual offerings cannot bring them any help. Maudgalyayana, disciple of the Buddha, 'wishing to save his father and his mother and to show his gratitude for the benefit they had done him in nursing and nourishing him, gazed upon the universe with the eye of understanding; he saw that his dead mother had been born among famished demons; she could neither drink nor eat and her skin was stuck to her bones . . . he filled his bowl with food and went to feed her; when his mother took the food, she covered it with her left hand and with her right hand rolled it into balls; before the food could enter her mouth it was turned into burning coals.' Out of pity for the pious son the Buddha decided that on the fifteenth day of the seventh moon 'good men and women' should 'for their kinsmen in the direct line for seven generations . . . bring together the foods of a hundred flavours and the five sorts of fruit, bowls for washing, scents and oils, stoves and lamps, beds and bedding, assemble all that is good and fine in the world, place it in a vessel (the vessel of Avalambama) and make of it an offering to the assembly of monks of high virtue in the ten regions. At the same time the assembly of all the holy ones, those who in the mountains attain samadhi (state of contemplation), those who beneath the trees behave according to the rule . . . , those who have heard the voice, those who have understood the causes, the bhiksus (monks) in whom are present in strength the Bodhisattvas of the ten regions, all those in a word who form part of the great assembly will, with *one* heart, receive the food from the bowl. As for the conduct of the *assembly of the holy ones who embody all purities by the observance of the prohibitions, its virtue is immense.* When the offering to these classes of monks has been made at the *moment when they begin to confess the sins of each* (of them), *at that very moment the kinsmen (of those making the offerings) will be delivered and will be* quite naturally *clothed and fed . . .* , they will enter into the refulgence of heavenly flowers and will receive endless joy.' Thus, 'thanks to the benefaction of the power of the merits of the Triratna (the three jewels: the Buddha, the Law, the Church) and thanks to the power of the divine force of the assembled monks', a pious son could wash away the sins of his parents, save them, and feed them simply by an offering of clothing and food made to the bhiksus when they wash away their own sins.[120] The Avalambama ceremony[121] has made for the success of Buddhism among the Chinese people. Not only did it offer ample satisfaction to filial piety, but still more it made good a flaw in official religion. Peasant communities ensured regular incarnation to the souls of the dead by waving flowers over the waters; the feudal lords propitiated the unworshipped *kuei* by sacrifices. The Empire failed in this great duty of State: ensuring peace to the dead—and that, during periods of disturbance when there were numerous souls made cruel, vindictive, and bold by violent and premature death. Just as Taoism had to be called to the aid of official religion, abstract and impoverished as it was, so that the forces of Nature might continue their good offices to the Chinese, so Buddhism established its prestige by taking upon itself the burden of pacifying the world of the dead to the benefit of the nation. The ceremony of offerings carried out on the fifteenth day of the seventh moon answered so well to a national need that it quickly became a festival regulated according to the most ancient beliefs. That day nobody failed to float out upon the waters fruit rinds or flowers with little lights stuck in them; that was called: gathering together the *Kuei*. Later, people thought that the rite was only for the souls of the drowned, for whom the lights served to show the way to reincarnation: yet it was the central rite of a general festival of the dead and of reincarnation.

How could the monks be reproached with not practising filial piety? And how could they be refused the alms they claimed as a tithe owed to them for their ascetic labours? If they were fed and clothed, it was they who gave food and clothing to the dead. They did more than that: they caused the dead to share in the salvation that in the first place they appeared to seek for themselves alone. Their assembly formed a church militant and triumphant in which, by freeing themselves from sin, the monks liberated all beings from suffering, and 'with one heart' associated them with 'the immense virtue' and blissful glory of a communion of Saints. Such was the supreme prayer of one who, renouncing all worldly goods in favour of those who had not recognized the vanity of desire, was very near to becoming a Buddha: 'I desire that it may come to pass that all living beings attain salvation and need no longer endure the sufferings of old age, sickness, and death.'[122] What the assembly of Saints could achieve he who attained supreme Saintliness could achieve by himself alone. There was a saviour of the world in every Buddha. But the founder of the religion, Çakyamuni Buddha, promised salvation only by the practice of the Law and the intercession of the Church; adoring him merely opened up the long ascetic way that allowed men to escape the cycle of rebirth. The Chinese preferred to pay their devotions to Maitreya Buddha and especially Amitabha Buddha; the latter, assisted by the Bodhisattva Kuan-yin (Avalokiteçvara), reigned in the Western Paradise. Amitabha had vowed to give enlightenment to all those whom he chose, and to receive into his Pure Kingdom all people who, repentant sinners, would ask at the moment of their dying to be reborn there. Indeed, he sat enthroned upon a magnificent lotus and about him, in the heart of the lotus flowers, saw blossoming the perfectly white souls freed from the world by his mercy. Kuan-yin hearkened to the appeals of the wretched and freed them from all suffering. When the pilgrim Fa-hsien returned from his long voyage, it was Kuan-yin who saved the holy books and the faithful believers from shipwreck in a tempest. It was enough to invoke her to be saved from brigands and demons; the prisoner's irons fell away; the snakes were without poison and the thunder without danger; one obtained easy childbirth and fine children. The piety of women was directed to Kuan-yin, who was the source of all mercy, led souls to Paradise, and granted their wishes to mothers. Most often Kuan-yin was represented with feminine attributes, sometimes with the thousand arms signifying her power of intercession, sometimes surrounded by children, sometimes moving under a rain of flowers, carrying a flag and incense pot, dressed in a flowing robe and humbly followed by the little faithful soul she was leading to the Pure Land.

The only one to compete with her for popular devotion was the Buddha of Medicine; he for his part sat enthroned, bowl in hand, surrounded by his ten generals. The saviour Buddhas and Bodhisattvas, whose images were brought from India to China across the sea or the deserts of Asia, formed a numberless pantheon. With the traditions of Gandhara art, a distant reflection of Greek beauty was to be found in their features: the smile of Apollo, the complex grace of composite deities.[123] The images of Buddhist gods, painted or in sculpture, greatly helped religious propaganda: the Chinese had never before had to do with gods so concrete and so close. Over long periods, in much-frequented and beautiful spots, devotion was responsible for the digging of great grottoes where the faithful might arrange niches and install their chosen Buddhas. In this fashion the grottoes of the thousand Buddhas of Yün-kang, Lung-men,[124] Tun-huang, and Szechwan were constructed. The visible god, made individual and particular by his personal attributes, represented in one of the ritual attitudes of a monk, served to edify the public; and an inscription bore witness to the piety of the makers of the offerings and their confidence in the *ex voto*. If in the earliest period of Buddhist art in China, under the Tungus dynasty of the Wei, the gods still kept some individual features along with their beauty, a mediocre uniformity quite soon became the rule. Similarly, the votive inscriptions contained only stylized clauses and were of an absolute monotony. The donors asked the god for the salvation of the world, of the Emperor, of the Dowager Empress, of the Crown Prince, and of seven generations of their own kin; they asked to be reborn in the Pure Land;[125] as for private prayers, they were as usual those of the sick asking to be cured, or of soldiers who begged for an end to their service, or of officers beseeching that they might be saved from war. Some inscriptions (undated) show that T'ai Shan tended to become a Buddhist deity. The only moving note was that of filial piety; but it was nevertheless expressed in classical and Confucian set phrases: 'They brought up their children . . . , the benevolence of the mother is like unto the summit of Heaven; how can it be repaid? The father and mother embrace the child and gently divert it with their singing . . . When it is thirsty, the mother gives it drink; if it were not her child, she would not give it suck.'

These inscriptions seem in general to have been the work of people in easy circumstances; it is almost impossible to know to what extent Buddhism spread in the countryside. It suffered some violent persecutions: in 444, in 626, in 845; none endured or succeeded in weakening it; the persecution of 845 lasted barely two years during which time a little more than 250,000 monks were secularized. A reform of the discipline in the seventh century, and especially the introduction in the eighth century of the art of efficacious spells and gestures, tantras and mudras, added to the power of the religion. Thenceforth Buddhism and Taoism vied in their protection of the Chinese against an army of demons, of souls of things, trees, graveyards, fords, wells, ancient objects, souls of hanged men, of drowned men, of undecomposed corpses, and so on. Buddhism lived by the sale of amulets and incantations. At least it aroused in the upper classes a revival of the mystical spirit from which art profited, and among the middle classes, perhaps too among the common people, a renewal of the beliefs, or at least the practices, relative to the dead and the hereafter.

It is a wonder that Buddhism could gain acceptance in China. For that to happen there had to be an exceptional concatenation of circumstances and the weakening of the State under pressure from the Barbarians. It is still more remarkable that Chinese civilization and orthodox belief were able to resist the effects of the social disintegration of which that foreign faith took advantage, a disintegration that was further to reinforce the scarcely tempered individualism of Chinese Buddhism. The literati kept careful watch: they had in the highest degree the feeling of public responsibility and for national traditions. They were aware that monastic institutions and the mystical spirit represented a danger for the State by ruining the old rules of filial piety and the foundations of conformity. Han-yü addressed a remónstrance, which has deservedly remained famous, to the Emperor Hsien-tsung who wished to send someone in search of a relic of the Buddha; it was written with eloquence and vigour by a man who saw clearly. Wise and educated as he was, how could the Emperor lend credence to Buddhist superstitions? Easy to lead astray, difficult to enlighten, the people would not get to the bottom of things; if they saw the relic being honoured they would think that the Son of Heaven had become a Buddhist: how would the common people not become Buddhist? They would flock into the monasteries. National manners would be ruined and foreigners would laugh at China; for the Buddha was only a barbarian, who knew not the Chinese tongue or how to wear Chinese dress, who knew nothing of the teaching of the Sages, who had disregarded his duties as son and subject. Let the executioner be given these bones that no Ancient would have dared come near without having the pollution expelled from them by the peach-wand of the official exorcists. If the Buddha came to know of it and could do anything about it, then let him take his revenge: Han-yü took the full responsibility upon his own shoulders and dedicated himself wholeheartedly to the protection of the Empire against superstition and ruin.[126] That energetic petition was the model for the numerous pamphlets by which the literati defended national traditions.

The literati were victorious. None of the religious revivals seriously affected the ancient beliefs of China. Their principal effect was to increase, along with the number of Gods, the indifference to dogma. The Chinese finally adopted a sort of superstitious positivism which accepted all religious formulae to the extent that they showed themselves effectual, which made use of all of them to some degree to try them out—for, after all, they might at a given moment, in a special case, and for a particular individual, be good for some purpose—but which at bottom was concerned only with respecting tradition. That syncretic pragmatism, if I may so put it, found doctrinal expression in Sung philosophy. A school of orthodox thinkers, whose theories were summed up by Chu Hsi in the twelfth century, elaborated a composite system of evolutionist bent, but in which rationalism was the chief feature, under the influence of subjectivist Buddhism and Taoist monism. Its main object seems to have been to free the mind from the terror of death and the fear of ghosts and demons. The World had its Norm by which it developed in a regular fashion; every species had its Law which placed it on a higher or lower rung on the ladder of the concrete manifestations of the universal Norm; every man had his Portion, that is to say, a particular power of understanding and life. All individuation was fated to perish: in the extreme, an ephemeral survival was possible, but the soul must disperse and return into Matter-Norm in which it merely shared. Different beings could not but act, and must act only, in accordance with that immanent semi-material Reason. The system eliminated all mysticism and accorded value to religious practices only in virtue of their traditional character.[127] In the sixteenth century, Wang Yang-ming,[128] almost wholly abandoning the metaphysical part of the system, gave an innate sense of good, characteristic of the gentleman and supposedly identical with heavenly Reason, as the sole foundation of the moral life. The sole duty and unique principle of truth and peace was to know one's heart. This moral subjectivism, more or less accommodated to traditionalism and rounded off by a marked taste for all evolutionist philosophy, still seems in our own day to inspire the sentiments of the educated Chinese in regard to things religious.

Conclusion

Religious Sentiment in Modern China

Geographers repeatedly say that there are 400 million Buddhists in China; those who know China a shade less badly assert that the Chinese practise three religions. Indeed, one may see quite enough quite ugly images which carry the legend: the three religions. They represent Lao Tzu, the Buddha, and Confucius. Confucius is never in the place of honour; in the middle there is either Lao Tzu or the Buddha: a sign that the image is of Buddhist or Taoist make. Each of the two unofficial religions agrees to tolerate the other on condition that it occupy the better place and in order to gain the advantage of a reconciliation with orthodox doctrine.* In fact the current formula, 'the three religions are but one religion', serves only to point to a basic indifference to any kind of dogma. The Chinese are not divided up into followers of one or another of the three faiths; in circumstances fixed by tradition they appeal at the same time to Buddhist or Taoist priests, even to literati or officials. Not only do they never submit to a dogmatic parti pris, but when they have recourse to specialists, they do not at all show towards them the veneration of the sort due to the members of a clergy.

In the towns, except for those in lowly occupations, the men have been to school. They read the newspapers or listen to them being read. All are more or less imbued with the Confucian spirit. They have respect for traditional practices, little or no disposition to mysticism, and a bent for the positivism that excludes faith, if not superstition. They follow custom: it requires that in such and such circumstances, at funerals for instance, certain services must be sought from professionals. In a courtyard next to yours[129] you hear a Buddhist mass being

---

* In a model prison in Peking, dating from 1912, there is a meeting hall. Behind the preacher's pulpit are placed five images representing Christ, Lao Tzu, Confucius, John Howard, and Mohammed. Too much importance should not be given to this syncretism based upon five religious elements. The fact that the Buddha is missing means nothing, nor the presence of John Howard either.

sung for a dead man: do not imagine that the dead man had faith in
the Buddha or that someone among his kin is a Buddhist, or even that
the family is more or less vaguely tied to the Buddhist faith by its
traditions. You will soon hear the music and voices of a Taoist mass
and, if your neighbours are the sort of people who do things on a grand
scale, bonzes and tao-shih[130] will take turns at their masses night
and day. When the moment comes to *dot* the dead man's tablet,[131]
it is a literatus who will be called in. The service asked of him is a
religious service, quite different from that which we ask of a scholar
in giving him the task of composing an epitaph.[132] His stroke of the
writing brush will give the tablet all that makes it a sacred object and
the centre of the ancestor cult. It all happens as though the literatus,
acting in the name of the body of officials, in the name of the State,
authorized the family to possess an Ancestor. At the very moment
when he makes the dot he is, we might say, a priest; the moment after,
he is nothing but a layman: his position in society, it is true, makes
him at all times respectable, but nothing would be more deprived of
sense than to consider the body of literati as a clergy. There exists a
Buddhist clergy and a Taoist clergy. One finds a small number of
administrators, of scholars, and of ascetics among them; the public
is hardly aware of them. It sometimes employs humble servants; it
does not honour them. It is taken for granted that bonzes and tao-
shih have all the vices: they appear on the theatre stage as robbers,
liars, gluttons, and lechers. It is not at all a matter of the onlookers
taking a minor anticlerical pleasure in these serious charges. It falls
to tao-shih and bonzes to be employed as rascals because they apparently
are so, and not because they form a low class of clergy who are derided
and feared at the same time. Their bad reputation does not prevent
their being used, but the relations one has with them are not those of a
believer or unbeliever with a priest whose calling it is to bury the dead,
who, once his job is done, remains a priest, hated or honoured, and,
finally, whose person is rarely a matter of indifference, while the
practices for which he is paid may well be. They are the relations between employer and casual employee: once the exorcism is over,
what does the exorcist matter? Respect goes to the practice and not
to the practitioner. Bonzes and tao-shih are men with devices;[133]
in some cases they can hardly be over-used: the Chinese then call
in all those who possess the traditional secrets of all the formulae
which have been or are assumed to be effectual. For the average man
in the towns, the Buddhist or Taoist priests are not even sorcerers: they
are specialists.

One might think that the women have more regard, and a more
personal regard, for them; but the favour which they enjoy has nothing
to do with their being sanctified; the blind man led into the courtyard

of the house to tell fortunes does not earn less veneration or fear: he owes nothing to the Buddha, to Lao Tzu, to the frequenting of things sacred which properly belong to a religion. A Chinese woman asks for children or any blessing she desires from the Heavenly Weaving Maiden, when it is her festival, from Kuan-yin or the Princess of Coloured Clouds, when a fair draws her to a temple where the image of one of these two goddesses is to be seen; her devotion is expressed uniformly by kneelings and prostrations that do not differ from those made by the beggar-woman to the Excellency who passes by. To what religion does the god belong? She cares not at all; she knows only that, depending on the place, in order to burn incense it is necessary to address herself to a bonze or a tao-shih: he appears less like a priest than a sexton. But the women do not have recourse to him only on fixed occasions; they often need his devices. Those of which he possesses the formulae do not perhaps inspire more confidence than those recommended by the advertisements in the newspapers; the difference is that the owner of the secret is not anonymous; he enjoys a personal prestige which brings him close to the sorcerers.

In the countryside, bonzes and tao-shih make a living out of a monopoly: they serve the local temple. It is of no importance that the god has been enfeoffed to such and such a pantheon, that the server has a shaven head or wears a hat: every server is only an intermediary imposed by custom, every god only a local god. By means of some small offerings the peasant protects himself from the enmity of the one and meets the traditional demands of the other. He is not by that a Buddhist or Taoist or both at the same time: he pays up one or more tithes. In this fashion he obtains a peace analogous to that in which the government leaves him when he has performed his corvée and paid his taxes. Suppose that the government creates a new tax or that some religion favours the area with a new temple: without bothering his head any more about theology than about the form of the government, the peasant will end up, more or less by habit, by docilely bringing his tribute to the tax collector or to the owner of the cult. If religion were defined by the more or less explicit adherence by individuals to a dogma, and their more or less great respect for a clergy, it would equally be false to say that the Chinese practise two or three religions or that they practise one. Indeed, in China there exist as almost definite beliefs only those about Ancestors, and if anyone deserves the title of priest, it is a layman: the paterfamilias.

Neither dogma nor clergy presides over the religious life of the Chinese. It consists in a host of small practices—they are religious practices, for they are obligatory: but it is very difficult to know the extent to which each man ascribes efficacy to each of them—and in a mass of vague beliefs; they are religious beliefs, for they are collective:

but it is very difficult to say what faith each of them inspires in each man.

The person who dresses a corpse never fails to place a sort of winnowing-basket under his feet;[134] in some areas arrows must be shot over the bridal procession: there is a season when the children are made to play with kites; when an important person sets off by train one never forgets to let off firecrackers. Must one think that the Chinese still feel the need to propitiate the gods of travel, that they imagine that the autumn must be celebrated by a festival of ascension, that they consider it impossible to transport a betrothed girl without acting out a ritual fight, and that they still think of respecting the divinity of Mother Earth? In fact, the employees who salute the departure of their employer with a salvo quite simply wish to do him honour: just as a European expresses his homage to a lady traveller of quality by bringing her flowers into her compartment. Chinese boys have a season for kite-flying as French boys have one for playing at prisoner's base. When one shoots arrows over a wedding sedan-chair, one does not think any more about it than the King of England when he throws paper hoofs[135] over his daughter's coach, and the busybody among us who would not dress a corpse without lighting a candle has perhaps more metaphysical preoccupations than has the Chinese perched over his winnowing-basket.[136]

There are innumerable customs in China analogous to those I have taken as examples. Religious practice is made up of the sum of these observances, which in the West seem to be worldly, for they appear to be distinguished from religious duties as these are defined by catechisms. At first sight, the distinction between the sacred and the profane is less appreciable in China than among us.[137] Thus, according to observers, the Chinese are said to be the most practical or the most superstitious people in the world: it will rarely be said, on the other hand, that they are a religious people. In reality, almost all of them observe the sum total of customary practices out of the spirit of tradition and a taste for conformity; it is a general fidelity that constitutes the national religion. As for the trust that each may have in a given usage, it varies from individual to individual, and probably, for the same individual, from moment to moment. If the child of a person who knows the benefits of vaccination has the smallpox, he will paste red paper over his windows, for that is a traditional remedy, and one would reproach oneself for having failed to use it. A modern-minded bride will refuse to allow herself to be carried, veiled in red, in a closed sedan-chair, also red; she will get into a motor car where she will be seen by everybody clad in a dress of western cut: she wishes so to show her disregard of prejudice. It is a ritual prejudice that keeps red for brides and white for people in mourning; the cushions in the car and the bride's dress will be pink; they will be of the palest pink imaginable: they will not be white. You may be sure that neither the young woman nor the father of the sick child, nor doubtless many a Chinese, believes in the efficacy of red or white: they observe or know how to adjust the rules of an ancient symbolism to current taste, but they would not wish to disobey them in every respect; they feel their obligatory character, and if they violated them they would be vaguely afraid of having given a hold to Misfortune.

In general one can say that the system of Chinese practices is not an assemblage of superstitious rules, each of them being deliberately used to obtain a particular advantage. Only a general obedience to those rules is valid; they form a body of age-old conventions the observance of which frees life from undefined risks. These risks are not ordinarily thought of in the realistic and common form of a hell to come. What one wishes to avoid is at once less concrete and more practical: by a host of small acts that one performs routinely and without giving them thought, one succeeds in eliminating all mystical care from daily preoccupations.

Taken up with an infinite number of minor practices which are religious in nature and poorly defined in their bearing, the life of the Chinese seems oriented to an almost completely secular ideal. Those for whom the religious spirit is made up of the great ideals of faith may say that the Chinese are deprived of it; they do not lack it however: but it is of quite another kind. Its basis is the feeling which, with more or less refinements and nuances, animates all individuals, namely, a profound conviction of the value of the moral tradition. In 1919 some Chinese in Peking, admittedly very conservative, were invited to dine at the Hôtel des Wagons-lits; they knew perfectly well that western customs allow men and women to dance in couples, that many of their fellow-countrymen of both sexes had taken to this custom, and that after dinner they would be offered the spectacle of such a dance. Twenty bars of a two-step had scarcely been danced when they were seen to get up in a body, salute their host, and leave him on his own; it must have been very hard for them to flee in this manner, but how were they to withstand the sight of the disordered movement of an American dance? That would have meant exposure to the contamination of barbarism. A well-ordered ballet would probably not have outraged them. Some years earlier, a new bishop was being enthroned in the Cathedral. Some members of the court had been invited to the ceremony; a specialist explained its meaning and details to them. They showed not the least surprise at the mysteries revealed to them, but they were visibly interested by the pomp of the ceremonial acts: these were well-ordered rites. They remained attentive, calm, and cool: they in no way feared being sullied by the contagion of a foreign faith. A bold-spirited Chinese asked me one day to explain the dogma of transubstantiation; he found it very odd. So I took him to hear a mass. I had warned him that there is a moving moment when everybody refrains from looking at the altar, but that if he wanted to see the actions of the officiant he was quite free not to lower his head, that I for my part should not lower mine, and that in any case this practice was customary and not obligatory. He lowered his head very conscientiously.[138] A system of rites is necessary; any rite may be beneficial; no belief is of true interest: the different systems of belief matter little.

Yet, if we are to trust observers, one belief appears to dominate Chinese life: the belief in spirits which, according to them, is deeply rooted and common to all classes of the Nation. It is true that the combined efforts of the Buddhist and Taoist theologians have given China a vast pantheon of gods and demons; it is also true that the literati have never resolutely taught the vanity of belief in gods or in the survival of souls. The majority professed a prudent agnosticism; many were pure sceptics; some harshly mocked public credulity; all strove to render it harmless; none (except perhaps Wang Ch'ung who, in the first century of our era, explained alleged apparitions of spectres by the objective power of cursing and who denied any kind of survival)[139] has really tried to destroy the faith in ghosts, in propitious or more often maleficent spirits. That faith which almost nobody has dared to attack head on—probably for fear of undermining the realistic beliefs which seemed necessary for the popular cult of the Ancestors—can be taken as a firm and lasting popular faith. It seems alive to go by what one reads in some of the newspapers, where the stories of *Kuei* persecuting a neighbourhood and making work for the police, the accounts of haunted houses and all sorts of beings and enchanted objects are current themes of reporting. And one may also hear it told that such and such a fashionable actress has just died as a result of the terror caused her by an avenging *Kuei*. A feature common to all these stories of *Kuei* offered as *news* is that there is an attempt to give them authority by reference to an historical account: that account is taken from a few collections of anecdotes. Accounts of *Kuei* form a literary genre with its own rules, and if the formula 'once upon a time' is replaced in them by a minutely precise date, it is noticeable that these accounts all have the character of a tale. To what extent do they allow credence? To what extent are they imagined, recounted, and listened to as illustrations of the Virtue of the literati or priests, a Virtue that is well known to be enough to cause evil spirits to disperse? To what extent does mockery come into it? It is impossible to say. When I was in the army I had a comrade, a Parisian and a craftsman, very practical-minded. Several times he told me, and always with the same details, that he knew a baker's wife who had given birth to a litter of puppies; the poor woman had even gone to prison for it. I was never able to guess whether my friend was joking: he seemed to be quite convinced, gave the date and place, and experienced some pleasure when his story met with success. If a Chinese had heard him, and along with him all his comrades who each of them had a great deal to say on the ghosts of their country, what would the Chinese have thought of French beliefs? Would he have said that in France, as in China, many things happen that can be explained only by the actions of ghosts? Would he have said that the French and the Chinese believe in all sorts of *Kuei*? Would he have said that in all places there exists a literature of stories, that their subject-matter is everywhere more or less the same, that they point to certain traditional needs of the imagination rather than to the present state of belief, and that if China has an impressive mass of such stories it is because his fellow-countrymen like telling them and have all the time to do so? I do not know at all, and I do not know whether the Chinese inhabit the haunted world of their tales.

Do they believe more deeply in *Kuei* than in deities? The idea they have of the reality of the closest of their gods, Lao T'ien Yeh (a sort of kindly supreme god) or the Kitchen God,[140] certainly varies with social class: it would seem that it varies among them more or less as among us there is variation by age in the idea that children have of the reality of Father Christmas. It does not seem that there ever enters into Chinese beliefs anything that resembles definite conviction or manly adherence. As soon as the Gods are conceived in a distinct fashion (I am thinking of the Gods of China) they tend to become plain imaginative or speculative creations and no longer to possess any reality other than that lent them by some power of mental play. It is not absurd to think that the belief in *Kuei* (which gives Chinese religion the appearance of an animist religion) corresponds to nothing other than a literary expression, and which is often sly, of a vague and potent idea, namely, that the world is made up of the interaction of indeterminate and ubiquitous magico-religious forces. That was the idea that Lieh Tzu had in mind when he analysed the notion of *Cosmic Continuum* by means of fables. I am quite willing to believe that it is still today the substantial basis of Chinese thought. It serves to give as much a positive as a mystical direction to practice or speculation. When everything is wonderful, nothing is miraculous. The Chinese have no more need of a religion of miracles than they are disposed to be surprised by the miracles of science. The most moving of inventions never give them anything but an impression of déjà-vu. Centuries ago their mechanics made aeroplanes fly and Taoist curers knew how to inspect the internal organs of the human body. It matters little whether one proceeds by interpsychic action or makes use of instruments: it is enough to have the device[141] or to employ someone who possesses it. Such a mental set in practice gives a perfect freedom of manner. I know a sinologist who envied his servants their tranquillity at the telephone. The Chinese are no more anxious when faced by an apparatus whose workings they know than they are about deities or spirits whose modes of conduct are known to them through tradition. All things can without exception be handled by the aid of appropriate formulae and suitable practices. If one does not know them, one calls in a specialist. But one does not feel the need to pass on to a clergy the burden of caring for things divine: the latter do not cause so much concern as to harm practical activity.

If in a world that is created by the criss-crossing of sacred forces the Chinese live without apparent religious preoccupations, their existence is none the less governed by sentiments, barely conscious it is true, which are by nature religious in the strictest sense of the term. These sentiments are roughly the same as those that dominated the lives of their ancestors. The idea of an active solidarity between man and the world has remained powerful: everyone feels the need for an organization of existence congruent with the order of things, and in consequence oriented, if I may so put it, in time and space: whence the importance of the calendar and geomancy (*feng-shui*).[142] In vain has the Bureau of Astronomy published elegant ephemera adorned with the portraits of famous men of all races; despite the tendency that can otherwise push the Chinese to set up a positivist cult of great men, the respected calendar is the calendar on the ancient model: it fixes the auspicious and inauspicious days and allows one to know at what moments nature requires one to stay at home, at what moments it allows journeys and undertakings. It is highly plausible that the pleasure taken in eating the first vegetables and fruits in season results in China more than anywhere else from the satisfaction gained from the accomplishment of a duty to share closely in the life of nature. That obligatory participation still involves a constant care for spatial orientation: thence comes the fortune of those specialists called *geomancers*. They are not consulted merely to know whether such and such a site is suitable for a tomb or a house being built. They also know the procedures by which it is possible to transform an orientation that is actually irregular into an orientation that will be correct in religious law; for that, it is enough to put up screens and build mounds, or to modify the appearance of the earth (for the form of the unevenness of the ground has a symbolic value) or by means of appropriate emblems to ascribe qualities to the directions of immediately adjacent space. It is a duty to submit as a matter of course to the influences of Nature: one cannot sleep or arrange one's furniture in an arbitrary fashion. These customs are taken as Chinese characteristics: one could find their equivalent in any country, but in China they have the character of specifically religious obligations. They can be taken as being significant of an agrarian civilization; yet they have resisted centuries of urban life. That life comes more and more under Western influences; it is possible that the duties of spatial and temporal orientation are little by little being transformed into simple traditional customs to be unsupported by any belief. Soon after the establishment of the Republic Yüan Shih-k'ai felt the need to make the politicians of the South realize that Peking was not a secure place; besides, the people liable to tax took advantage of the newness of the regime by not paying up; the soldiery nevertheless demanded their pay. One evening the troops pillaged and burnt some districts. Now, since the fall of the Manchus the central gate to the South, hitherto reserved to the Emperor, had been open to the public. South is the Direction of Fire. The rumour ran in the city that fire had got into Peking through the incautiously opened gate. It was closed up and in fact the fires went out. I could not say how many people accepted the diplomatic fiction suggested to them. Since then, traffic needs have caused the South gate to be opened wide and widened; Peking is not on fire; it is true that they have been careful to keep a gate tower as a screen—or as a decoration.[143]

If it can be said that in the big cities the duties imposed upon man to maintain his solidarity with the natural world are losing their value, there is little chance that for a long time hence the peasants will feel that obligation less. In both town and countryside the obligations resulting from the bond of mutual belonging between an individual and his native soil continue to be strictly respected. The idea of autochthony inspires one of the two greatest religious duties of the Chinese: that of being buried in his native soil. The respect for that duty is imposed upon foreigners. In all the contracts for the export of labour there is a regular clause for the repatriation of corpses. An American woman dies on board ship; her husband pleads for her body to be kept; the captain foresees how bad that burial at sea will look; nevertheless he orders it; there are certainly some coffins on board, but they are the contractual property of the Chinese in the engine-room: even if only one of them were removed there would be a strike. When a colony of people of some importance belonging to the same province live in a Chinese town, an association is formed to take care of transporting the dead back to their native soil. This conveying of the dead is not based upon quite artificial sentiments as among us, in which ostentation plays a part; it is governed by a simple and deeply held belief: the substance of a dead man belongs to his native soil.

The other great duty imposed upon everyone is not to let one's family die out. Celibacy remains shameful and the greatest misfortune for a woman is not to have a son. The fear of lacking male posterity is one of the greatest obstacles encountered by the campaign against the institution of secondary wives. The feeling that the worst disaster is to see a line and its cult disappear constitutes the most realistic element existing in Ancestor worship: among the Chinese bourgeoisie it would have nothing but the value of a symbolic commemoration of family traditions if the duty to perpetuate the line were not translated into emotions of a religious character. It happens that these emotions are revealed in reactions that astonish Westerners. A Chinese learning that his whole family has been massacred far from where he is, congratulates himself first on not having been present and on having escaped the misfortune. It would be very foolish to see in that the naïve expression of a quite selfish insensitivity. Far from thinking of himself, the Chinese thinks at once, with manly stoicism, of his line; he is happy that some hope has been preserved for it; that does not mean at all that he would not sincerely prefer his father and his older brother to have been saved in place of him.

Some simple and deep-lying beliefs, heritage from an ancient peasant past, animate the religious life of the Chinese; they suffice to give meaning to the life of the humblest of them; among the more cultivated, religious feeling is manifested by an inner effort of personal cultivation along the line taken by national tradition. According to all, the formalism inspired by an age-old symbolism is enough to free life from the preoccupation with holy powers. Everybody conceives those powers as basically immanent. There is no need at all to throw the care for religious things on to the shoulders of a clergy; there is no temptation to place a world of gods above the world of men.[144] No religious revival has succeeded in noticeably modifying these attitudes of the Chinese towards the sacred. Will other revivals manage to change them? It seems that the problem has relevance at the present day, since there are missionaries in China and since some Chinese put circulars about in which we may read the question: 'Do we need a Religion?' (sc. a new religion).

After the Buddhists, the Nestorians, the Mazdeans, and many others, the Catholics have come to offer a new religion to the Chinese. Catholic propaganda formerly profited from the attraction of then new scientific and technical knowledge, all the prestige of which went to the missionaries alone; it profited from the subtle fervour of the Jesuits in the most fortunate period of their Order; still today it has the most devoted missionaries, those who doubtless (save for the orthodox: they are very few) are the most moved by fraternal feelings. At the beginning, its progress was incomparably less brilliant in China than in Japan; since the persecutions have stopped, the regularity of the progress has been remarkable but so also has been its slowness. The wealth of

Catholic dogma has only little prestige for the Chinese: revelation, holy books received upon the mountain, incarnation of a God in a Virgin Mother, resurrection of the dead, paradise, hell, redemption from punishment, all that they know. If dogma has neither attraction nor importance for them, for the missionaries it is a hindrance, since it must be clear, fixed, unalterable: the times of Gregory the Great are gone. Catholic rites being beautifully ordered, they might seduce the Chinese, if it were not that the converts were commanded to use only them and put aside all others. The most serious difficulties are moral: the Chinese cannot see how the authority of a paterfamilias, which is absolute,[145] could accommodate itself to the pre-eminent authority claimed by a spiritual director. Finally, it does not seem easy to give an idea of what prayer ought to be for a true believer to people for whom only stereotyped formulae are efficacious. Catholic missionaries do not appear to count on numerous conversions among Chinese nourished on Confucian thought; indeed, there are reasons why those Chinese show as much aversion from Catholicism as their forbears manifested in regard to Buddhism. While seeking to gain followers among the influential classes of the country, Catholic propaganda is principally directed to the common people: it hopes, by concerning itself with education from an early age, to bring up perfect believers in the second or third generation. The mode of recruitment is inspired by a precise knowledge of native life; the Chinese have the habit of forming groups of clients: to protect them against the abuse of local authority or to support them in their lawsuits, they could not have better patrons than the Catholic missionaries. These display an untiring devotion which, accompanied by a sense of economic reality, allows the Mission to take root in Chinese soil. Conversions are the fruit of patience: there are no examples of mass conversion produced directly by preaching.

The ideal of the Catholic Missions is to propagate the dogmas of their religion in all their orthodox rigour. The task of the Protestant Missions, in which the American element increasingly dominates, might seem made easier by the less definite nature of belief in the reformed churches. If preoccupation with dogma seems from day to day to take on more importance in the religious thought of the United States, it is far from being placed in the forefront by the body of missionaries imported into China from America. The Protestant Missions offer themselves as humanitarian missions; they are rich in personnel and money; they busy themselves with public health and social assistance; they work chiefly in the towns; they try to organize social life there according to Anglo-Saxon principles: their meeting halls and recreation rooms are welcoming; they attract the English-speaking Chinese public, which is quite large; the lecture system pleases the natives who all have the taste for talk; the discussion bears only upon a few themes of moral rhetoric: war on opium, on drink, on prostitution, on polygamy. In Peking, where a very large effort has been made (there are nearly 200 missionaries there aided by 350 native auxiliaries), Anglicans and Protestants have gathered in fewer than 5,000 followers. The Catholics have about 10,000. Peking has more than 800,000 inhabitants (according to the census of 1918).

There are quite a number of Muslims in North-West China (about 25,000 in Peking); in 1914 they unsuccessfully asked for verses from the Koran to be introduced into the school-books alongside Confucian teachings. The importance of Islam in China is political not religious.[146] The same is true of Lamaistic Buddhism. A few Buddhist sects practising the cult of Amitabha have a small number of followers: 'In my whole life I shall never forget' (the speaker is a Jesuit Father) 'the feeling I experienced when I watched a young Amidist mother at her devotions . . . , she first closed her eyes and deeply meditated, her lips murmuring the act of repentance and request. Then she lined up two little children . . . who, perfectly trained, did in the most serious possible manner what their mother had done . . . I wonder if there are not among these Amidists . . . many souls who worship the true God.' A Buddhist society which has some branches in the country has 10,000 members in Peking: it holds two meetings a year and appears to function chiefly as a temperance association.[147]

The figures I have given may indicate the missionary power that the religions imported into China have at the present time. Is Taoism capable of revival? About ten years ago, there were still Taoist tracts being distributed in the streets. I took advantage of one of these windfalls with the gratitude that a stranger in Paris, curious to know French beliefs, might have for a leaflet put out by the temperance society. Despite their respect for written paper, I did not then see any of the Chinese going about their business, or even any of those strolling along with their pet birds in cages, hurry up to the man who was distributing the leaflets. Taoist thought does not appear to inspire any sect. Yet it corresponds to certain deep dispositions of the national mind. If some great social crisis arose in China it cannot be said that Taoism would not play a role in it.

The official cults are finished. Since 1916 no sacrifice has been made to Heaven. A bandstand has been put up in the enclosure where the spring ploughing used to be carried out, and one can see Chinese families spending their afternoons seated in the shade of the ancient grove of the Earth God. Will the cult of Confucius survive? Free-thinking parliamentarians determinedly fight against it. It is defended by a *Confucian Society* which has undertaken to make the teachings of the Master obligatory. That Society is conservative in cast.

Chinese of bold opinions refuse to accept the principle of State morality. Some among them have founded independent schools, certain of them called 'Auguste Comte Schools'. Comte is written in Chinese in two words: one means virtue, the other is the surname of Confucius.

Admittedly, the virtue of Confucian teaching is to nourish a practical spirit whose ideal might be defined by the formula Order and Progress. Many schools are being set up in China, often lodged in the disused outhouses of religious buildings. Education begins to reach the humblest classes of society. It imbues them with the sentiments proper to a morality that has only human ends. That morality, whose tradition was kept up by the literati for the benefit of the Chinese bourgeoisie and whose principles were established by the ancient ritualists, has always had the merit of freeing men from the weight of the Gods; it could not formerly free them from the weight of traditional rites. Until quite recently Chinese children were enchantingly wise, but they were too wise. One has now only to be present at a ball game or when school empties out to ascertain that the fear no longer weighs upon them of not preserving the integrity of the bodies bequeathed to them by their parents. They remain gentle and shrewd: they have a wide-awake air. They are taught things and no longer actions and formulae. They are lively, bold, prepared for action and free thought. One day I saw some of them running out of their classrooms,[148] which had been set up in the outhouses of an old Buddhist temple, a corner of which had been left to the officiating priests. As they were playing, the little urchins bumped into a priest coming out of his quarters absent mindedly. They did not seem much frightened but their pretty smiles offered an apology. The bonze, however, was angered, and the lay teacher took some pleasure in going to the aid of his pupils. Some idlers came up. The exchange between the two men did not last long; it was ended when a certain expression, *turtle egg*,[149] struck one's ears. All this took place in the twilight of a winter nearing its end, in a charming corner of old Peking, on the high open court in front of the Mahakala Miao.[150] In the approaching nightfall there was doubtless no evil spirit, for the only little bell still hanging from one of the corners of the roof did not tinkle. The new season about to arrive could be felt in the mildness of the evening. The time had perhaps come for retreat and meditating upon supreme renunciation: the bonze's yellow robe disappeared behind a wall in ruins.

Editorial Notes

1. I have modified my translation of Granet's version of this passage in the light of standard English renderings. Cf., e.g., Arthur Waley, trans., *The Analects of Confucius*, Allen and Unwin, London, 1938, p. 194.

2. The text has *seigneuries*. To translate that term as 'seigniories' and match it with 'seignior' would have the advantage of preserving in 'seigniorial' the ambiguity of Granet's *seigneurial*: pertaining to both 'domains' (as I have in the end decided to call them here) and their lords. But that trio of terms would, I think, look highly artificial. My choice of 'domain' is in fact justified by Granet's usage in the lectures he gave in 1936 on Chinese feudalism: *La féodalité chinoise*, published posthumously in 1952. There he employs both *domaine* and *seigneurie*, appearing to favour the former. 'L'expression "*Tchong kouo*" [*Chung-kuo*], vaut aujourd'hui pour la Chine entière . . . Mais avant l'unification de la Chine, le mot "*kouo*" avait le sens précis de "*principauté*", de "*fief*", de "*domaine seigneurial*"' (p. 37). 'Est seigneur (*Kiun*) qui possède un Domaine (*Kouo*) comprenant terres et vassaux . . .' (p. 105). In English works on China the word *kuo* is in this context often rendered as 'state' or 'principality'. I am not of course concerned here to debate with Granet the sense in which it is true that China knew feudalism, and how far one is justified in taking over for China a language deriving from European institutions. Granet was, needless to stress, aware of the problem: see *La féodalité chinoise*, pp. 19–23. On the issue cf. Derk Bodde, 'Feudalism in China', in Rushton Coulborn, ed., *Feudalism in History*, Princeton University Press, Princeton, N. J., 1956. . . . Granet was in his student days much preoccupied with European feudalism (cf. Introductory Essay above, pp. 8f.), and paid attention to the works on both European and Japanese feudalism reviewed in the *Année Sociologique*. Cf. Fauconnet's review of Georges Appert, 'Un code de la féodalité japonaise au XIIIᵉ siècle', 1900, in *Année Sociologique*, vol. 4,

1899–1900, pp. 404–406, and Durkheim's review of Fukuda Tokuzo, *Die gesellschaftliche und wirstchaftliche Entwickelung in Japan*, 1900, in *Année Sociologique*, vol. 5, 1900–1, pp. 342–347, especially pp. 346f. where Durkheim draws an analogy between Japanese and European developments. In one of his own rare book reviews, Granet was himself later to write of J. Calmette, *La société féodale*, 1923, in *Année Sociologique*, n.s., vol. 1, 1923–24, p. 663: 'On s'étonne du peu d'importance accordée aux croyances qui soutiennent le régime féodal: il n'est à peu près rien dit ni de l'honneur ni de ses emblèmes (blason . . .).' In this book Granet sometimes translates *Chung-kuo* (China) as either *la Confédération chinoise* or *la Chine confédérée*, according to whether the accent is to be put upon the unity of the country vis-à-vis the non-Chinese world or upon the plurality of a country made up of linked political units sharing a common culture. Cf. *Danses et légendes*, 1926, p. 73, fn. 1.

3. The second edition, 1951, has an anonymous footnote here to draw the reader's attention to the fact that the book was written in 1922. Granet was himself later to write on the subject of Taoism in 'Remarques sur le Taoïsme ancien', 1925, *La civilisation chinoise*, 1929, and *La pensée chinoise*, 1934. Cf. note 102 below.

4. The first edition has *troisième*, but the error is corrected in the second.

5. That is, because in the chapter on peasant religion Granet expounds his own highly original (and we may say, brilliantly imaginative) research, and in the concluding chapter he makes use of his own observations in China.

6. Granet is referring here to the *Shih Ching*, 'The Book of Odes' or 'The Book of Songs', as it is commonly known in English. That was the source upon which he worked to marvellous effect in *Fêtes et chansons anciennes de la Chine*, 1919, many of the conclusions of which are incorporated in the first chapter of this book.

7. The distinctiveness *and* complementarity of urban and rural society form a chief feature of Granet's sociology of China. It may well be thought that he overdrew the contrast between town-dwellers and countrymen, at least for the post-Han dynasties. (On the interpenetration of town and country in modern China, see my papers 'On the Sociology of Chinese Religion', in Arthur P. Wolf, ed., *Ritual and Religion in Chinese Society*, Stanford Univ. Press, Stanford, Calif., 1974, and 'The Politics of an Old State: A View from the Chinese Lineage', in John Davis, ed., *Choice and Change: Essays in Honour of Lucy Mair*, London School of Economics Monographs on Social Anthropology no. 50, Athlone Press, London, 1974.) It would require a highly expert assessment of the archaeology and early history of China to decide how far Granet's view of the ancient system of urban-rural

relations is still tenable. For recent expressions of opinion, see e.g. Paul Wheatley, *The Pivot of the Four Quarters, A Preliminary Enquiry into the Origins and Character of the Ancient Chinese City*, Edinburgh University Press, Edinburgh, 1971, especially pp. 478f.; Joseph R. Levenson and Franz Schurmann, *China: An Interpretive History, From the Beginnings to the Fall of Han*, University of California Press, Berkeley, etc., 1969; Judith M. Treistman, *The Prehistory of China, An Archeological Exploration*, The Natural History Press, for the American Museum of Natural History, Doubleday, Garden City, N.Y., 1972; Cho-yun Hsu, *Ancient China in Transition, An Analysis of Social Mobility, 722–222 B.C.*, Stanford University Press, Stanford, Calif., 1965; Jacques Gernet, trans. Raymond Rudorff, *Ancient China, From the Beginnings to the Empire*, Faber and Faber, London, 1968 (but this last work is perhaps too heavily influenced by Granet to form a check upon his views). It is interesting to compare Granet's interpretations of early China with those, framed in a more narrowly sinological setting, by his contemporary Henri Maspero. Cf. Henri Maspero and Etienne Balazs, *Histoire et institutions de la China ancienne des origines au XIIe siècle après J.C.*, ed., Paul Demiéville, Presses Universitaires de France, Paris, 1967, pp. 1–39.

8. In this statement we are afforded a striking example of the difficulty faced by the ordinary reader in assessing Granet's assertions of fact. The statement is not repeated (or withdrawn) in his splendid lecture 'La droite et la gauche en Chine', 1933, but it is several times mentioned in his earlier work: *La polygynie sororale*, 1920, p. 28, in *Etudes sociologiques sur la Chine*; 'La vie et la mort', 1920–21, p. 206, fn. 1, in *Etudes sociologiques; Danses et légendes*, 1926, p. 6; and *La civilisation chinoise*, 1929, p. 209. In fact, the assertion is made upon the basis of one brief passage in the Han dynasty text *Po Hu T'ung*. In *La polygynie sororale, loc. cit.*, Granet cites the classical formula to the effect that the rites do not go down to the common people, and in a note says: 'L'opposition entre les usages nobles et plébéiens est bien marquée pa Ho HIEOU (I *b*). Le *Po hou t'oung* (chapitre du "Mariage") note (et c'est un fait curieux et important) que les familles rustiques donnaient la préférence à la gauche parce qu'elles prenaient pour modèle l'ordre céleste, tandis que les familles distinguées, suivant l'ordre terrestre, préféraient la droite.' But according to Tjan Tjoe Som, this reading of the Chinese text is false. Tjan's version of the relevant passage goes: 'The adherents of the Principle of Substance model themselves on Heaven, and reverence the left. The adherents of the Principle of Form model themselves on Earth, and reverence the right.' Granet translates (mistranslates, in Tjan's view) as 'les familles de gens simples, rustiques' and 'les familles distinguées' what Tjan renders, respectively, as 'adherents of the Principle of Substance' and 'adherents of the Principle of Form'. See

Tjan Tjoe Som, *Po Hu T'ung*, *The Comprehensive Discourses in the White Tiger Hall*, vol. I, Brill, Leiden, 1949, pp. 252, 351. Even if Granet were to be granted his translation, it would still seem to be a slender base upon which to erect the general statement about a systematic difference in preference for the side of the body between nobility and peasantry. I can find no repetition of the statement in Granet's work after 1929, and it may perhaps be concluded that he silently retracted an over-enthusiastic interpretation made in his early studies. For a recent sinological treatment of the question of 'laterality' see Paul Demiéville, 'Gauche et droite en Chine', in Demiéville, *Choix d'études sinologiques (1921–1970)*, Brill, Leiden, 1973 (originally published in 1968).

9. Here Granet is referring as briefly as possible to the highly debatable (and hotly debated) question of the ethnic components of Chinese civilization. Cf. his *Danses et légendes*, 1926, pp. 3f., 8ff., and *La civilisation chinoise*, 1929, pp. 163f. For a recent comment on Granet's views see Jaroslav Průšek, *Chinese Statelets and the Northern Barbarians in the period 1400–300 B.C.*, D. Reidel Publishing Company, Dordrecht, 1971, p. 13; and for an example of one kind of reconstruction allowed by the complex and fragmentary evidence, see Wolfram Eberhard, trans. E. W. Dickes, *A History of China*, 2nd edn., Routledge and Kegan Paul, London, 1960, pp. 7–36.

10. Cf. note 8 above. The formula comes from the *Li Chi*.

11. Granet's *Fêtes et chansons*, 1919 (the groundwork for which had been prepared in 'Coutumes matrimoniales de la Chine antique', 1912, written while he was a student in Peking) is devoted to a reconstruction of ancient Chinese rural society upon the basis of songs (drawn for the most part from the *Kuo Feng* section) in the *Shih Ching*. Cf. note 6 above. A philological case against Granet's ingenious interpretation is made in Bernhard Karlgren, 'Glosses on the Kuo Feng Odes', *Bulletin of the Museum of Far Eastern Antiquities*, Stockholm, no. 14, 1942, p. 75; it seems to me to rest in part on a doubtful view of the relation between popular and learned poetry, but the argument is not one into which a non-sinologist ought to venture. See also note 32 below.

12. As an example of the poetic sources for Granet's statements about ancient life see, for the building of houses, the poem translated at pp. 282f. in Arthur Waley, trans., *The Book of Songs*, Allen and Unwin, London, 1969 (first published 1937), and at pp. 130f. in Bernhard Karlgren, trans., *The Book of Odes*, the Museum of Far Eastern Antiquities, Stockholm, 1950.

13. Based upon the song given the title 'Le manche de hache', *Fêtes et chansons*, 1919, p. 125 (trans. E. D. Edwards, *Festivals and Songs of Ancient China*, 1932, p. 120), in which the following lines are to be found (in Edwards's version of Granet's translation):

How is the hemp to be grown?
The furrows must be crossed (E. to W. and N. to S.)
How is a wife to be taken?
Her parents must be informed.
How are the boughs to be cut?
With no axe it cannot be done.
How is a wife to be taken?
With no match-maker none can be had.

Cf. the corresponding translations in Karlgren, *The Book of Odes*, p. 66, and Waley, *The Book of Songs*, pp. 67f.

14. By the time he wrote *La civilisation chinoise*, 1929, Granet had come to make his model of ancient peasant society more complex by adding to it a men's house organization (see *op. cit.*, p. 198), which in turn was one of the sources of *confréries*, men's associations (*ibid.*, chap. IV). And cf. *Danses et légendes*, 1926, pp. 52, 291, 333. The development of *confréries* formed a link between peasant society and the feudal system to follow on from it. Of this intermediate stage Granet writes (*Danses et légendes*, p. 52): 'That setting was certainly highly complex and made up, if I may so put it, of different layers. In it are to be found vestiges of Totemism and traces, quite faint, of an organization whose *characteristic features* were: the existence of *confréries* (linked, it would seem, with a classification by compass points and winds)—the custom of men's houses (linked, it would appear, with a distribution of the male population by age-classes, as well as a distinction between active and honorary members);—finally, the religious character of the winter season.' On totemism, see especially *Danses et légendes*, pp. 602–606. Potlatch also appears; see especially *Danses et légendes*, pp. 611–615. Mana was part of Granet's vocabulary when he wrote his first paper on a Chinese subject; see below, note 20. The insertion of *confréries* into the model is pointed out by Mrs. S. C. Humphreys, 'The Work of Louis Gernet', *History and Theory, Studies in the Philosophy of History*, vol. 10, no. 2, 1971, pp. 179, 195. That paper on Granet's fellow-Durkheimian, his analogue in Greek studies, admirably demonstrates the intellectual consequences of the *Année Sociologique* school for the interpretation of ancient civilizations. Cf. note 8 to the Introductory Essay, above, pp. 4f. Note Durkheim's review of Heinrich Schurtz, *Altersklassen and Männerbünde*, Berlin, 1902, in *Année Sociologique*, vol. 6, 1901–2, pp. 317–323. On the other hand, of course, it was not only within a Durkheimian setting that the late nineteenth-century and early twentieth-century stock of anthropological rubrics was made to embrace Chinese data. See e.g. Wilhelm Koppers, 'Die Frage des Mutterrechts und des Totemismus im alten China', *Anthropos*, vol. 25, 1930, and Martin Quisdorp, 'Männergesellschaft und Altersklassen

im Alten China', *Mitteilungen des Seminars für orientalische Sprache an der Königlichen Friedrich-Wilhelms-Universität zu Berlin*, vol. 18, Berlin, 1915.

15. Granet here sees ancient Chinese kinship as resting essentially upon the double distinction of age and generation, but at the same time embodying early on a unilineal principle, to begin with matrilineal and then later patrilineal. (Cf. Granet, *La polygynie sororale*, 1920, pp. 28–30 in *Etudes sociologiques*. There, at p. 30, he says that there are grounds for believing that in the beginning each local community consisted of a pair of family groups, marriage exchanges taking place between them, that hypothesis being based upon an analysis of early Chinese kinship terminology. See below, note 16.) Yet I think it might just possibly be argued that Granet is here showing some slight hesitation in characterizing early Chinese kinship as matrilineal, and that his final views, expressed in *Catégories matrimoniales et relations de proximité dans la Chine ancienne*, 1939 (his last work published while he lived), according to which the ancient form of Chinese kinship lacked a unilineal principle and rested upon a four-section marriage system, fully expressed his initial doubt about the primitive matriliny fashionable at the time of his basic sociological education. See *Catégories matrimoniales*, pp. lf., 5, 95, 96, 97, 102, 167f., 176, etc.

16. Primordial matriliny. See above, note 15. Cf. *La civilisation chinoise*, 1929, pp. 183f. The patrilocality of residence evident in the *Shih Ching* is countered by ascribing that rule of residence to feudal times (when of course the poems were recorded) and by reading into the (officially disapproved) institution of married-in sons-in-law (which has persisted to our own day) a relic of ancient matrilocality. The argument for the 'femininity' of the house is more interesting, if no more convincing: the furnishings were (and are still, for the new conjugal bedroom) provided out of the wife's dowry. But that fact needs to be more fully analysed in relation to the structure of the transactions between the two families involved. Cf. Maurice Freedman, *Rites and Duties, or Chinese Marriage*, Bell, London, 1967, pp. 7, 13.

17. Cf. Granet, *Fêtes et chansons*, 1919, p. 97, 'Les tiges de bambou', which Edwards (*Festivals and Songs*, pp. 91f.) translates as:

> The slender bamboo stalks
> Are for fishing in the Ch'i!
> Do I not think of thee?
> But afar one cannot go.
>
> The Ch'uan spring is on the left,
> On the right the river Ch'i!
> A girl, when she goes to be married
> Leaves afar her brothers and parents.

The river Ch'i is on the right
The Ch'uan spring on the left.
A smile shows the flash of teeth . . .
The charms tinkle on the way . . .

The river Ch'i flows on, flows on.
Oars of cedar . . . boats of pine . . .
In my chariot I roam
To dissipate my sorrow . . .

Cf. Karlgren, *op. cit.*, p. 41, and Waley, *op. cit.*, p. 47. And for another song on the same theme, see 'L'arc-en-ciel', *Fêtes et chansons*, p. 44 (*Festivals and Songs*, pp. 42f.); cf. Karlgren, *op. cit.*, p. 33, and Waley, *op. cit.*, p. 61 (where, however, the interpretation is somewhat different).

18. See above, note 13.

19. In Durkheim's work see especially *Les formes élémentaires de la vie religieuse, Le système totémique en Australie*, Alcan, Paris, 1912, pp. 498f. 'We know that positive worship tends naturally to take periodic forms; that is one of its distinctive features. Doubtless, there are rites that men perform on occasion, in order to cope with passing situations. But these episodic practices never play other than a secondary role, and in the religions specially under study in this book they are even almost exceptional. What in essence constitutes the cult is the cycle of festivals which recur regularly at fixed periods. We are now in a position to understand where that trend to periodicity stems from; the rhythm followed by religious life merely expresses the rhythm of social life, and it springs from it. Society can revive the view (*sentiment*) it has of itself only on condition that its members congregate. But it cannot hold its gatherings continuously. The exigencies of life do not allow it to remain indefinitely in a state of being gathered together; it disperses, then, in order to congregate afresh when it once more feels the need to do so. The regular alternation of sacred and profane times is in accordance with these necessary alternations. Since in origin the object of the cult, at least its apparent object, is to make regular the course of natural phenomena, the rhythm of cosmic life has marked the rhythm of ritual life. That is why, for a very long time, festivals have been seasonal . . . But the seasons merely furnished the outer framework of that organization, not the basis upon which it rested; for even the cults that aimed at only spiritual ends remained periodic. So that the periodicity was due to other causes. As seasonal changes are critical periods for nature, they are natural occasions for assemblies and, in consequence, religious ceremonies . . . That rhythm is . . . liable to vary in form according to the society. Where the period of dispersal is long and the dispersal extreme, the period during which society congregates is in turn

much prolonged, and veritable excesses of collective and religious life result. One festival follows another for weeks or months, and ritual life sometimes reaches a sort of frenzy . . . Elsewhere, on the other hand, these two phases of social life followed each other at closer intervals, and the contrast between them was then less marked. The more societies develop the less they seem to tolerate stressed intermissions.' (Cf. Joseph Ward Swain, trans., *The Elementary Forms of the Religious Life*, Allen and Unwin, London, 1954, first published 1915, pp. 349f.) On the theme, cf. Marcel Mauss (with H. Beuchat), 'Essai sur les variations saisonnières des sociétés eskimos, Etude de morphologie sociale', *Année Sociologique*, vol. 9, 1904–5, especially, pp. 65, 96ff., 125. See Granet, *La pensée chinoise*, 1934, pp. 109ff., noting in particular the sentence, p. 110, 'Une société ne peut durer sans se recréer'; and his 'La sociologie religieuse de Durkheim', 1930.

20. In the text the word *vertu* (often *Vertu*) is nearly always meant to convey a particular sense of the Chinese *te* or *tao-te*. In his first published sinological exercise ('Coutumes matrimoniales', 1912, p. 67, in *Etudes sociologiques*) Granet wrote: 'L'ordre parmi les hommes, comme l'ordre dans la nature, sont l'effet du *tao tö*, de la vertu, du mana, de l'influence efficace de l'empereur.' The meaning is effectiveness, power, energy, capacity. In his exposition of Taoism later in the text (see p. 122) Granet says that *Tao-te* designates the Power of Realization characterizing every religious force and, in particular, princely authority. *Tao* is reserved to the prince, but *te* may represent its delegated or specialized use. The French *vertu*, as the Latin *virtus* from which it derives, covers the Chinese range of meaning (from moral correctness to efficaciousness) better than its English cognate. And cf. Granet, *La pensée chinoise*, 1934, pp. 301ff.; the footnote at p. 301 is especially interesting for the light it casts upon Granet's style of sociological reasoning: 'All I have read' since drawing the analogy with *mana* in 'Coutumes matrimoniales', 'has confirmed me in the idea that the analogy was correct. Just as the concept of *mana* remains latent in the most archaic societies and begins to be expressed only in more developed civilizations, so the idea of *tao*, latent in China from the time when the Yin and the Yang Emblems were conceived, emerged only at the moment when the Chinese adopted a hierarchical organization: it bears its stamp.'

21. The text has *mouette*, but Granet is translating a Chinese word, *chü*, which is conventionally rendered 'osprey' in English. See Edwards, trans., *Festivals and Songs*, p. 109.

22. Note Granet's keen sense of the structure of a complex language made up of speech and gesture. He was obviously inspired by the Durkheimians in this as in other respects, and Lucien Lévy-Bruhl's *Les fonctions mentales dans les sociétés inférieures*, Alcan, Paris, 1910, was one of the works from which he derived his ideas about language.

Lévy-Bruhl, *op. cit.*, pp. 175ff., deals with sign language. Cf. note 31 below. Granet carried the notion of *langage* as structure into the realm of mourning ritual in a paper published in the same year as that in which he wrote *La religion des Chinois*: 'Le langage de la douleur d'après le rituel funéraire de la Chine classique'. Rituals were to be seen as language in which the elements (to quote from the text to which the present note refers) take 'from their place in the total design a special syntactic function'. Cf. the concluding sentences of 'Le langage de la douleur', p. 242 in *Etudes sociologiques*: 'Et c'est pourquoi les gestes de la douleur se sont ordonnés en une suite de rites qui sont aussi un système de signes. Ils constituent une technique et une symbolique; ils forment un langage qui a ses besoins d'ordre, de correction, de clarté, qui a sa grammaire, sa syntaxe, sa philosophie, et, je dirais aussi, sa morale.'

23. The speaker was one of Confucius's disciples. See Granet, *Danses et légendes*, 1926, p. 327.

24. Granet's derivation, in the Durkheimian manner, of Chinese categories from states of social order is better exemplified in a passage in *La pensée chinoise*, 1934, pp. 24ff. 'The category of Order or Totality is the supreme category of Chinese thought; its symbol is Tao, an essentially concrete emblem . . . The notion of Tao goes beyond notions of force and substance; and Yin and Yang, which indiscriminately have the values of forces, substances, and kinds (*genres*), are yet again something else, since these emblems have as a whole the function of classifying and animating the antithetical aspects of universal Order . . . Chinese thought seems completely governed by the joint ideas of order, totality, and rhythm . . . The notions to which Chinese attribute a categorial function depend essentially upon the principles on which the organization of their society rests: they represent a sort of institutional base for Chinese thought, and their analysis merges (as we shall see for example in the case of ideas of Time, Space, and even Number) with a study of social morphology. But these key ideas did not all become explicit at the same point in history . . . If Yin and Yang form a *pair* and appear to preside jointly over the rhythm lying at the base of universal Order, then it is because their conception springs from a period of history when a principle of rotation sufficed to regulate social activity shared between two complementary groupings. The concept of Tao goes back to a less ancient era; it could become explicit only at the moment when the structure of society was more complex and in settings where there was reverence for the authority of Chieftains who were entitled to offer themselves as the sole originators of the order in the universe . . .'

25. The first edition reads: '. . . et son activité, qui est d'ordre inférieur . . . .', while the second edition alters the last word to 'intérieur'.

26. From the *Li Chi*. See Granet, *Fêtes et chansons*, 1919, p. 199, fn.

27. See above, notes 15 and 16.

28. See *La civilisation chinoise*, 1929, p. 205, for Granet's justification of the concept of Mother Earth and his citation of contrary views. And note, as a probable source of many echoes, Mauss's critical review of A. Dietrich, *Mutter Erde: ein Versuch über Volksreligion*, 1905, in *Année Sociologique*, vol. 9, 1904–5, pp. 264–268, especially p. 264: 'M.D. part de l'observation de trois rites romains: le dépôt de l'enfant nouveau-né sur la terre; l'enterrement de l'enfant non brûlé; le dépôt du mourant sur le sol.'

29. Cf. Granet, 'Le dépôt de l'enfant sur le sol', 1922. And cf. note 28 above.

30. Cf. Mauss's review of L. Marillier, 'L'origine des dieux', 1899, in *Année Sociologique*, vol. 4, 1899–1900, pp. 256f., to which Granet paid attention: 'In the course of this work M. Marillier has several times the occasion to raise objections to any hypothesis which would derive the notions of gods from over-simple origins (*principes*) . . . We too believe that the evolution of religion has never taken the form of a movement from the simple to the complex; but that is not to say that it started from a multiplicity of simple elements, each distinct from the others, a plurality of heterogeneous sources. It moves from the diffuse complex to the differentiated complex, from a confused unity made up of indistinguishable parts, to an organized unity.'

31. Granet here seems to begin with a view that makes thought depend upon language and then to switch to the idea that thought changes language. He was in *La pensée chinoise*, 1934, to write fully on the Chinese language; in 1920 he had published a paper entitled 'Quelques particularités de la langue et de la pensée chinoises'. In that paper he acknowledges his debt to Lévy-Bruhl's *Les fonctions mentales* (cf. note 22 above), referring especially, pp. 102 fn. in *Etudes sociologiques*, to pp. 187ff. in Lévy-Bruhl's book. And cf. *Fêtes et chansons*, 1919, p. 94, fn. 4.

32. On ancient Chinese folklore see Derk Bodde, 'Myths of Ancient China', in Samuel Noah Kramer, ed., *Mythologies of the Ancient World*, Anchor Books, Doubleday, Garden City, N.Y., 1961; Bernhard Karlgren, 'Legends and Cults in Ancient China', *Bulletin of the Museum of Far Eastern Antiquities*, no. 18, 1946 (noting the criticism, somewhat tempered by praise, of Granet, at pp. 346f.); and Henri Maspero, 'Légendes mythologiques dans le *Chou King*', *Journal Asiatique*, vol. 204, Jan.–March, 1924.

33. Cf. notes 2 and 7 above.

34. Cf. *La civilisation chinoise*, 1929, p. 209.

35. Cf. Joseph Needham, *Science and Civilisation in China, vol. 3: Mathematics and the Sciences of the Heavens and the Earth*, Cambridge University Press, Cambridge, 1970, p. 244.

36. Cf. *La civilisation chinoise*, 1929, p. 289.

37. Cf. *La polygynie sororale*, 1920, pp. 31–34 in *Etudes sociologiques*.

38. I have translated 'le lot des femmes' as 'bevy of wives', borrowing a usage proposed by I. Schapera: see J. A. Barnes, *Marriage in a Changing Society, A Study of Structural Change among the Fort Jameson Ngoni*, The Rhodes-Livingstone Papers, no. 20, Oxford University Press, Cape Town, 1951, p. iii.

39. Cf. *La polygynie sororale*, 1920, pp. 34–50 in *Etudes sociologiques*.

40. Early on in his studies of Chinese kinship Granet made a distinction between *filiation* and *affiliation*. In his account of the work of the *pensionnaires* at the Fondation Thiers during Granet's second year there, the Director (obviously basing himself upon what Granet had written about his own researches) reported: 'M. Granet, dealing with the law of persons in feudal society, is chiefly concerned with two problems: the morphology of feudal groupings, and the relationships of both family and feudal government . . . M. Granet has separated off a part which . . . deals with the organization of the Chinese family. He notes especially that, in China, entry into the family does not follow from the fact of birth alone, but is achieved by a series of investitures carried out at certain critical stages, by means of which the tie of kinship is set up between the child and larger and larger groups. Kinship does not consist in a personal tie between two individuals, but in the relationship of dependence in which two individuals stand to the same group. It is a matter not of filiation but of affiliation.' *Annuaire de la Fondation Thiers 1911*, n.s., Imprimerie Gaignault, Issoudun, 1911, pp. 9f.

41. Quoted from one of the 'Praise-songs of Lu': see *Fêtes et chansons*, 1919, p. 79, fn. 1 (*Festivals and Songs*, p. 75, fn. 1).

42. Cf. William Edward Soothill, *The Hall of Light, A Study of Early Chinese Kingship*. Lutterworth Press, London, 1951, pp. 57f.; Karlgren, 'Legends and Cults', p. 262; and J. Needham, *op. cit.*, pp. 186f.

43. See Soothill, *op. cit.*

44. See *La pensée chinoise*, 1934, p. 197.

45. From the *Shih Ching*. See *Danses et légendes*, 1926, p. 233, fn. 1.

46. See *Danses et légendes*, 1926, p. 231, fn.1, and p. 233, fn. 1.

47. See Karlgren, *The Book of Odes*, pp. 224ff.

48. See Granet, 'La vie et la mort', 1920, pp. 219f. in *Etudes sociologiques*.

49. Cf. Karlgren, *The Book of Odes*, p. 31, and Waley, *The Book of Songs*, p. 77.

50. *Fêtes et chansons*, 1919, pp. 192f.

51. *Danses et légendes*, 1926, pp. 450–456 ('Le dévouement de T'ang').

52. *La civilisation chinoise*, 1929, pp. 179f. (where the translation differs slightly); cf. Waley, *op. cit.*, p. 162, and Karlgren, *op. cit.*, pp. 250f.

53. *Danses et légendes*, 1926, p. 121, fn. 3.

54. Cf. James Legge, trans., *The Sacred Books of the East, The Texts*

of Confucianism, Part III, The Lî Kî, I–X, Clarendon Press, Oxford, 1885, pp. 449–454.

55. *La civilisation chinoise,* 1929, p. 393.

56. Cf. 'Le langage de la douleur', 1922, pp. 224–235 in *Etudes sociologiques.*

57. Cf. Legge, trans., *The Sacred Books of the East, The Texts of Confucianism, Part IV, The Lî Kî, XI–XLVI,* 1885, p. 210.

58. *La civilisation chinoise,* 1929, p. 397. The reference is to the *Li Chi.*

59. Cf. Legge, trans., *op. cit.,* pp. 239f.

60. See notes 15 and 16 above.

61. That is, Granet is here assuming two intermarrying matrilineally recruited groups. In such a system I am a member of my mother's group but not my father's (hence, in Granet's language, he is not my kinsman, *parent*); and my father's father must belong to the same group (moiety) as my mother.

62. Cf. note 40 above. Granet is arguing that the father's father remains a kinsman, in the sense in which the father is not, because of a transfer into the patrilineal (agnatic) system of the linkages constructed in the previous matrilineal system. See note 61 above. The models used were derived from Granet's understanding of primitive kinship, especially Australian, as he studied it directly in the ethnographic writings and in the papers and reviews in the *Année Sociologique.* The welding together of kinship theory with his theory of Chinese feudalism allowed Granet ingeniously to construct a model of ancient Chinese agnation in which, in accordance with the *chao-mu* order in the arrangement of the ancestor tablets (see note 67 below), patrilineal descent so to say skipped a generation, leaving the men in immediately adjacent generations to be tied by bonds of enfeoffment.

63. That is, because in the sacrifice the son represented his father's father.

64. The *chao-mu* order. See below, note 67.

65. See above, note 62.

66. That is, the *wu fu* system of mourning, based, so far as agnates are concerned, on a five-generation group. See e.g. Han-yi Fêng, *The Chinese Kinship System,* Harvard University Press, for the Harvard-Yenching Institute, Cambridge, Mass., 1948 (reprinted from *Harvard Journal of Asiatic Studies,* vol. 2, no. 2, July 1937), pp. 38–43; and Maurice Freedman, *Lineage Organization in Southeastern China,* London School of Economics Monographs on Social Anthropology no. 18, Athlone Press, London, 1958, pp. 41–45.

67. See *La polygynie sororale,* 1920, pp. 40f. in *Etudes sociologiques*: 'But why was the collaboration necessary in the temple service? The rules for the organization of the cult sprang almost entirely from a

particular arrangement of the ancestral temple. The tablets of the worshipped ancestors were arranged by alternate generations, those of the father and the great-grandfather being to one side of the building, and those of the grandfather and the great-great-grandfather to the other. That arrangement, in the texts called the *chao-mu* order of the ancestral temple, involved kinsmen falling into two groups, the members of two successive generations never belonging to the same group; that is explained by an ancient state of the Chinese family in which, as a consequence of uterine filiation, the son could not be in the same group as his father, while the grandson was necessarily in the same group as his paternal grandfather, marriage taking place obligatorily between cousins who were offspring of brothers and sisters. It followed from that that a man was not qualified to render on his own the ritual honours to all his ancestors; he could offer them validly only to his grandfather and great-great-grandfather, for he belonged to the same half of the kinship group as they: but if his marriage was normal, if his wife was the daughter of his father's sister, that woman (who was necessarily a member of the same group as her maternal uncle, that is, her father-in-law)'—but if Granet is postulating, at the origin of the marriage system, two intermarrying moieties, a man's 'father's sister's daughter' is at the same time his 'mother's brother's daughter'; in *La civilisation chinoise*, 1929, pp. 186f., Granet writes of men marrying their mothers' brothers' daughters, but see *ibid.*, pp. 247–250— 'was perfectly qualified for the priesthood of the cult of the father and the great-grandfather. And we see that the collaboration in priesthood of the two spouses was, in effect, obligatory because it sprang, as the Chinese authors preserved its tradition, from ancient prescriptions about exogamy, themselves consequences of the rule governing the separation of the sexes. We see too that, in order to acquire a wife who might be a true collaborator, it was necessary for her to belong to the same generation as her husband. Thence came the obligation to marry at a fixed age, which amounted to requiring that spouses be of the same age-set (*promotion*), thence the scorn for irregular unions, and thence the prohibition of marriage when, two families being already linked by matrimonial alliance, the woman and the man she was to marry were classified in different generations by virtue of the alliance established.' I have omitted the footnotes in translating this passage, but one of them, referring to the phrase 'that is explained by an ancient state of the Chinese family', poignantly reads: 'It is hoped that the reader will provisionally accept the explanation which I here sketch in outline: it will be justified in *La famille chinoise des temps féodaux*.' Cf. *Fêtes et chansons*, 1919, p. 87, fn. 8, where Granet speaks of that work appearing soon, and *Danses et légendes*, 1926, p. 4, fn. 1, where he writes that the book is 'tout préparé', having formed the basis of his courses at the

Sorbonne in 1922–23 and 1923–24. *La famille chinoise* . . . is one of the great unwritten books of the social sciences, taking its place alongside such named and aborted monographs as Malinowski's *The Psychology of Kinship*. Of course, although the great book was never composed (except in Granet's head, for when he spoke of it being ready he almost certainly meant that it was clearly formed in his mind), he was later to take up many of its themes in *La civilisation chinoise*, 1929, especially pp. 182–190, 368–405, and above all in *Catégories matrimoniales et relations de proximité dans la Chine ancienne*, 1939. That last work greatly complicates and develops his earlier ideas about ancient Chinese kinship and marriage, and in such a fashion as to make an impact upon kinship theory in general via Lévi-Strauss. See also his notes for his unwritten book, *Le Roi boit*: R. A. Stein, 'Présentation de l'œuvre posthume de Marcel Granet: "Le Roi boit" ', *Année Sociologique*, third series, 1952, especially p. 60: '*L'ordre des générations*. Mariages entre cousins (non agnats): alliances répétées (confirmées): lévirs et co-époux. Alliances simples et alliances redoublées (inversion du sens des circuits d'alliances).' . . . This is not the place for a technical commentary upon Granet's work on kinship and marriage (it is a very big subject), but I should like to say that despite Lévi-Strauss's labours, much remains to be done in respect both of the nature of Granet's arguments and the sources upon which he drew. It is also perhaps worth saying that I think Lévi-Strauss errs in laying stress upon what he takes to be the paradox that Granet, in *Catégories matrimoniales*, 1939, contributed to kinship theory when he imagined that he was merely rediscovering the kinship system of ancient China. See Claude Lévi-Strauss, trans. James Harle Bell and John Richard von Sturmer, ed. Rodney Needham, *The Elementary Structures of Kinship*, Eyre and Spottiswoode, London, 1969, pp. 311f. Granet was certainly more closely in touch with current anthropological writing than might appear to be the case (see Introductory Essay above, pp. 25f.); and, more important, he took what he had to say about China, in this as in every field, as a contribution to the study of mankind at large. It is wrong, I suggest, to speak of Granet as 'a specialist who perhaps exceeds his proper role' (*ibid.*, p. 311); as I have tried to show in my Introductory Essay, Granet chose the status of sinologue not to confine himself to China but in order to make general statements, however oblique and furtive, about humanity.

68. The text has 'membres de la même promotion'.

69. Cf. *La civilisation chinoise*, 1929, p. 304.

70. Cf. Legge, trans., *The Sacred Books of the East*, *The Texts of Confucianism, Part IV*, pp. 228f.

71. Cf. note 108 below.

72. Note the remark in Bodde, 'Myths of Ancient China', p. 372,

that writers on Chinese mythology tend to use the word 'euhemerism' to mean exactly the opposite of what is usually intended by it.

73. Cf. *Danses et légendes*, 1926, pp. 563f. On the mythology dealt with in this and the following paragraphs compare the study by a pupil of Granet, Max Kaltenmark, 'Notes à propos du Kao-mei', *Annuaire 1966–1967 Ecole Pratique des Hautes Etudes, Ve Section—Sciences religieuses*, vol. 74, Paris, 1966.

74. Cf. *Fêtes et chansons*, 1919, pp. 166f.

75. In *Danses et légendes*, 1926, Granet criticizes this use of the term *doublet* and says that he ought here to have written *thème mythique*.

76. Cf. Waley, *The Book of Songs*, p. 241, and Karlgren, *The Book of Odes*, pp. 200f.

77. Cf. 'Le dépôt de l'enfant sur le sol', 1920, pp. 171–183 in *Etudes sociologiques*, and *Danses et légendes*, 1926, pp. 294, fn. 1, 429, 468, fn. 2, etc.

78. Cf. note 31 above.

79. *Cf. Fêtes et chansons*, 1919, p. 196.

80. Cf. *La pensée chinoise*, 1934, pp. 487f. The quotation is from the *Ta Hsüeh*, 'The Great Learning'. See *La pensée chinoise*, p. 337, for Granet's characterization of the style of reasoning.

81. Cf. note 144 below.

82. Here as elsewhere in Granet's discussion of Confucius and Confucianism it is necessary to consult what he was later to write in *La pensée chinoise*, 1934. Uncharacteristically for a French work of the period, the book is well indexed, as are *Danses et légendes*, 1926, and *La civilisation chinoise*, 1929. It is interesting to compare what Granet writes on Confucius with what his master said on the subject: Edouard Chavannes, 'Confucius', *La Revue de Paris*, vol. 10, no. 4, 15 Feb. 1903. The tone is very similar. For a useful survey of the Confucian literature see Wing-tsit Chan, *A Source Book in Chinese Philosophy*, Princeton University Press, Princeton, N.J., Oxford University Press, London, 1963, chaps. 2–6.

83. Now in second place, *yin* and *yang* were, on Granet's analysis, historically prior, *tao* being latent and not realized until society had taken a particular form. See note 20 above.

84. See *La pensée chinoise*, 1934, pp. 168–173, 193–195, 244–249, 305–314.

85. See Book II ('Les idées directrices') of *La pensée chinoise*, 1934.

86. On rites and music, see *La pensée chinoise*, 1934, pp. 408–415.

87. See 'Le langage de la douleur', 1922, p. 238 in *Etudes sociologiques*.

88. See above, p. 91, and note 73 above.

89. On T'ai Shan and the *feng-shan* sacrifices cf. *La civilisation*

chinoise, 1929, pp. 450–452, and Edouard Chavannes, *Le Tai Chan*, *Essai de monographie d'un culte chinois*, Leroux, Paris, 1910.

90. Cf. note 62 above.

91. In a review (which Granet read) of Maurice Courant, 'Les associations en Chine', 1899, Durkheim had made the point (*Année Sociologique*, vol. 3, 1898–99, pp. 380f.) that Roman and Chinese *patres-familias* differed in their power: the Chinese *paterfamilias* was the head of a 'community' more than a proprietor. It is worth noting that in another review of a work by Courant (*En Chine*, 1901, in *Année Sociologique*, vol. 6, 1901–2, pp. 368f.) Durkheim, while remarking upon the analogies between the Roman family and the Chinese, points out what he takes to be elements of uterine organization in the latter: 'Nevertheless, the uterine family must have strongly affected the domestic organization of the Chinese; for in addition to the wife keeping up religious relations with her family, the husband himself enters the family of his wife, but as a distant kinsman. When his parents-in-law die, he wears the fifth degree of mourning . . . We are not told whether there is any trace of taboo between him and his mother-in-law. The information would have been of great interest . . . This situation of the widow is even so important that we should be tempted to see in it a consequence of the traces left by the uterine family.'

92. Cf. note 91 above. Although in *Catégories matrimoniales*, 1939, Granet was to drop the idea of a primordial unilineality in Chinese kinship (see note 15 above), he for long retained from the earlier phase of Durkheimian sociology the notion that the special position of the mother's brother in a patrilineal system is evidence of some pre-existing matrilineal organization.

93. From the 'Doctrine of the Mean'. Cf. Chan, *op. cit.*, p. 104.

94. Granet is here referring to *feng-shui*, Chinese geomancy, a subject upon which he in fact wrote little, for although its roots lie deep in ancient Chinese thought and practice, *feng-shui* flowered only after the period of history with which Granet was chiefly concerned. See p. 151 for another reference to the subject, this time by name. Cf. *La civilisation chinoise*, 1929, p. 278, and *La pensée chinoise*, 1934, pp. 118, fn. 5, 387. Cf. Maurice Freedman, 'Geomancy', *Proceedings of the Royal Anthropological Institute of Great Britain and Ireland 1968*, London, 1969.

95. On these symbols see Edouard Chavannes, *La sculpture sur pierre en Chine au temps des deux dynasties Han*, Leroux, Paris, 1893, pp. 33ff., and the same author's *Mission archéologique dans la Chine septentrionale, Tome I*, Leroux, Paris, 1913, pp. 167ff., 191. The calendar tree is that which grew by the Ming T'ang; see p. 68 above. The fish with paired eyes is Granet's (because Chavannes's) 'poisson aux yeux accouplés'; it was 'Deux poissons accolés et n'en faisant qu'un' (Chavannes, *La sculpture*, p. 36).

96. See Chavannes, *Mission archéologique*, pp. 99–101.

97. See Chavannes, *La sculpture*, pp. 9f., and William Frederick Mayers, *The Chinese Reader's Manual*, American Presbyterian Mission Press, Shanghai, and Trubner, London, 1874, p. 113 (entry no. 337).

98. See Chavannes, *Mission archéologique*, p. 145, and *La sculpture*, p. 24.

99. See Chavannes, *La sculpture*, pp. 25f.

100. See *ibid.*, p. 21.

101. Cf. *La civilisation chinoise*, 1929, p. 493.

102. Cf. note 3 above. For Granet's later writing on the subject, see especially *La pensée chinoise*, 1934, pp. 501–551, but it is certainly true, as Max Kaltenmark has observed (in his 'Préface', p. 3, to Henri Maspero, *Le Taoïsme et les religions chinoises*, Gallimard, Paris, 1971), that Granet published far less on Taoism than he taught in his courses. Cf. the work of his contemporary in Paris, Henri Maspero, *Le Taoïsme* = *Mélanges posthumes sur les religions et l'histoire de la Chine*, vol. 2, Publications du Musée Guimet, Bibliothèque de Diffusion, vol. 58, Civilisations du Sud, S.A.E.P., Paris, 1950 (republished in Maspero, *Le Taoïsme et les religions chinoises*, 1971), and that of one of his pupils: Max Kaltenmark, 'Le Taoïsme religieux', in Henri-Charles Puech, ed., *Histoire des religions, I, Les religions antiques—La formation des religions universelles et les religions de salut en Inde et en Extrême-Orient*, Encyclopédie de la Pléiade, Gallimard, Paris, 1970. And cf. Holmes Welch, *The Parting of the Way, Lao Tzu and the Taoist Movement*, Methuen, London, 1958.

103. For convenient references see Wm. Theodore de Bary *et al.*, *Sources of Chinese Tradition*, vol. 1, Columbia University Press, N.Y. and London, 1964, chaps. 4 and 11; and Chan, *op. cit.*, chaps, 7, 8, and 18.

104. Cf. *Danses et légendes*, 1926, p. 87 fn.

105. From the *Lieh Tzu*. See *La pensée chinoise*, 1934, p. 524.

106. From the *Chuang Tzu*. See *La pensée chinoise*, 1934, p. 526. It is perhaps the best-known of Chinese metaphysical problems. Cf. E. R. Hughes, trans. and ed., *Chinese Philosophy in Classical Times*, Everyman's Library, no. 973, Dent, London, Dutton, N.Y., 1942, p. 184, and Chan, *op. cit.*, p. 190.

107. Cf. *La pensée chinoise*, 1934, p. 530.

108. The text reads: ' . . . d'autres de simples indigitations préposées à des moments de la vie ou à des aspects de la Nature.' Granet is here using the word *indigitations* to correspond to the Latin *indigetes*, assumed to be Roman Gods of occasion. *Indigitamenta* were taken to be the calendars listing them. They caught the attention of the Durkheimian reviewers. See Mauss's review of H. Usener, *Götternamen*, 1896, in *Année Sociologique*, vol. 1, 1896–97, pp. 240–247 (which Granet marked

in his copy). At p. 246 Mauss writes: 'La découverte par M.U. de ces deux genres de dieux, dieux spéciaux, dieux occasionels, est une des celles qui passeront dans la tradition scientifique.' In fact, the matter is complex, and that interpretation of *indigetes* and *di minuti* was rejected by G. Wissowa, whose *Religion und Kultus der Römer*, 1902, was reviewed by Hubert in *Année Sociologique*, vol. 6, 1901–2, pp. 237–242. At p. 238 Hubert writes: 'La plupart des *indigitations* . . . sont rattachées à quelque nom divin qui répond à une image plus complexe.' Hubert reviewed Wissowa's book a second time, *ibid.*, pp. 290–292. Cf. M. Cary *et al.*, eds., *The Oxford Classical Dictionary*, Clarendon Press, Oxford, 1949, p. 452; and Kurt Latte, *Römische Religionsgeschichte*, C. H. Beck'sche Verlagsbuchhandlung, Munich, 1960, pp. 43ff.

109. See Edouard Chavannes, 'Le jet des dragons', in Senart and Cordier, eds., *Mémoires concernant l'Asie orientale*, vol. 3, Leroux, Paris, 1919.

110. Chavannes, *op. cit.*, note 32 at p. 201.

111. Because of its relatively late appearance as a feature of Chinese culture, Granet paid little attention to Buddhism in his writings. There are passing references to it in *La civilisation chinoise*, 1929, at p. 158, and in *La pensée chinoise*, 1934, at pp. 551, 581. See also 'L'esprit de la religion chinoise', 1929, p. 253 in *Etudes sociologiques*. This section of *La religion des Chinois* therefore occupies a most important place in Granet's writings as a whole. Had he lived to complete *Le Roi boit*, he would have published more on Buddhism, for it would have appeared in his account of T'ang life . . . The remark against which this note stands is not as rash as might at first appear. For modern work on the subject, see e.g. Paul Demiéville, 'Le Bouddhisme chinois' in Puech, ed., *op. cit.*; Arthur F. Wright, *Buddhism in Chinese History*, Stanford University Press, Stanford, Calif., and Oxford University Press, London, 1959; E. Zürcher, *The Buddhist Conquest of China, The Spread and Adaptation of Buddhism in Early Medieval China*, revised edn., Sinica Leidensia XI, Brill, Leiden, 1972; Kenneth K. S. Chen, *Buddhism in China, A Historical Survey*, Princeton University Press, Princeton, 1964. And cf. Henri Maspero, 'Le Bouddhisme' and 'Comment le Bouddhisme s'est introduit en Chine', in Maspero, *Mélanges posthumes* . . . , vol. 1, *Les religions chinoises*, Publications du Musée Guimet, Bibliothèque de Diffusion, vol. 57, Paris, 1950 (and in *Le Taoïsme* . . . , *op. cit.*). For the Chinese Buddhist literature see Chan, *op. cit.*, chaps. 20–26.

112. See Henri Maspero, 'Le songe et l'ambassade de L'Empereur Ming, Etude critique des sources', *Bulletin de l'Ecole Française d'Extrême-Orient*, vol. 10, 1910.

113. See Paul Pelliot, ' "Meou Tseu, ou les doutes levés" traduit et annoté,' *T'oung Pao*, vol. 19, no. 5, 1918–19, published 1920.

114. *Parinirvāṇa:* the final escape from 'the bonds of trouble and vexation'.

115. See Edouard Chavannes, *Cinq cent contes et apologues extraits du Tripiṭaka chinois,* vol. 1, Leroux, Paris, 1910, pp. 330–335.

116. See Chavannes, *Cinq cent contes . . .* , vol. 3, 1911, pp. 155–157.

117. See Chavannes, *Cinq cent contes . . .* , vol. 1, pp. 72–75.

118. There are six *pāramitā:* cardinal virtues.

119. The Sutra of Sudāna. See Chavannes, *Cinq cent contes . . .* , vol. 3, pp. 362–395.

120. See Edouard Chavannes, *Contes et légendes du Bouddhisme chinois,* Les Classiques de l'Orient, Bossard, Paris, 1921, pp. 199–205.

121. Cf. Arthur Waley, *Ballads and Stories from Tun-huang, An Anthology,* Allen and Unwin, London, 1960, pp. 216–235.

122. Cf. Edward Conze *et al.,* eds., *Buddhist Texts through the Ages,* Bruno Cassirer, Oxford, 1954, p. 131 ('The Bodhisattva's infinite compassion').

123. The text has 'Panthées', for which there is no simple English equivalent. *Panthée* means an image embodying the attributes of several deities.

124. On the Yun-kang and Lung-men grottoes, see Chavannes, *Mission archéologique,* part 2.

125. See e.g. Chavannes, *op. cit.,* p. 352.

126. Han Yü, 786–824: cf. de Bary *et al., op. cit.,* pp. 371ff.

127. Cf. *ibid.,* chap. 16, and Chan, *op. cit.,* chap. 34.

128. Cf. de Bary *et al., op. cit.,* pp. 514–526, and Chan, *op. cit.,* chap. 35.

129. Granet's personal observations begin at this point. It will be recalled that he spent two years in Peking in 1911–13, as a student, and a few months there in the spring of 1919 after his military service in Siberia.

130. That is, Buddhist and Taoist priests.

131. The dotting of the tablet (whenever possible by a man of high standing) associates the soul of the dead man with it. A red dot is imposed on the tablet with a writing-brush.

132. When Granet died the scholar who composed his epitaph was Mauss.

133. The text has 'des hommes à recettes'. By *recette* Granet is trying to render in one word the Chinese term *shu* which Mathews (*Mathews' Chinese-English Dictionary,* revised American edn., Harvard University Press, Cambridge, Mass., 1963, p. 833, character no. 5889) translates as 'A Device; an artifice. A trick, a mystery. Art, method.' Obviously the slang term 'gimmick' would be an admirable English (or at any rate American) equivalent, but it would look very much out of place in a version of Granet's French.

134. Granet has taken this ethnographic scrap from De Groot, as one can tell from 'Le dépôt de l'enfant sur le sol', 1922, p. 170 in *Etudes sociologiques*. What De Groot says, however, is that 'a large shallow tray of wicker work' is placed beneath 'a wooden form or chair' where the principal mourner, the eldest son, sits while he is being dressed in the clothes which, once assembled in this fashion, will be transferred to the corpse: J. J. M. de Groot, *The Religious System of China, Its Ancient Forms, Evolution, History and Present Aspects, Manners, Customs and Social Institutions Connected Therewith*, vol. 1, Brill, Leiden, 1892, p. 67. It is not therefore the actual dresser of the corpse who has the tray interposed between him and the ground. Moreover, what De Groot reports about Amoy custom only doubtfully serves as a description valid generally for China. Granet many times in his writings calls upon De Groot for ethnographic data; they were not the sort of information he was himself inclined to collect.

135. The text has 'des sabots de papier'. Is this a misreading of 'paper horseshoes', i.e. confetti?

136. See note 134 above.

137. Cf. 'L'esprit de la religion chinoise', 1929, but written in 1924, p. 257 in *Etudes sociologiques*: '. . . in China, the sacred and the profane have never taken to themselves sharply separated domains. It is not enough to say that one abuts the other: depending on the circumstances, the same act will either be accompanied by religious emotions or be carried out in a practical spirit.' Like many others trying to adhere to Durkheimian principles, Granet clearly has difficulty in applying the distinction between sacred and profane.

138. Granet is here evidently referring to the same man and the same occasion mentioned in *La polygynie sororale*, 1920, pp. 3f. in *Etudes sociologiques*.

139. See e.g. Hughes, *op. cit.*, pp. 324–327.

140. The conventional, but not quite accurate enough, English version of Tsao-chün, the god of the cooking-place.

141. See note 133 above.

142. See note 94 above.

143. Cf. *La féodalité chinoise*, 1952 (but written between 1936 and 1940), pp. 8ff.

144. This is a tribute from a freethinker. The otherness that Granet always noted in Chinese civilization (and which was one of the main reasons for his being attracted to it, even as it provided him with a generalizable case of Humanity) was compounded of both good and bad points. The rational and intellectual limitations imposed upon the Chinese by their system of thought, as he interpreted it, had as their compensation a deep-lying humanism reflected in Chinese religious attitudes. See especially *La pensée chinoise*, 1934, pp. 338f.: 'The

greatest merit' of Chinese thought 'is never to have separated off the human from the natural, and always to have conceived the human in thinking of the social. If the idea of Law (*Loi*) never developed and, in consequence, the observation of nature was abandoned to empiricism and the organization of society to the system of compromise, the ideal of Rule, or rather the notion of Models, by allowing the Chinese to preserve a supple and plastic conception of Order, has not led them to imagine over and above the human world a world of transcendental realities. Completely imbued with a concrete view of nature, their Wisdom is resolutely humanist.' And see *ibid.*, pp. 584ff., where Granet places emphasis upon China as an exemplar of moral wisdom to its Far Eastern neighbours, and brackets China's reliance upon wisdom and reasonableness with its rejection of both law (*loi*) and God; p. 586: 'Insisting upon the fact that the Chinese do not willingly submit to any constraint, even simply dogmatic, *I shall confine myself to characterizing the spirit of Chinese mores by the formula*: neither God nor Law.' Given the nature of Chinese religion and, as I have called it elsewhere ('On the Sociology of Chinese Religion.' *op. cit.*), its polymorphism, it was easy enough for Granet to find his own religious tastes matched in those of the Chinese scholars whom he knew or read; but one may well conclude that his characterization of Chinese religion as a whole wrote up the agnostic and wrote down the ecstatic.

145. But see note 91 above.

146. Granet was to give a lecture on Chinese Islam a few years later: 'L'Islam et la Chine', 1927. There he repeats, p. 54, the statement made in the footnote at p. 144 about the presence of the image of Mohammed in the model prison in Peking.

147. For a modern account of Chinese Buddhism in this century, see Holmes Welch, *The Practice of Chinese Buddhism 1900–1950*, Harvard University Press, Cambridge, Mass., 1967. And see, for twentieth-century Chinese religion in general, Wing-tsit Chan, *Religious Trends in Modern China*, Columbia University Press, N.Y., 1953.

148. In Granet's own copy of *La religion des Chinois* he has written the words 'Mars 1919' in the margin at this point.

149. A vigorous term of abuse.

150. P'u Tu Ssu, the great Lama temple, about a quarter of a mile from the south-east corner of the Forbidden City. Built on a platform, it rises some 15 feet above the neighbouring houses. See Juliet Bredon, *Peking, A Historical and Intimate Description of its Chief Places of Interest*, Kelly and Walsh, Shanghai, etc., 1922, pp. 182–187, for a description of the temple as it was in the period when Granet knew it.

Bibliography

Part 1: Works by Marcel Granet

This list includes every item I have so far been able to find, other than short book reviews. The abbreviation *YK* stands for Yang K'un, 'An Introduction to Granet's Researches', in Chinese, listed in Part 2 of the Bibliography below. *ES* represents *Etudes sociologiques sur la Chine*, 1953.

1911   *Contre l'Alcoolisme, Un Programme socialiste*, Les Cahiers du Socialiste no.11, Librairie du Parti Socialiste, Paris.

1912   'Coutumes matrimoniales de la Chine antique', *T'oung Pao*, vol. 13, pp. 516–558. Reprinted in *ES*.

1914   'Programme d'études sur l'ancienne religion chinoise', *Revue d'histoire des religions*, vol. 69, March-April, pp. 228–239.

1919   *Fêtes et chansons anciennes de la Chine*, Bibliothèque de l'Ecole des Hautes Etudes, Sciences religieuses, vol. 34, Leroux, Paris. The 2nd edition, 1929, differs from the 1st by restoring the original English version of the Hakka song recorded by Eitel, at pp. 297ff. Trans. E. D. Edwards, *Festivals and Songs of Ancient China*, Routledge, London, 1932. There is a Japanese translation, 1938, by Ushida Chio, which I have not seen; see *YK*, item 78. For mention of another English translation see *YK*, item 66.

1920   *La polygynie sororale et le sororat dans la Chine féodale. Etude sur les formes anciennes de la polygamie chinoise*, Leroux, Paris, Reprinted in *ES*.

1920   'Quelques particularités de la langue et de la pensée chinoises', *Revue philosophique de la France et de l'étranger*, vol. 45, nos. 1 and 2, Jan.–Feb, pp. 98–128, and nos. 3 and 4, March–April, pp. 161–195. Reprinted in *ES*.

1920 'La vie et la mort, Croyances et doctrines de l'antiquité chinoise', *Annuaire 1920–1921 Ecole Pratique des Hautes Etudes, Section des Sciences religieuses*, Imprimerie Nationale, Paris, pp. 1–22. Reprinted in *ES*.

1922 'Le langage de la douleur d'après le rituel funéraire de la Chine classique', *Journal de Psychologie normale et pathologique*, vol. 19, no. 2, 15 Feb., pp. 97–118. Reprinted in *ES*.

1922 'Le droit et la famille', *Journal de Psychologie normale et pathologique*, vol. 19, no. 10, 15 Dec., pp. 928–939 (review article on Fauconnet, *La responsabilité;* Davy, *La foi jurée*; and Westermarck, *The History of Human Marriage*).

1922 'Le dépôt de l'enfant sur le sol. Rites anciens et ordalies mythiques', *Revue Archéologique*, vol. 14, pp. 305–361. Reprinted in *ES*.

1922 *La religion des Chinois*, Science et civilisation, Collection d'exposés synthétiques du savoir humain, Gauthier-Villars, Paris. 2nd edition 1951, Bibliothèque de Philosophie Contemporaine, Presses Universitaires de France. Trans. ed. Bianca Candian, *La religione dei cinesi*, Adelphi, Milan, 1973.

1925 'Chansons d'amour de la vieille Chine', *Revue des Arts Asiatiques*, vol. 2, no. 3, Sept., pp. 24–40.

1925 'Remarques sur le Taoïsme ancien', *Asia Major*, Leipzig, vol. 2, fasc. 1, pp. 146–151. Reprinted in *ES*.

1926 *Danses et légendes de la Chine ancienne*, 2 vols., Travaux de l'Année Sociologique sous la direction de Marcel Mauss, Alcan, Paris. The edition of 1959, Presses Universitaires de France, is an exact reprint. Italian version in preparation by Adelphi, Milan.

1926 'L'Extrême Orient', chap. IV, Livre Xe in Maxime Petit, ed., *Histoire générale des peuples de l'antiquité à nos jours*, Larousse, Paris, vol. II, pp. 399–408, and 'Chine', part of chap. II, Livre XVe, in vol. III, pp. 325–330.

1927 'L'Islam et la Chine', in Maréchal Lyautey, Gaudefroy-Demombynes, Paul Boyer, Marcel Granet, *et al.*, *L'Islam et la politique contemporaine*, Alcan, Paris, pp. 35–56.

1927 *L'Institut des Hautes Etudes chinoises de Paris*, [Paris], 7pp. The Address inaugurating the Institut.

1928 'L'expression de la pensée en chinois', *Journal de Psychologie normale et pathologique*, vol. 25, no. 8, 15 Oct., pp. 617–656.

1928 'La civilisation chinoise' (part II of a survey entitled 'Les études orientales à Paris'), *Annales de l'Université de Paris*, vol. 3, no. 6, Nov.– Dec., pp. 543–550.

1929 'L'esprit de la religion chinoise', *Scientia, Revue internationale de synthèse scientifique*, Milan, May, pp. 329–337. Reprinted in *ES*.

1929 'Changhai', p. 127, 'Chang-ti', p. 127, and 'Chine', pp. 222–224 (excluding section on Beaux-arts) in *Larousse du XXe siècle*, vol. 2, Librairie Larousse, Paris.

1929 *La civilisation chinoise, La vie publique et la vie privée*, Bibliothèque de Synthèse Historique, L'Evolution de l'Humanité, no. 35, La Renaissance du Livre, Paris. Reprinted with bibliographical additions by P. Demiéville (for 1929–47) and Jeanne-Marie Boch-Puyraimond, Albin Michel, Paris, 1968. Trans. K. E. Innes and M. R. Brailsford, *Chinese Civilization*, Routledge and Kegan Paul, London; Knopf, New York; 1930. Italian translation by G. Casella, *La civittà cinese antica*, Einaudi, Turin, 1950 and 1968, which I have not seen. Polish translation by M. J. Künstler, *Cywilizacja chińska*, Państwowy Instytut Wydawniczy, Warsaw, 1973.

1930 'La sociologie religieuse de Durkheim', *Europe*, no. 86, 15 Feb., pp. 287–292 (part of symposium, 'L'œuvre sociologique d'Emile Durkheim', by Bouglé, Davy, Granet, Lenoir, and Maublanc).

1931 'Les problèmes du Pacifique', in *Quinze ans de l'histoire universelle 1914–1929*, Librairie Aristide Quillet, Paris, pp. 621–646.

1931 'L'Institut des Hautes Etudes chinoises', *Annales de l'Université de Paris*, vol. 6, no. 6, Nov–Dec., pp. 514–517.

1931 'Japon', pp. 153–155 (but only main sections of the piece are by Granet) in *Larousse du XXe siècle*, vol. 4, Librairie Larousse, Paris.

1932 Speech on the teaching of sociology, *Bulletin de l'Institut Français de Sociologie*, vol. 2, fasc. 3, pp. 98–107.

1933 'La droite et la gauche en Chine', *Bulletin de l'Institut Français de Sociologie*, vol. 3, fasc. 3, pp. 87–116. Reprinted in *ES*. Trans. Rodney Needham, 'Right and Left in China', in Rodney Needham, ed., *Right and Left: Essays on Dual Symbolic Classification*, University of Chicago Press, Chicago and London, 1973.

1934 'La mentalité chinoise', in Lahy-Hollebecque, ed., *L'évolution humaine des origines à nos jours*, vol. 1, Librairie Aristide Quillet, Paris, pp. 371–387.

1934 *La pensée chinoise*, Bibliothèque de Synthèse Historique, L'Evolution de l'Humanité, no. 35bis, La Renaissance du Livre, Paris. Reprinted with bibliographical additions by P. Demiéville (for 1934–47) and Jeanne-Marie Boch-Puyraimond, Albin Michel, Paris, 1968. Trans. Manfred Porkert, *Das chinesische Denken, Inhalt, Form, Charakter*, R. Piper, Munich, 1963. Trans. G. Cardona, *Il pensiero cinese*, Adelphi, Milan, 1971. I have not seen the German and Italian translations. For a Chinese translation see *YK*, item 6.

1937 'Les Chinois et nous', *Les Nouvelles Littéraires*, 30 Oct., p. 1. I have not seen this piece.

1937   'A propos du conflit sino-japonais. Les Chinois et leurs voisins', *Les Nouvelles Littéraires*, 6 Nov., p. 8, and corrigenda 11 Dec., p. 8.

1938   'La civilisation chinoise', *Les Cahiers Rationalistes*, no. 67, April, pp. 106–121.

1939   *Catégories matrimoniales et relations de proximité dans la Chine ancienne*, Alcan, Paris; and as *Annales Sociologiques*, Série B, Sociologie religieuse, fasc. 1–3

1939   'Confucius (551–479)', in Sébastien Charléty, ed., *Les grandes figures*. Librairie Larousse, Paris, pp. 35–40.

1952   *La féodalité chinoise*, Instituttet for Sammenlignende Kulturforskning, Serie A: Forelesninger 22, Aschehoug, Oslo (with a Foreword by Alf Sommerfelt).

1952   [*Le Roi boit*]: R.-A. Stein, 'Présentation de l'œuvre posthume de Marcel Granet: "Le Roi boit"', *Année Sociologique*, 3rd series, pp. 9–105 (but published 1955).

1953   *Etudes sociologiques sur la Chine*, Bibliothèque de Sociologie Contemporaine, Presses Universitaires de France, Paris (with Preface by Louis Gernet, and Introduction by R.-A. Stein).

Part 2: Other works cited

AS represents *Année Sociologique*.

ANDLER, Charles,	*Vie de Lucien Herr (1864–1926)*, Rieder, Paris, 1932.
Annuaire, Ecole Pratique des Hautes Etudes [1914–1915],	Paris, 1914.
Annuaire, Ecole Pratique des Hautes Etudes, Section des Sciences religieuses, 1920–21, 1921–22,	Paris, 1920, 1921.
Annuaire, Ecole Pratique des Hautes Etudes, Section des Sciences religieuses, 1922–23 to *1940–41 et 1941–42,* and *1950–51,*	Melun, 1922 to 1941, and 1950.
Annuaire de la Fondation Thiers 1910, 1911, 1912,	n.s., Imprimerie Gaignault, Issoudun, 1910, 1911, 1912.
BARNES, J. A.,	*Marriage in a Changing Society, a Study of Structural Change among the Fort Jameson Ngoni*, The Rhodes-Livingstone Papers no. 20, Oxford University Press, Cape Town, 1951.

BARY, Wm. Theodore de, *et al.*,
Sources of Chinese Tradition, vol. 1, Columbia University Press, N.Y. and London, 1964.

BODDE, Derk,
'Feudalism in History', in Rushton Coulborn ed., *Feudalism in History*, Princeton University Press, Princeton, N.J., 1956.

————
'Myths of Ancient China', in Samuel Noah Kramer, ed., *Mythologies of the Ancient World*, Anchor Books, Doubleday, Garden City, N.Y., 1961.

BOUILLIER, Henry,
Victor Segalen, Mercure de France, Paris, 1961.

BREDON, Juliet,
Peking, a Historical and Intimate Description of its Chief Places of Interest, Kelly and Walsh, Shanghai, etc., 1922.

CARY, M., *et al.*, eds.,
The Oxford Classical Dictionary, Clarendon Press, Oxford, 1949.

CHAN, Wing-tsit,
Religious Trends in Modern China, Columbia University Press, N.Y., 1953.

————
A Source Book in Chinese Philosophy, Princeton University Press, Princeton, N.J., Oxford University Press, London, 1963.

CHAVANNES, Édouard,
La sculpture sur pierre en Chine au temps des deux dynasties Han, Leroux, Paris, 1893.

————
'Confucius', *La Revue de Paris*, vol. 10, no. 4, 1903.

————
Le Tai Chan, Essai de monographie d'un culte chinois, Leroux, Paris, 1910.

————
Cinq cent contes et apologues extraits du Tripiṭaka chinois, vol. 1, Leroux, Paris, 1910.

————
Mission archéologique dans la Chine septentrionale, Tome I, Leroux, Paris, 1913.

————
'Le jet des dragons', in Senart and Cordier, eds., *Mémoires concernant l'Asie orientale*, vol. 3, Leroux, Paris, 1919.

CHAVANNES Édouard (*cont.*)   *Contes et légendes du Bouddhisme chinois*, Les Classiques de l'Orient, Bossard, Paris, 1921.

CHEN, Kenneth K. S.,   *Buddhism in China, A Historical Survey*, Princeton University Press, Princeton, N.J., 1964.

CONDOMINAS, Georges,   'Marcel Mauss, Père de l'ethnographie française, I, A l'ombre de Durkheim', *Critique*, no. 301, 1972.

CONZE, Edward, *et al.*, eds.,   *Buddhist Texts through the Ages*, Bruno Cassirer, Oxford, 1954.

DE GROOT, J. J. M.,   Trans. C. G. Chavannes, *Les fêtes annuellement célébrées à Emoui (Amoy), Etude concernant la religion populaire des Chinois*, Annales du Musée Guimet, vols. 11 and 12, Paris, 1886.

————   *The Religious System of China. Its Ancient Forms, Evolution, History and Present Aspects. Manners, Customs and Social Institutions Connected Therewith*, 6 vols., Brill, Leiden, 1892–1910.

DEMIÉVILLE, Paul,   'W.–A. Jablonski (1901–1957)', *T'oung Pao*, vol. 45, nos. 4–5, 1957.

————   'Le Bouddhisme chinois', in Henri-Charles Puech, ed., *Histoire des religions, I, Les religions antiques— La formation des religions univer-selles et les religions de salut en Inde et en Extrême-Orient*, Encyclopédie de la Pléiade, Gallimard, Paris, 1970.

————   'Gauche et droite en Chine', in Paul Demiéville, *Choix d'études sinologiques (1921–1970)*, Brill, Leiden, 1973 (originally published in R. Kourilsky and P. Grapin, eds., *Main droite et main gauche, Norme et latéralité*, Relation et sciences de l'homme, Paris, 1968).

————   'Aperçu historique des études sinologiques en France', in Paul Demiéville, *Choix d'études sinolo-giques (1921–1970)*, Brill, Leiden,

DEMIÉVILLE, Paul (*cont.*)   1973 (originally published in *Acta
                                      Asiatica*, vol. 11, 1966, Tokyo).
DUMÉZIL, Georges,   *Mythe et épopée**. *L'idéologie des trois
                                      fonctions dans les épopées des peuples
                                      indo-européens*, Gallimard, Paris,
                                      1968.
DURKHEIM, Émile,   Review of M. Courant, 'Les associa-
                                      tions en Chine', *AS*, vol. 3,
                                      1898–99.
————   Review of Fukuda Tokuzo, *Die
                                      gesellschaftliche und wirtschaftliche
                                      Entwickelung in Japan*, *AS*, vol. 5,
                                      1900–1.
————   Review of M. Courant, *En Chine*, *AS*,
                                      vol. 6, 1901–2.
————   Review of H. Schurtz, *Altersklassen
                                      und Männerbünde*, *AS*, vol. 6,
                                      1901–2.
————   *Les formes élémentaires de la vie
                                      religieuse, Le système totémique en
                                      Australie*, Alcan, Paris, 1912.
————   Trans. J. W. Swain, *The Elementary
                                      Forms of the Religious Life*, Allen
                                      and Unwin, London, 1954.
DURKHEIM, Émile, and   Trans. and ed. Rodney Needham,
  Marcel Mauss,   *Primitive Classification*, Cohen and
                                      West, London, 1963.
EBERHARD, Wolfram,   Trans. E. W. Dickes, *A History of
                                      China*, 2nd edn., Routledge and
                                      Kegan Paul, London, 1960.
FAUCONNET, P.,   Review of Appert, 'Un code de la
                                      féodalité japonaise au XIIIe siècle',
                                      AS, vol. 4, 1899–1900.
————   'Enseignement de la Sociologie',
                                      *Bulletin de l'Institut Français de
                                      Sociologie.*, 1ère Année, 1930–31.
————   'L'enseignement de la Sociologie',
                                      *Bulletin de l'Institut Français de
                                      Sociologie*, 2e Année, Fasc. 1, 1931.
FÊNG Han-yi,   *The Chinese Kinship System*, Harvard
                                      University Press, for the Harvard-
                                      Yenching Institute, Cambridge,
                                      Mass., 1948 (reprinted from

FÊNG Han-yi (*cont.*)   *Harvard Journal of Asiatic Studies*,
                         vol. 2, no. 2, July 1937).

FREEDMAN, Maurice,   *Lineage Organization in Southeastern
                         China*, London School of Economics
                         Monographs on Social Anthro-
                         pology no. 18, Athlone Press,
                         London, 1958.

————   'Sociology in and of China', *The
                         British Journal of Sociology*, vol. 13,
                         no. 2, 1962.

————   'A Chinese Phase in Social
                         Anthropology', *The British Journal
                         of Sociology*, vol. 14, no. 1, 1963.

————   *Rites and Duties, or Chinese Marriage*,
                         Bell, London, 1967.

————   Geomancy', *Proceedings of the Royal
                         Anthropological Institute of Great
                         Britain and Ireland 1968*, London,
                         1969.

————   'The Politics of an Old State: A
                         View from the Chinese Lineage',
                         in John Davis, ed., *Choice and
                         Change: Essays in Honour of Lucy
                         Mair*, London School of Economics
                         Monographs on Social Anthro-
                         pology no. 50, Athlone Press,
                         London, 1974.

————   'On the Sociology of Chinese
                         Religion', in Arthur Wolf, ed.,
                         *Ritual and Religion in Chinese
                         Society*, Stanford University Press,
                         Stanford, Calif., 1974.

GERNET, Jacques,   Trans. R. Rudorff, *Ancient China,
                         From the Beginnings to the Empire*,
                         Faber and Faber, London, 1968.

GERNET, Louis,   'Préface' to Marcel Granet, *Etudes
                         sociologiques sur la Chine*, 1953.

GERNET, Louis, and   *Le génie grec dans la religion*, Albin
   André Boulanger,   Michel, Paris, 1970 (original edn.,
                         La Renaissance du Livre, Paris,
                         1932).

GRANET, Marcel,   Review of J. Calmette, *La société
                         féodale, AS*, n.s., vol. 1, 1923–24.

HSU Cho-yun,   *Ancient China in Transition, An*

Hsu Cho-yun (*cont.*)

HUBERT, H.,

HUGHES, E. R., trans. and ed.,

HUMPHREYS, S.C.,

JABLONSKI, Witold,

KALTENMARK, Max,

KARLGREN, Bernhard,

trans.,

KOPPERS, Wilhelm,

Analysis of Social Mobility, 722–222 B.C., Stanford University Press, Stanford, Calif., 1965.

Review of G. Wissowa, *Religion und Kultus der Römer*, *AS*, vol. 6, 1901–2.

Chinese Philosophy in Classical Times, Everyman's Library, no. 973, Dent, London, Dutton, N.Y., 1942.

'The Work of Louis Gernet', *History and Theory, Studies in the Philosophy of History*, vol. 10, no. 2, 1971.

'Marcel Granet and his Work', *The Yenching Journal of Social Studies*, Peking, vol. 1, no. 2, 1939.

'Notes à propos du Kao-mei', *Annuaire 1966–1967 Ecole Pratique des Hautes Etudes, Ve Section— Sciences religieuses*, vol. 74, Paris, 1966.

'Le Taoïsme religieux', in Henri-Charles Puech, ed., *Histoire des religions, I, Les religions antiques— La formation des religions univer-selles et les religions de salut en Inde et en Extrême-Orient*, Encylopédie de la Pléiade, Gallimard, Paris, 1970.

'Préface' to Henri Maspero, *Le Taoïsme et les religions chinoises*, Gallimard, Paris, 1971.

'Glosses on the Kuo Feng Odes', *Bulletin of the Museum of Far Eastern Antiquities*, Stockholm, no. 18, 1942.

'Legends and Cults in Ancient China', *Bulletin of the Museum of Far Estern Antiquities*, Stockholm, no. 18, 1946.

The Book of Odes, The Museum of Far Eastern Antiquities, Stockholm, 1950.

'Die Frage des Mutterrechts und des

KOPPERS, Wilhelm (*cont.*) Totemismus im alten China', *Anthropos*, vol. 25, 1930.

LANGLOIS, Ch. V., 'Agrégation d'Histoire et de Géographie, concours de 1907', *Revue Universitaire*, vol. 16, pt. 2, no. 9, 1907.

LATTE, Kurt, *Römische Religionsgeschichte* (*Handbuch der Altertumswissenschaft*, 5th Section, pt. 4), C. H. Beck'sche Verlagsbuchhandlung, Munich, 1960.

LEACH, E. R., *Rethinking Anthropology*, London School of Economics Monographs on Social Anthropology no. 22, Athlone Press, London, 1961.

LEGGE, James, trans., *The Sacred Books of the East, The Texts of Confucianism, Part III, The Lî Kî, I–X*, Clarendon Press, Oxford, 1885.

————— ————— *The Sacred Books of the East, The Texts of Confucianism, Part IV, The Lî Kî, XI–XLVI*, Clarendon Press, Oxford, 1885.

LEVENSON, Joseph R. and Franz Schurmann, *China: An Interpretive History, From the Beginnings to the Fall of Han*, University of California Press, Berkeley etc., 1969.

LÉVI-STRAUSS, Claude, 'French Sociology', in Georges Gurvitch and Wilbert E. Moore, eds., *Twentieth Century Sociology*, the Philosophical Library, N.Y., 1945.

————— 'Ce que l'ethnologie doit à Durkheim', *Annales de l'Université de Paris*, vol. 30, no. 1, 1960 (reprinted in Claude Lévi-Strauss, *Anthropologie structurale deux*, Plon, Paris, 1973).

————— Trans. J. H. Bell and J. R. von Sturmer, *The Elementary Structures of Kinship*, ed. R. Needham, Eyre and Spottiswoode, London, 1969.

LEVY, Marion J., Jr., 'Granet, Marcel', *International Encyclopedia of the Social Sciences*, vol. 6, ed. David L. Sills, Macmillan

LEVY Marion J., Jr. (*cont.*)

LÉVY-BRUHL, Henri, and Free Press, Chicago, 1968.
Memorial address on Marcel Granet,
5 Dec. 1955, unpublished.

LÉVY-BRUHL, Lucien, *Les fonctions mentales dans les sociétés inférieures*, Alcan, Paris, 1910.

Livret de l'étudiant, Année scolaire 1922–1923, L'Université de Paris et les établissements parisiens d'enseignement supérieur, Bureau de renseignement à la Sorbonne, Paris.

Livret de l'étudiant, Année scolaire 1929–1930, L'Université de Paris . . . , Presses Universitaires de France, Paris.

LUKES, Steven, 'Mauss, Marcel', *International Encyclopedia of the Social Sciences*, vol. 10, ed. David L. Sills, Macmillan and Free Press, Chicago 1968.

——— *Émile Durkheim, His Life and Work, a Historical and Critical Study*, Allen Lane, the Penguin Press, London, 1973.

'Marcel Granet', *AS*, third series, 1940–48, vol 1.

MASPERO, Henri, 'Le songe et l'ambassade de l'Empereur Ming, Etude critique des sources', *Bulletin de l'Ecole Française d'Extrême-Orient*, vol. 10, 1910.

——— 'Légendes mythologiques dans le *Chou King*', *Journal Asiatique*, vol. 204, 1924.

——— *Mélanges posthumes sur les religions et l'histoire de la Chine*, vols. 1, 2. Publications du Musée Guimet, Bibliothèque de Diffusion, vols. 57, 58. Civilisations du Sud, S.A.E.P., Paris, 1950 (republished in Henri Maspero, *Le Taoïsme et les religions chinoises*, Gallimard, Paris, 1971).

MASPERO, Henri, and Etienne Balazs, *Histoire et institutions de la Chine ancienne des origines au XIIe siècle après J.C.*, ed. P. Demiéville,

MASPERO, Henri, and   Presses Universitaires de France,
  Etienne Balazs (*cont.*)   Paris, 1967.
Mathews' Chinese-English   revised American edn., Harvard
  Dictionary,   University Press, Cambridge,
                                Mass., 1963.
MAUSS, Marcel,   Review of H. Usener, *Götternamen*,
                                AS, vol. 1, 1896–97.
————   Review of L. Marillier, 'L'origine des
                                dieux', *AS*, vol. 4, 1899–1900.
————   Review of A. Dietrich, *Mutter Erde:*
                                ein Versuch über Volksreligion, *AS*,
                                vol. 9, 1904–5.
————   Review of J. J. M. de Groot, *The*
                                Religious System of China, vol. 5,
                                AS, vol. 11, 1906–9.
————   'Essai sur le don, Forme et raison de
                                l'échange dans les sociétés
                                archaïques', *AS*, second series, vol.
                                1, 1923–24.
————   *Œuvres 3. Cohésion sociale et divisions*
                                de la sociologie, ed. Victor Karady,
                                Editions de Minuit, Paris, 1969.
MAUSS, Marcel, with   'Essai sur les variations saisonnières
  H. Beuchat,   des sociétés eskimos, Etude de
                                morphologie sociale', *AS*, vol. 9,
                                1904–5.
MAYERS, Wm. Frederick,   *The Chinese Reader's Manual*,
                                American Presbyterian Mission
                                Press, Shanghai, Trubner, London,
                                1874.
MESTRE, Édouard,   'Marcel Granet (*1884–1940*)',
                                Annuaire 1940–1941 et 1941–1942,
                                Ecole Pratique des Hautes Etudes,
                                Section des Sciences religieuses,
                                Imprimerie Administrative, Melun,
                                1941.
MILLS, C. Wright,   'The Language and Ideas of Ancient
                                China: Marcel Granet's Contribu-
                                tion to the Sociology of Knowledge',
                                in *Power, Politics and People, The*
                                Collected Essays of C. Wright Mills,
                                ed. Irving Louis Horowitz, Oxford
                                University Press, London, N.Y.,
                                1963.

NEEDHAM, Joseph,   *Science and Civilisation in China,*
                                vol. 3, *Mathematics and the Sciences*
                                of the Heavens and the Earth,
                                Cambridge University Press,
                                Cambridge, 1970.

NEEDHAM, Rodney, ed.,   *Right and Left: Essays on Dual Symbolic*
                                Classification, University of Chicago
                                Press, Chicago and London, 1973.

PELLIOT, Paul,   ' "Meou Tseu, ou les doutes levés"
                                traduit et annoté', *T'oung Pao,*
                                vol. 19, no. 5, 1918–19.

POIRIER, Jean,   'Histoire de la pensée ethnologique',
                                and 'Ethnologie juridique', in Jean
                                Poirer, ed., *Ethnologie générale,*
                                Encyclopédie de la Pléiade, N.R.F.,
                                Paris, 1968.

PRŮŠEK, Jaroslav,   *Chinese Statelets and the Northern*
                                Barbarians in the Period 1400–300
                                B.C., D. Reidel Publishing
                                Company, Dordrecht, 1971.

QUISDORP, Martin,   'Männergesellschaft und Altersklassen
                                im alten China', *Mitteilungen des*
                                Seminars für orientalische Sprache an
                                der Königlichen Friedrich-Wilhelms-
                                Universität zu Berlin, vol. 18, 1915.

RADCLIFFE-BROWN, A. R.,   'The Comparative Method in Social
                                Anthropology', in A. R. Radcliffe-
                                Brown, *Method in Social Anthro-*
                                pology, ed. M. N. Srinivas,
                                University of Chicago Press,
                                Chicago, 1958 (reprinted from
                                Journal of the Royal Anthropological
                                Institute of Great Britain and
                                Ireland, vol. 81, Pts. 1 and 2, 1951).

SEGALEN, Victor,   *René Leys,* N.R.F., Gallimard, Paris,
                                1971 (originally published 1922).

SKINNER, G. William, ed.,   *Modern Chinese Society, An Analytical*
                                Bibliography, 1. Publications in
                                Western Languages 1644–1972,
                                Stanford University Press,
                                Stanford, Calif., 1973.

SOOTHILL, William Edward,   *The Hall of Light, A Study of Early*
                                Chinese Kingship, Lutterworth Press,
                                London, 1951.

STEIN, R.-A.,   'Edouard Mestre (1883–1950)', *Annuaire 1951–1952, Ecole pratique des Hautes Etudes, Section des Sciences religieuses*, Paris, 1951.

———   'Présentation de l'œuvre de Marcel Granet: "Le Roi boit"', *AS*, third series, 1952, published 1955.

———   'Introduction' to Marcel Granet, *Etudes sociologiques sur la Chine*, 1953.

TING, V. K.,   'Prof. Granet's "La Civilisation Chinoise"', *The Chinese Social and Political Science Review*, vol. 15, no. 2, 1931.

TJAN Tjoe Som,   *Po Hu T'ung, The Comprehensive Discourses in the White Tiger Hall*, vol. 1, Brill, Leiden, 1949.

TREISTMAN, Judith M.,   *The Prehistory of China, An Archeological Exploration*, The Natural History Press, for the American Museum of Natural History, Doubleday, Garden City, N.Y., 1972.

VANDIER-NICOLAS, Nicole,   Memorial address on Marcel Granet, 5 Dec. 1955, unpublished.

WALEY, Arthur, trans.,   *The Analects of Confucius*, Allen and Unwin, London, 1938.

———   *Ballads and Stories from Tun-huang, An Anthology*, Allen and Unwin, London, 1960.

——— ———   *The Book of Songs*, Allen and Unwin, London, 1969.

WELCH, Holmes,   *The Parting of the Way, Lao Tzu and the Taoist Movement*, Methuen, London, 1958.

———   *The Practice of Chinese Buddhism 1900–1950*, Harvard University Press, Cambridge, Mass., 1967.

WHEATLEY, Paul,   *The Pivot of the Four Quarters, A Preliminary Enquiry into the Origins and Character of the Ancient Chinese City*, Edinburgh University Press, Edinburgh, 1971.

WRIGHT, Arthur F.,   *Buddhism in Chinese History*,

WRIGHT, Arthur F. (*cont.*)   Stanford University Press, Stanford,
                                     Calif., and Oxford University
                                     Press, London, 1959.

YANG K'un,   'Marcel Granet: An Appreciation',
                                     *The Yenching Journal of Social
                                     Studies*, Peking, vol. 1, no. 2, 1939.

————   'An Introduction to Granet's
                                     Researches', in Chinese, *Peking
                                     University School of French Studies,
                                     Social Science Quarterly*, Peking,
                                     1943.

YU Ping-yuen,   *Chinese History, Index to Learned
                                     Articles, Volume II, Based on
                                     Collections in American and
                                     European Libraries*, Harvard-
                                     Yenching Library Bibliographical
                                     Series I, Harvard University,
                                     Cambridge, Mass., 1970.

ZÜRCHER, E.,   *The Buddhist Conquest of China, The
                                     Spread and Adaptation of Buddhism
                                     in Early Medieval China*, revised
                                     edn., Sinica Leidensia XI, Brill,
                                     Leiden, 1972.

Index